*Getting Started w.....*

# Microsoft®
# Word
## for the Apple® Macintosh®

Version 5

# Getting Started with

# Microsoft®
# Word

## for the Apple® Macintosh®

### Version 5

**Michael Boom**

PUBLISHED BY
Microsoft Press
A Division of Microsoft Corporation
One Microsoft Way
Redmond, Washington 98052-6399

Library of Congress Cataloging-in-Publication Data

Boom, Michael.
    Getting started with Microsoft Word for the Apple Macintosh / Michael Boom.
       p.    cm. -- (Getting started right series)
    Includes index.
    ISBN 1-55615-378-3 : $19.95 ($24.95 Can.)
    1. Microsoft Word (Computer program)  2. Word processing--Computer
programs.  3. Macintosh (Computer)--Programming.   I. Title.
    II. Series.
Z52.5.M52B658     1992                    91-39266
                                          CIP

Printed and bound in the United States of America.

1 2 3 4 5 6 7 8 9  AGAG  6 5 4 3 2 1

Distributed to the book trade in Canada by Macmillan of Canada, a division of Canada
Publishing Corporation.

Distributed to the book trade outside the United States and Canada by Penguin Books Ltd.

Penguin Books Ltd., Harmondsworth, Middlesex, England
Penguin Books Australia Ltd., Ringwood, Victoria, Australia
Penguin Books N.Z. Ltd., 182-190 Wairau Road, Auckland 10, New Zealand

British Cataloging-in-Publication Data available.

**Acquisitions Editor:** Marjorie Schlaikjer
**Project Editor:** Mary Ann Jones
**Technical Editor:** Jim Fuchs

*To my mother, Diana, and my father, Ken,*
*for putting up with having their names*
*stuck in the front of yet another book.*

# Contents

# Acknowledgments

I'd like to thank the diligent folks at Microsoft Press who shepherded *Getting Started with Microsoft Word for the Apple Macintosh* from first drafts to the book you hold in your hands. Thanks in particular to Marjorie Schlaikjer, who suggested the scope and shape of the book (rectangular with pages, always popular); to Jim Fuchs, who tenaciously checked out all the technical details against Word version 5 as it evolved through beta stages; to the Microsoft Press Proof department, and especially Alice Copp Smith, who ruthlessly eliminated widows, orphans, and other unsightly blemishes; and to Megan Sheppard and Mary Ann Jones, tag-team editors who massaged the flab from the text.

Thanks also to my wife, Lynn, whose gracious support during deadline pressures made it possible each day for me to put my nose back to the digital grindstone with a smile on my face.

# Introduction

This is a simple book about a complex program. It's aimed squarely at teaching you the ins and outs of Microsoft Word version 5 without going into needless detail. To that end, it concentrates on Word's most useful features and teaches the simplest, most practical methods for getting work done. It sidesteps esoteric features loved by a small percentage of Word's users (and happily ignored by the rest), and focuses instead on practice sessions that give you hands-on experience with the techniques you're reading about.

Even if you're a Word novice or haven't used Word version 5 before, this book will have you writing a business letter by the end of Chapter 2. Before you start, however, you should know some Macintosh fundamentals: how to turn the Mac on and off, how to use the mouse, how to work with menus, and how to perform other standard Macintosh activities. You'll find good tutorials for these simple techniques in the documentation that came with your Macintosh.

If you've already had some experience with Word, you can start at a level that suits you. The book is divided into three progressive sections:

- Section I, "The Bare Essentials," is for first-time Word users. It shows you how to start Word, gives you a brief tour of its parts, and then shows you how to enter, edit, format, and print a business letter.

- Section II, "For Everyday Work," teaches the Word skills you need to produce a variety of standard documents such as business memos and reports with columns of figures. It shows you how to control the appearance of characters and paragraphs, and it introduces you to Word's writing and editing tools. It also teaches you techniques for effectively saving and printing documents.

- Section III, "For Special Documents," delves into some of the more advanced features of Word used for such documents as multipage reports, invitations with pictures, and multicolumn newsletters. It teaches you how to add headers and footers to the page, how to draw and insert graphics, and how to arrange text in snaking columns. It also shows you how to control the amount of text on each page, how to view your documents for page layout, and how to organize text within a table.

If you've just bought Word and haven't yet installed it on your Macintosh, turn to the complete instructions for installation in the appendix at the back of the book. Read them first to install Word, and then begin with Chapter 1.

One quick technical note before you start: The examples and pictures throughout the book describe Word as it runs on a Macintosh with System 7 software, the most recent system software available. If you run your Mac with earlier system software, Word's operation might deviate in minor details from a few of the descriptions, but not by much. Press on, and you shouldn't have any trouble working through the practice sessions in this book.

Enjoy yourself with the practice sessions. And don't forget to experiment on your own—Word is full of features to make your writing work go faster and look better.

# Section I

# The Bare Essentials

# Chapter 1

# A Tour of Word

This chapter is your first step in getting started with Microsoft Word for the Apple Macintosh, version 5. It's simple. You start Word, look at its parts, poke through its menus, and then quit Word. Along the way, you see how Word's commands are grouped in menus and learn how to use the keyboard to choose commands. You'll find out how to get help within Word and set up Word to work for the examples in this book. While you're doing all this, you'll also learn the names of Word features that we'll use throughout the rest of this book.

## STARTING MICROSOFT WORD

Before you can start Word, it must be installed on your Macintosh. If you haven't already installed Word, turn to the Appendix of this book for installation instructions.

To start Word, your Mac must be turned on and the desktop must appear on screen, showing the disks available to your Macintosh. You start Word just as you start any other standard application for the Mac: You first find its icon and then double-click on it.

### PRACTICE

**Starting Word**

1. If you can't see the contents of your hard disk, double-click on its icon to open its window. Look in the window for a folder labeled *Word 5.0* or simply *Word*.

2. Double-click on the Word folder to open it, and then look in the folder for the Microsoft Word icon. (Figure 1-1 shows a typical open Word folder.)

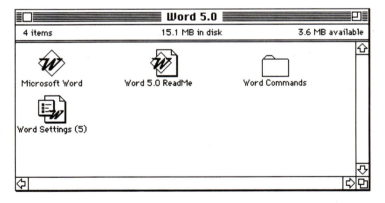

FIGURE 1-1. *The Word folder on a hard disk contains Word and its associated files.*

3. Double-click on the Microsoft Word icon to start Word. Word is loaded from the disk.

## WORD'S PARTS

After you start Word, it appears on the desktop with an empty document window (shown in Figure 1-2). You'll see Word's menus in the menu bar at the top of the screen, and a small Word icon at the right end of the menu bar, which shows that you're currently working with Word.

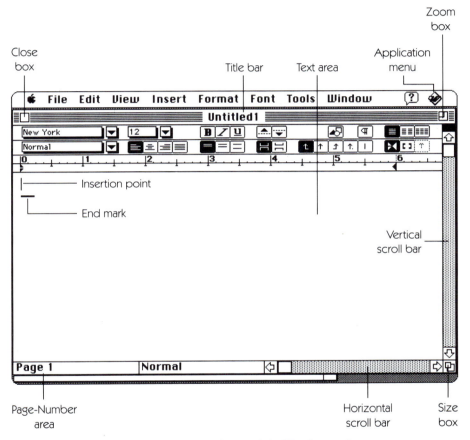

**FIGURE 1-2.** *A Word document window and the Word menu bar appear when you start Word.*

## The Document Window

The document window on the screen contains a single Word document that's empty and untitled for now, waiting for you to fill it with text and give it a name. The document window fills the screen on standard 9-inch Mac monitors; on larger monitors, Word takes advantage of the larger screen, usually enlarging the document window to fill the screen from top to bottom but leaving a strip of open space on the right side of the screen.

The document window probably looks familiar to you, because it uses these standard Macintosh window elements:

- A *title bar* on top that shows the name of the document (currently "Untitled1"). You can put the pointer on the title bar and drag the window to a new location.

- A *close box* in the upper left corner that you can click on to close the window.

- A *zoom box* in the upper right corner that you can click on to quickly shrink or enlarge the window.

- A *size box* in the lower right corner that you can drag to resize the window.

- A *vertical* and a *horizontal scroll bar* on the right and bottom borders that you can click on to display other areas of the window.

The document window also contains Word-specific elements, described in the following sections, that are designed to perform word processing tasks.

## The Insertion Point and the End Mark

The large white expanse filling the center of the document window is the *text area*, where text appears as you type. In the upper left corner of the text area is a small, blinking vertical line called the *insertion point*. It marks the spot where you enter text. Try typing something now, and watch the insertion point as you type. It moves across the text area from left to right, inserting characters as it moves.

The short, thick horizontal line at the left edge of the text area, immediately below the text you enter, is the *end mark*. It marks the end of the document and moves downward as you fill the text area with text.

## The Ribbon and the Ruler

The Ribbon and the Ruler are two horizontal strips of buttons and controls located just below the title bar. The Ribbon (shown in Figure 1-3) controls the appearance of characters in a document. You can use its controls to choose a font (a set of characters with a distinctive appearance); set the size of characters; add emphasis such as bold, italic, or underlining; and create superscript and subscript characters, as in $3^2$ and $H_2O$. You can also use the Ribbon to insert a picture, set up text in columns on the page, and display nonprinting characters such as spaces between words and paragraph marks at the end of each paragraph.

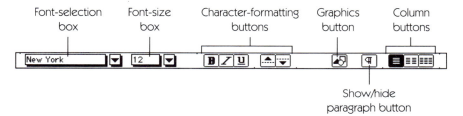

**FIGURE 1-3.** *The buttons and controls in the Ribbon control character appearance, set columns of text, and display nonprinting characters.*

The Ruler (shown in Figure 1-4), which is just beneath the Ribbon, controls the appearance and properties of paragraphs. The Ruler's bottom half is the *measure,* which measures the width of the page and (using markers along the measure's length) sets paragraph indents, which control the width of paragraphs. The controls above the measure set paragraph alignment (centering text or aligning it at the left or the right side of the paragraph), line spacing within the paragraph, and spacing between paragraphs. You can also set tab stops along the measure, and change the Ruler to show different information for special purposes.

The Ribbon and the Ruler duplicate features you can find in Word's menus. The advantage of the Ribbon and the Ruler over menus is that they're quick and easy—you can see the control you want and, with a single click, change the appearance of part of your document. You'll learn in later chapters how to turn off both the Ruler and the Ribbon to allow more room on the screen for displaying the contents of your document.

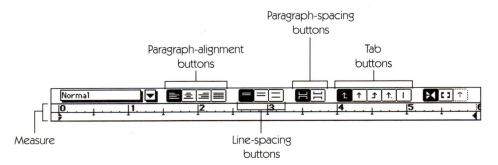

**FIGURE 1-4.** *The Ruler controls the appearance of paragraphs of text in a document.*

## The Page-Number Area and the Style Area

The *Page-Number area* and the *Style area* share the bottom of the document window with the horizontal scroll bar. Both areas display information about the document displayed in the window.

The Page-Number area shows what page of the document you're viewing. Word documents can run up to hundreds of pages in length and can be divided into many different sections. The Page-Number area shows the section number (if there are sections) and the page number of the page you're currently viewing. The Page-Number area can also display messages from Word about current status, such as Word's progress in saving a document, and can prompt you to type information when you use a keyboard shortcut to change the font, apply a style, or perform another Word action.

The Style area shows the name of the style applied to different paragraphs or text blocks.

## USING WORD'S MENUS

Word's menus work like menus in any other Macintosh program—you open a menu by clicking and holding on the menu, and dragging downward. You choose a command by releasing the mouse button when the command you want is highlighted. You can also choose a command by pressing the appropriate key combination. (Key combinations are usually shown after the command in the menu.) For example, you can press Command-P to choose Print from the File menu.

The following sections offer a few more facts that you might not know about Word's menus.

## Choosing Menu Commands with the Keyboard

Word users who don't want to use a mouse and don't like memorizing keyboard shortcuts can open menus and choose commands using the keyboard. Pressing the decimal-point key on the numeric keypad highlights the menu bar so that you can open a menu. Each press of the left-arrow or right-arrow cursor key opens the menu to the left or right along the menu bar. After you open a menu, pressing the up-arrow or down-arrow cursor key highlights a different command, and pressing Return chooses the highlighted command. If you want to abandon the menus without choosing a command, press Esc.

If your keyboard has a numeric keypad, try using the keyboard method now to select a menu command.

### PRACTICE

#### Choosing commands with the keyboard

1. Press the decimal-point key on the numeric keypad. The menu bar is highlighted.

2. Press the 1 key on the numeric keypad. The File menu opens.

3. Press the right-arrow cursor key several times. At each press, the current menu closes and the menu to its right opens. Stop pressing as soon as the rightmost menu closes and the Apple menu at the far left of the menu bar opens.

4. Press the down-arrow cursor key once to highlight the About Microsoft Word command.

5. Press Return to choose the highlighted command. The menu closes, and the About Microsoft Word dialog box appears.

6. Press Esc to close the dialog box.

## Navigating Through Different Menu Sets

A Macintosh with System 7 can run several programs simultaneously; you can work with one program at a time, switching back and forth among them as you see fit. The menus in the menu bar are associated with the program you're currently using. If you know you're running Word but can't find the menus, a different program is currently active. You can easily switch back to Word by moving the pointer to the Application menu on the far right of the menu bar and opening the menu there. This menu lists every program currently running. Choose Word, and Word's menus (and any open Word document windows) appear again.

## WORD'S MENUS

Word groups commands into logical menu families to help you find the commands you need. Open each of Word's menus and become acquainted with the commands Word has to offer.

### The Apple Menu

The Apple menu is displayed at the far left of the menu bar; its icon is an apple with a bite taken out of it. If you open it, you'll find a list of programs that you can run by choosing one from the menu. You're likely to find programs such as Calculator, Chooser, and Key Caps, handy utilities you might want to use during a Word session. While you're using one of these utilities, the menu bar changes to show the utility's menus. When you're done with the utility, quit by choosing its Quit command or by closing its window.

When Word is the active program, the Apple menu also contains the About Microsoft Word command, which opens a dialog box that gives you information about the version of Microsoft Word you're running.

### The File Menu

You'll find four sections of commands in Word's File menu. The first section includes document control commands—commands that save your documents on disk, load documents from disk, start new documents, and sort through previously saved documents. The second section includes printing commands—commands that show how your document will look on paper before you print, commands that control page size, and commands that send a document to your printer when you're ready. The third section (which appears only if you've given a command to show it) shows the last few documents you worked on so that you can quickly reopen them. The final section, Quit, quits Word and returns you to the desktop.

## The Edit Menu

The commands in the Edit menu remove, copy, and move blocks of text and graphics in your document. They also help you edit pictures, find and replace specific instances of text, go to a specific page, and paste in text and pictures from a collection of text and pictures called called a *glossary*. The last set of commands in the menu are for advanced users and, among other things, link Word documents to files created by other programs.

## The View Menu

The commands in the View menu change the appearance of your Word document. The first three commands let you alternate between a view of text unbroken by pages, a view that shows the bare bones of the document in outline form, and a view that shows page edges and page location of all document text. The two commands that follow let you turn the Ribbon and Ruler off or turn them on to make more room for text in your document window. And the commands after that open the Print Merge Helper (an advanced feature for printing many customized copies of a single document), locate voice annotations (recorded audio comments), and display nonprinting characters on the screen. The last three commands open special windows in which you can create headers, footers, and footnotes.

## The Insert Menu

The commands in the Insert menu insert special elements into your Word document: a voice annotation; a page break that forces following text to appear at the top of a new page; a section break that lets you mix types of page layout within a single document; a table that organizes text in rows and columns; a footnote that adds information at the bottom of the page or at the end of a document; the current date; and special symbols such as • or $\pi$. Other commands in the Insert menu help you mark a document for an index and a table of contents and then add an automatically generated index or a table of contents to your document. And other commands let Word import material from another file on disk, create a picture, or anchor a picture or text block on the page so that other text flows around it.

## The Format Menu

The commands in the Format menu control the appearance of different parts of your document. They start at the smallest unit—characters—and proceed upward to larger units—paragraphs, document sections, and finally to the entire document. The Border command controls borders around paragraphs and tables. Other commands here allow you to control the appearance and shape of tables, set a frame (a fixed picture or piece of text) on the page, and define and use styles, which are collections of formatting instructions. The last set of commands in the Format menu are character-formatting commands that add or remove emphasis in text.

## The Font Menu

The commands in the Font menu control the size and appearance of the characters in your document. The commands at the bottom of the menu offer you all the fonts available on your Macintosh. (The list will be short or long, depending on how many fonts are in the System folder). The commands above the fonts set the size of the characters and can change the default font (the font that Word starts with in a new document).

## The Tools Menu

The commands in the Tools menu help you to write and to customize Word so that it best suits your needs. The first five commands start powerful writing tools: a spelling checker to catch misspellings; a grammar checker to check on writing style; a thesaurus to suggest alternative words; a hyphenator to correctly break long words at the end of a line; and a word counter that tallies up words, sentences, paragraphs, and other elements within a document. The next four commands are useful utilities that automatically number or renumber paragraphs (very useful in an outline), sort paragraphs alphabetically, calculate the results of mathematical expressions within text, and repaginate a document so that you can see page breaks.

The last two commands are for customizing Word. The first lets you set Word's operating characteristics, and the last lets you choose the commands you want to see in Word's menus.

## The Window Menu

Commands in the Window menu control document windows. The Help command at the top of the Window menu displays a window where you can get help for most of Word's features. The commands in the middle section display the contents of the Clipboard (a tool that holds blocks of text and graphics being cut and pasted) and create a new window for an existing document. The bottom section lists all the document windows currently open in Word. You can choose any one of the document windows listed (if you have more than one document open) to place that document window on top of the other document windows.

## The Help Menu and the Application Menu

The last two menus on the right side of the menu bar are standard Macintosh System 7 menus, the Help menu and the Application menu. The Help menu, labeled with a question mark in a balloon, provides on-screen help for standard Macintosh and Word-specific items. If you choose Show Balloons from the Help menu, a text balloon appears whenever you drag the pointer over a standard Macintosh or Word-specific item (such as a Ruler button) that explains what the item does. When you get tired of the balloons (they get annoying after a very short time), turn them off by choosing the Hide Balloons command from the Help menu. If you choose the Microsoft Word Help command, you'll see a window that contains Word topics. When you double-click on any of the topics, Word will give you help on that topic.

The Application menu, labeled with the icon of whichever program is currently active, lists all other running programs at the bottom half of the menu. To switch to another program, simply choose the program's name.

## USING WORD'S DEFAULT SETTINGS

The way that Word automatically operates—the font it uses in a new document, the measurements it uses in the Ruler, the commands it lists in its menus, and the way it handles many other similar operations—is controlled by its *default settings*. Whenever Word performs an action, it uses default settings unless you tell it to use others.

This book assumes that you're working with Word set to its original settings. Because any Word user (you or someone else) can customize Word to the point where you won't even recognize the standard menus, you'll need a good way to get back to original settings. To reset everything, follow these steps—but first ask any other people using your version of Word whether it will ruin their custom settings.

## Returning to Word's Default Settings

1. Choose the Commands command from the Tools menu to open the Command dialog box (shown in Figure 1-5).

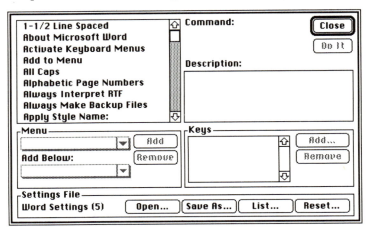

FIGURE 1-5. *The Command dialog box customizes Word by setting the commands and keyboard shortcuts available to its users.*

2. Click on the Reset button at the bottom right corner of the dialog box to open the Reset dialog box.

3. Click on Reset to Microsoft Standard Settings.

4. Click on the OK button to close the dialog box.

5. Click on the Close button to exit the Command dialog box.

## QUITTING WORD

When you finish using Word, choose the Quit command from the File menu. If you added text to any open documents or revised their contents in any way, Word displays a dialog box that asks whether you want to save your changes. Click on the Yes button to save the document changes and then quit Word; to quit Word without saving changes, click on the No button; click on the Cancel button to return to your document without quitting. After you quit Word, you return to the desktop, where you can start another application or turn off your Macintosh.

Now that you're familiar with Word's environment, it's time to move on to the next chapter, where you'll learn how to create and print a simple Word document.

# Chapter 2

# Creating a Business Letter

Now that you've had a chance to look at Microsoft Word version 5, it's time to roll up your sleeves and use it to do some real work— creating a business letter. Along the way, you'll get some answers to questions that almost everyone asks when they sit down for the first time at the keyboard with a new word processor: What do the keys on the keyboard do? How do I correct the mistakes I make as I type? How do I revise parts of my letter? How do I make my letter look professional? How can I save my letter to use again later? And finally, how do I get the letter from the screen onto the printed page?

## ENTERING TEXT

The first step in turning a blank page (or screen, in this case) into a business letter is to enter text: You simply press the keys and characters appear. The insertion point moves from left to right across the page and, when one line is full, automatically moves to a new line and continues entering characters.

The standard character keys are only part of entering text, however. You'll find a number of other keys on the keyboard that do more than simply enter characters—they move the insertion point around, move to different areas of your document, and insert special characters. Before you start entering your business letter, take a few minutes to get to know these other keys.

### The Keyboard Layout

Not all Macintoshes have the same keyboard. Figure 2-1 shows the keyboards most commonly used with Macs. The Plus keyboard comes with the Macintosh Plus, and the Portable keyboard comes with the Macintosh Portable. The remaining keyboards—the regular keyboard and the extended keyboard—are optional keyboards for the Classic, SE, and II families of Macs; you'll usually find one or the other with any of these Macs. Notice that the extended keyboard offers a row of function keys and other keys not found on the other keyboards, and that the Portable keyboard lacks the numeric keypad found on the right of the other keyboards. Despite the differences, most keys are common to all keyboards.

(A) The Macintosh Plus keyboard

*(continued)*

**FIGURE 2-1.** *Keyboards typically used with different Macintosh systems.*

**FIGURE 2-1.** *continued*

(B) The Macintosh Portable keyboard

(C) The regular keyboard

(D) The extended keyboard

## The character keys

The character keys are the majority of keys in the center of the keyboard. They are labeled with letters, numerals, and special symbols such as [ and =. When you press a character key, you enter a character in your document. You might be surprised to know that the space bar is also a character key; each time you press it, you enter a space character.

## The Tab key

The Tab key moves the insertion point to the next tab stop to the right. When you first start Word, tab stops are set at half-inch intervals. (You'll learn to set tab stops in Chapter 6, ''Aligning Text with Tabs.'')

## The Shift, Caps Lock, Control, Option, and Command keys

These five keys are modifiers: They work in conjunction with other keys. For example, pressing the A key by itself puts a lowercase *a* on the screen. If you hold down the Shift key and press the A key, you'll see an uppercase *A* on the screen. These are the modifier keys and their effects:

- The Shift key (labeled *shift*) used with character keys produces capital letters and also produces the upper symbols marked on some keys, such as @, %, and *.

- The Caps Lock key (labeled *caps lock*) also produces capital letters and, because it locks on, is especially useful for long strings of capital letters such as titles. Press Caps Lock once to turn it on and type capital letters; press it again to turn it off and type lowercase letters. Unlike the Shift key, Caps Lock doesn't produce upper key symbols such as those above numeral keys. Use the Shift key for those.

- The Command key (labeled with the clover symbol and, on most keyboards, also with the apple symbol) works with other keys to execute commands from the menus. For example, holding down Command and pressing S will save your document. These key combinations are called *keyboard shortcuts* for menu commands.

- The Option key (labeled *option*) works with some character keys to produce special characters such as •.

- The Control key (labeled *control* and not found on the Plus keyboard) is occasionally used for keyboard shortcuts.

You often use these modifier keys together for keyboard shortcuts. For example, holding down the Shift and Command keys together and then pressing B turns boldface type on and off in a Word document window. In this book, key combinations are shown with a hyphen between the key names. (For example, the keyboard shortcut for bold just described would appear as Shift-Command-B.)

### The Delete and Del keys

Use the Delete and Del keys to correct errors as you type. (Del is found only on the extended keyboard.) Pressing Delete deletes the character to the left of the insertion point; pressing Del erases the character to the right of the insertion point.

### The Return key

Use the Return key at the end of each paragraph to start the next paragraph at the beginning of a new line. *Don't* use it at the end of each line! Each time you press the Return key, Word inserts a special paragraph mark (usually invisible) that separates one paragraph from the next. You don't need to use Return for each line in a paragraph because Word automatically starts a new line when you type to the right edge of the page. You'll see how this works later when you start entering the text of the business letter.

## PRACTICE

### Learning the keyboard

*Take some time to play with the keyboard now—and enter whatever you want to, experimenting with the characters you can put on the screen. For now, use only the keys you've read about so far. If you have an extended keyboard, avoid the function keys at the top of the keyboard— they execute commands that you haven't learned yet.*

1. If you're not already up and running Word, you'll need to turn on your Mac and start Word. Word automatically opens a blank document window.

2. Press any character keys to put characters in the document window.

3. Press the Delete key to back up and erase some of those characters.

4. Hold down a character key. Your Mac should start repeating the character until you release the key.

5. Hold down the Shift key and see what characters you get as you press character keys.

6. Turn on Caps Lock and try typing letters and then numbers. You should get capital letters and numbers on the screen. Turn off Caps Lock when you're finished.

7. Hold down the Option key and try typing characters. You'll see some special characters—for example, Option-8 produces a bullet (•).

Now for some more useful keys.

### The Esc key

The Esc key is a bailout key—use it to escape from a process you started but don't want to finish. For example, if you open a dialog box and then decide you don't want to use it, simply press Esc to close the dialog box without any effect on the document.

### The cursor keys and cursor-movement keys

Cursor keys move the insertion point through text in a document. They won't move the insertion point outside of the text. To show you which direction each cursor key moves the insertion point, the keys are labeled with arrows: up, down, left, and right. Each time you press a cursor key, the insertion point moves one character left or right, or one text line up or down. Try them out now on the text you last entered.

Cursor-movement keys (available only on the extended keyboard) move the insertion point in larger jumps than do the cursor keys, as follows:

- *Home* moves the insertion point to the upper left corner of the text area.

- *End* moves the insertion point to the bottom right corner of the text area. At least, it will if there's any text there. If there isn't any text there, it moves the insertion point to the right of the last character in the text area.

- *Page Up* moves the insertion point to the top line of text on the previous screen.

- *Page Down* moves the insertion point to the top line of text on the next screen.

## The numeric keypad

The numeric keypad, shown in Figure 2-2, augments the standard keys on the keyboard to help you enter numbers and move the insertion point. To use the numeric keypad for entering numbers, you must first turn Num Lock mode on by pressing the Clear key in the upper left corner of the numeric keypad. The message *Num. Lock* appears in the page-number area at the bottom left of the document window to show that Num Lock is on. To use the numeric keypad to move the insertion point, press the Clear key again to turn Num Lock off.

**FIGURE 2-2.** *The numeric keypad.*

When Num Lock is on, you can use the numeric keypad to quickly enter numbers (0 through 9), operators (=, /, *, -, and +), and decimal points. The Enter key starts a new paragraph in the same way that the Return key does. (Be careful, though: it's not entirely the same! You'll find that when you use the Enter key in key combinations, it doesn't produce the same results that the Return key does.)

When Num Lock is off, the numeric keypad helps you move the insertion point around, performing the same functions as the cursor keys and cursor-movement keys. The keys on the numeric keypad also open menus and select commands from the menus. The numeric-keypad keys in this mode function as follows:

- *4* moves the insertion point one character to the left.

- *6* moves the insertion point one character to the right.

- *8* moves the insertion point one text line up.

- *2* moves the insertion point one text line down.

- *7* moves the insertion point to the left edge of the current text line.

- *1* moves the insertion point to the right edge of the current text line.

- *9* moves the insertion point to the top line of text on the previous screen (the same function as the Page Up key).

- *3* moves the insertion point to the top line of text on the next screen (the same function as the Page Down key).

- *0* moves the insertion point back to its previous location (useful when you jump around in a document and lose your last place).

- . (decimal point) selects the menu bar so that you can open a menu by using a keyboard command (as described in Chapter 1, ''A Tour of Word'').

- * (asterisk) scrolls the document one line down.

- + (plus sign) scrolls the document one line up.

- - (hyphen) extends the selection to a specified character. (You'll learn more about text selection in Chapter 4, ''Text-Editing Techniques.'')

## The function keys

The function keys (available only on the extended keyboard) execute commands with a single keystroke—for example, a single function key can insert text or print a document. Because function keys initiate actions that can alter your document, you shouldn't press a function key unless you know what it does. (If you're curious, you'll find a complete list of function-key operations and keyboard shortcuts in the *Microsoft Word User's Guide*.)

## The Help key

The Help key (which appears only on the extended keyboard and which is grouped with the cursor-movement keys) turns the pointer into a question mark. Use the question-mark pointer to click on a feature or to choose a menu item for which you want more information. Word then displays the Help window, which contains help text for that feature. If you don't have an extended keyboard, you can produce the same results by pressing the key combination Command-? (question mark).

## The Power On key

The Power On key (on only the regular and extended keyboards), labeled with a left-pointing wedge, turns the computer on. The Power On key works only with the Macintosh II family of computers.

## PRACTICE

### Entering text

*Enough keyboard theory! Try using your keyboard to enter the text of the business letter shown in Figure 2-3.*

1. Close the document you just used for keyboard experimentation: Click on its close box in the upper left corner of its window. When Word asks if you want to save it, click on the No button.

2. Open a new, empty document: Choose the New command from the File menu.

3. Type the date and address as shown in Figure 2-3. Press Return at the end of each line. (Pressing Return twice creates a blank line between paragraphs. That blank line is actually an empty paragraph.)

4. Type *Dear Mr. Petruchio:* and then press Return twice. If you make mistakes as you type, press the Delete key to delete the incorrect characters, and then type the correct text.

5. Type the first paragraph of the letter body, and then press Return twice at the end of the paragraph. (Remember—don't press Return to end lines within the paragraph!) Notice that when you type to the end of a line, Word moves the insertion point and the word you're typing to the beginning of the next line. This feature is called *wordwrap*; it lets you type without worrying about either running off the edge of the page or splitting words.

9/9/92

Mr. Orloff Petruchio
General Manager
Typecast, Inc.
4526 Ardentia Lane
Heater, CA 93265

Dear Mr. Petruchio:

I just received the first shipment of 10,000 videotape packages you
printed for us. We have a problem. The first paragraph on the back
of the package should read:

Helltax!

A Horror Film for the Entire Family...

When IRS auditor Nicholas Axolotl is possessed by demons, a week of
terror begins for the hapless Trunhill family. As blood oozes from
stones, each family member must endure merciless and probing
questions from disembodied voices about recent spending habits.
Realistic portrayals of disallowed deductions and dire fiscal
consequences will raise hairs on the back of every viewing adult
while putting the kids to sleep. A perfect film for families with
overactive children. Rated PG-13.

You mistakenly printed "A perfect film for families with radioactive
children" in the last sentence. This severely limits the market for
this movie, so we must have the entire run reprinted with
corrections. I've tried to contact you by phone, but have had no luck.
Your secretary tells me you're negoshiating contracts at the Film
Fresno Festival. I can't believe you did this to me, you poltroon!
Please call me immediately. We must fix this problem now.

Yours sincerely,


Pieter Geestliefde
Marketing Director
Goretax Films
Oakland, CA 94601

**FIGURE 2-3.** *Enter the text exactly as it appears in this example.*

*Note that Word's line breaks on your screen might not match the line breaks shown in Figures 2-3 and 2-4. This is because some printers can fit fewer characters in a line than others, and Word adjusts the text on the screen to match whatever printer you have set up. If your Mac is set up to use a dot-matrix printer such as the Apple ImageWriter, it won't show the same breaks as Figures 2-3 and 2-4, which were created for a laser printer.*

6. Type the rest of the document through the end of the line "Yours sincerely." Be sure to include any misspellings in the text (you'll correct them later), and remember not to press Return until the end of each paragraph.

7. To create blank space for a signature, press Return three times to first end the current paragraph and then create two empty paragraphs.

8. Type the name and address of the sender.

*As the text window fills up, text scrolls up off the top of the window so that you can enter new lines at the bottom. In the next section, you'll learn how to scroll back to see the text at the beginning of your document.*

## EDITING TEXT

Very few of us have perfect typing and spelling skills; we make mistakes as we go, and catch them later. Even when we do enter text without mistakes, we may have second thoughts about some of it and decide to make changes. That's when the ability to edit text is extremely important.

The simplest way to edit text is to move the insertion point to the characters you want to change, press the Delete (or Del) key to erase characters, and then type new text—which is fine for limited changes. For more extensive revisions, you'll want to select a full block of text and use Word's editing commands to edit the text. Let's start with simple editing.

### Moving the Insertion Point

As you learned in the last section, you can use the cursor keys to move the insertion point through text in the document. A faster way is to move the pointer to the desired position in the document window and then click the mouse button. The insertion point moves to the new position. If you click on a spot outside the text (but inside the document window), the insertion point goes to the text nearest the pointer. If you click outside the document window, the Finder or another application becomes active.

Sometimes your viewpoint doesn't include the text you want to edit. If so, you can use the scroll bar to move to another location, and then click on the desired text to move the insertion point there.

## Using the Vertical Scroll Bar

When you look at a Word document, think of the document as a single, long page of text that grows as you add more text and shrinks as you remove text. The document window shows only part of the document at one time, but you can see any other part of the document by using the cursor keys (Word scrolls the text to follow the insertion point) or by using the vertical scroll bar, shown in Figure 2-4, to rapidly move upward or downward in the document.

The key to the scroll bar is the *scroll box*: Drag the scroll box up to move to a preceding part of the document; drag it down to move to a following part. The length of the scroll bar represents the length of the entire document, and the scroll box's location represents your location within the document. To move to any section of the document, drag the scroll box to the approximate location you want to view.

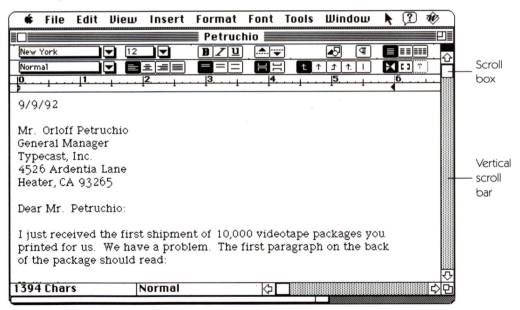

**FIGURE 2-4.** *Use the vertical scroll bar to rapidly move your viewpoint.*

If you want to fine-tune your location, you can use the vertical scroll bar in two other ways:

- Click on the up arrow or down arrow of the scroll bar to scroll the text one line down or up.

- Click on the shaded section of the scroll bar above or below the scroll box to scroll the text down or up by a full screen.

## PRACTICE

### Using the scroll bar

*Try using the scroll bar now on your business letter. If you haven't changed your location since you finished typing, the bottom part of the letter appears in the document window. Try moving up and down through the letter:*

1. Drag the vertical scroll box to the top of the scroll bar's shaded area. When you release the scroll box, you'll see the top of the document.

2. Click on the scroll bar below the scroll box. The scroll box moves down, and you'll see the text in the middle of the document.

3. Click once on the vertical scroll-bar up arrow. The text scrolls down one line.

4. Hold the mouse button down while pointing at the vertical scroll-bar up arrow. The text continuously scrolls down, one line at a time. Continue all the way to the top of the document.

Note one important fact about the scroll bar: When you use it to scroll the text, the insertion point remains in its original location. To move the insertion point to the new location, click on a character at the new location. If you move to a new location, leave the insertion point behind and out of sight, and then start typing, Word automatically scrolls the text back to the insertion point to keep you from typing in the dark.

The horizontal scroll bar along the bottom of the document window works in much the same way as the vertical scroll bar, but it scrolls text horizontally across the document rather than vertically. Most documents created for printout on 8½-by-11-inch paper don't show any text beyond the right edge of the text area, so you usually won't need to use the horizontal scroll bar. If you create documents that have wide text margins or if you shrink the size of the document window, you might need to use the horizontal scroll bar to scroll from side to side as you view text.

## PRACTICE

### Editing text

*If you typed the letter exactly as it is shown in Figure 2-3, it contains several mistakes. You may even find some of your own! Now's the time to correct them:*

1. Use the cursor keys or the vertical scroll bar to move to the end of the letter. You must be able to see the last full paragraph before the paragraph "Yours sincerely."

2. Place the insertion point between the "h" and the "i" of the word "negoshiating" in the last paragraph.

3. Delete the "h" and the "s" by pressing Delete twice.

4. Type *t* to replace the "sh."

*The text to the right of the insertion point moves to the left to fill in when you delete characters, and the text moves right to make space for new characters as you type. You can insert as much text as you want; Word pushes following text to the right and then to the beginning of the next line if necessary. Try it out. Insert the phrase* at your expense *at the end of the second sentence:*

5. Place the insertion point between the letter "s" and the period in the sentence that ends with the words "with corrections."

6. Type a space followed by *at your expense.*

*The rest of the text in the paragraph moves to the right and then down to following lines to accommodate the inserted phrase.*

## Selecting Text

Moving the insertion point is an effective way to correct small mistakes, but it's not an easy way to delete or move large sections of text. Word's editing commands are more efficient. To use them, you must first *select* the block of text you want to work on, which points out to Word the exact section of text you want to edit. The easiest way to select text is to use the pointer to indicate the beginning and end of the text block.

### Selecting text using the mouse

Move the pointer to the beginning (or end) of the text you want to select, and then drag the pointer (by holding down the mouse button) to the other end of the text. Word highlights the text as you drag. When you release the mouse button, the text remains highlighted. This highlighted text is called a *selected text block*. To drag to a section beyond the top or bottom of the screen, move the pointer to the top or bottom border of the document window; Word scrolls the text down or up in the indicated direction.

If you want to select a block of text without dragging the pointer, you can move the pointer to one end of the text block and click, hold down the Shift key, move the pointer to the other end of the text block, click again, and release the Shift key. Word highlights the text block. This process is called *extended selection*, and it allows you to select a very long text block. For example, you can click once at the beginning of a document and hold down the Shift key, use the scroll bar or cursor-movement keys to move far down the document, and then click again to define a very long text block.

### Selecting text using the keyboard

If you don't want to take your hands off the keyboard to select a text block, you can use the cursor and cursor-movement keys. First move the insertion point to the beginning (or end) of the text you want to select. Next hold down the Shift key and move the insertion point to the other end of the text, and then release the Shift key. As you move the insertion point, Word highlights the text block. The highlight remains when you release the Shift key.

## Deselecting Text

To *deselect* a block of text (remove the highlight), simply move the insertion point to a new location using the mouse or keyboard. When the insertion point appears, the text block selection disappears—it's no longer highlighted.

## Editing Commands

Selecting a text block is the first half of editing. The second half is choosing a Word command to edit the text in the block. The Edit menu contains most of the editing commands that work with selected text. The standard editing commands are Cut, Copy, and Paste—try them now.

### Using editing commands

*The first block of text you want to change is the sentence "I can't believe you did this to me, you poltroon!" which now seems a bit strong. To delete the sentence, first select it as shown in Figure 2-5. Try selecting the sentence using the mouse:*

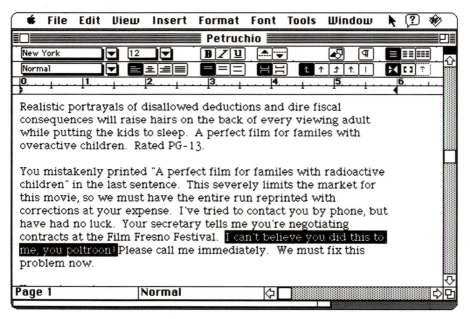

**FIGURE 2-5.** *The selected sentence is a text block to be deleted.*

1. Move the pointer to the spot immediately preceding the ''I'' at the beginning of the sentence.

2. Drag the pointer (by holding down the mouse button) to the spot immediately preceding ''Please'' at the beginning of the following sentence, and then release the button.

3. Choose the Cut command from the Edit menu. The sentence disappears from your letter, and the text following it moves to the left and up.

*Now try moving text from one location to another. The phrase "Film Fresno Festival," in the last paragraph, should read "Fresno Film Festival." To move the word "Film" to a new location behind the word "Fresno," take the following steps:*

4. Select the word ''Film'' and the space following it.

5. Choose the Cut command from the Edit menu. The word ''Film'' disappears from the letter.

6. Move the insertion point so that it immediately precedes the letter ''F'' of ''Festival.''

7. Choose the Paste command from the Edit menu. Word inserts ''Film'' between ''Fresno'' and ''Festival.''

## The Clipboard

When you use the Cut command, Word removes the text you selected and stores it in a part of memory called the *Clipboard.* The Copy command is similar: It instructs Word to create a copy of the selected text and place the copy in the Clipboard without removing the original text from the document. The Paste command instructs Word to insert the contents of the Clipboard into the document at the insertion-point location.

It's important to know that the Clipboard retains only one block of text at a time. When you use the Cut or Copy command on a new block of text, the old block in the Clipboard is removed from memory and disappears forever! If you want to see the contents of the Clipboard at any time, you can choose the Show Clipboard command from the Window menu, which opens the Clipboard window. Don't be fooled by the small size of the window; the

Clipboard can hold large blocks of text, limited only by the amount of available memory in your Mac.

# FORMATTING TEXT

Now that you've entered and edited your business letter, you can spruce up its appearance by emphasizing some of the words and by resetting selected paragraph margins to make some paragraphs stand out. Changing the appearance of your document this way is called *formatting*. Word offers four types of formatting that control the appearance of characters, paragraphs, document sections, and entire documents; but for most documents, all you'll need are character and paragraph formatting, which we'll look at now.

## Character Formatting

Character formatting changes the appearance of characters in a text block. You can use it to add emphasis to text by setting the text in boldface or italic, adding color, or underlining the text. You can also change the typeface, font, or spacing between characters. To help you perform character formatting, Word offers format controls in three places: the Ribbon at the top of the document window, a set of commands at the bottom of the Format menu, and the Character dialog box you open by choosing Character from the Format menu.

### Using the Ribbon

The Ribbon, shown in Figure 2-6, controls character formatting with the controls in its left and center. To add emphasis to text, first select the text, and then click on the B, I, or U buttons, which control boldface, italics, and underlining. One click turns on an emphasis, another turns it off. When an emphasis is on, Word highlights the corresponding button.

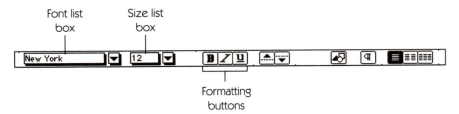

**FIGURE 2-6.** *The Ribbon controls character formatting.*

## PRACTICE

### Boldfacing with the Ribbon

*For some added punch, put the movie title "Helltax!" in boldface using the ribbon:*

1. Select the word "Helltax!" (including the exclamation point).

2. Click on the B button in the Ribbon. Word highlights the button to show that boldface is on, and "Helltax!" now appears in boldface, which you can see when you deselect the word.

## Using formatting commands

You can also format text in a selected block by choosing one of the commands at the bottom of the Format menu. These commands control emphasis and also control capitalization. Give them a try.

## PRACTICE

### Formatting with Format menu commands

1. Select the word "must" in the sentence at the end of the document that reads "We must fix this problem now."

2. Choose the Bold command from the Format menu. This turns the text into boldface characters.

3. Choose the Italic command from the Format menu. This turns the text into boldface italic characters.

4. Choose the Bold command once again from the Format menu. This turns boldface off, so the text is now in italic only.

5. Select a text block from the beginning of "H" in the title "Helltax!" extending through to the end of the word "Family..." in the line below.

6. Choose the Change Case command from the Format menu to open the Change Case dialog box. UPPER CASE is already selected in the dialog box.

7. Click on the OK button to close the dialog box and change the text to all capitals.

*Notice that you can combine types of emphasis. In this example, you combined boldface and italic for extra emphasis. Notice also that you can use keyboard shortcuts to execute some of these commands: For example, Shift-Command-B executes the Bold command; Shift-Command-I executes the Italic command.*

## Using the Character dialog box

The Character dialog box, shown in Figure 2-7, offers a third way to format characters. Although it takes a little more time to use, it gives you a few more options than either the Ribbon or the Format commands you just used. To open the Character dialog box, choose the Character command from the Format menu.

As you can see, the different areas of the Character dialog box offer some options not available anywhere else. For example, the Style box offers some new types of emphasis—Shadow, Strikethru, and others. The Color list box, which you can open by clicking on the box, offers eight colors you can apply

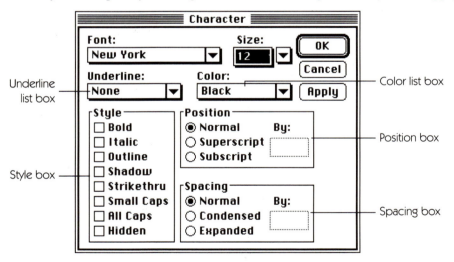

**FIGURE 2-7.** *The Character dialog box offers character-formatting options.*

to selected text. (You won't see the colors if you have a black and white monitor, but you can select them nonetheless for printing on a color printer.) The Underline list box gives you different kinds of underlining, the Spacing box lets you control the spacing between characters, and the Position box controls subscript and superscript characters. You won't need most of these for everyday work, but now you know where to find them if you do need them.

## PRACTICE
### Underlining with the Character dialog box

*Give the Character dialog box a try by underlining a word:*

1. Select the word "radioactive" in the sentence "A perfect film for radioactive children."

2. Choose the Character command from the Format menu to open the Character dialog box.

3. Click and hold on the Underline list box. The list opens to reveal the types of underlining available.

4. Drag the pointer down to the Single option and release the mouse button. The list closes, and *Single* appears in the list box.

5. Click on the OK button (or press the Return key) to close the dialog box. The word "radioactive" is now underlined with a single line.

*Note that if you click on the Cancel button in the dialog box or press the Esc key, the dialog box will close without applying any character formatting, even if you selected a formatting option.*

## Paragraph Formatting

Character formatting affects the smallest units of a document: characters. Paragraph formatting, the next level up, affects full paragraphs at a time, changing indents, line spacing, and other paragraph attributes. To use paragraph formatting, you must first select a text block, just as you do for character formatting. However, there's an important difference.

Because paragraph formatting affects only full paragraphs—all the text between the paragraph marks you insert by pressing Return—paragraph formatting will affect all of a paragraph even if the paragraph is not fully selected. For example, you might select only a word in a surrounding paragraph and then use paragraph formatting. *All* the text in the paragraph is affected. In fact, you can select a paragraph for paragraph formatting simply by putting the insertion point in the paragraph, or by including a single character of the paragraph in a text block.

### Setting indents

The Ruler, shown in Figure 2-8, contains controls for paragraph formatting. It uses markers along the measure to show you the left and right indents of the paragraph (or paragraphs) you select. The left indent marker is the lower half of the wedge at the left of the Ruler. The first-line indent marker is the upper half of the wedge, which shows the left indent of the first line of the paragraph. (This indent can be different from the left indent of the rest of the paragraph.) The right indent marker is the solid wedge at the right of the Ruler.

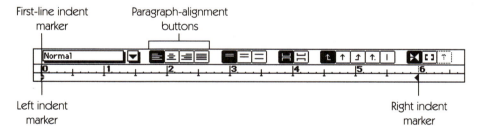

**FIGURE 2-8**. *The Ruler shows the indents of selected paragraphs.*

You can drag any of these markers to new locations on the Ruler to set new paragraph indents. The markers indent from the left and right margins, which are typically set 1.25 inches in from the edges of the paper. That means that the 0 mark on the Ruler is usually 1.25 inches in from the left edge of the paper, and the 6 mark is usually 1.25 inches in from the right edge of an 8½-by-11-inch piece of paper.

## PRACTICE

### Changing indents

*Change the left indent of the paragraph "9/9/92" so that it starts in the middle of the page as follows:*

1. Move the insertion point into the paragraph.

2. Drag the left indent marker (the lower half of the wedge on the left side of the Ruler) from the 0 mark to the 3 mark on the Ruler. The first-line indent marker (the upper half of the wedge) moves with the left indent marker as you drag it. The date now appears in the middle of the screen, aligned with the new left indent setting.

*Now try moving inward both left and right indents in the paragraph that describes the movie so that the paragraph is set off from the rest of the letter as a quotation:*

1. Place the insertion point anywhere in the paragraph that begins "When IRS auditor...."

2. Drag the left indent marker from the 0 mark to the 0.5 mark on the Ruler (halfway between the 0 and 1 marks).

3. Drag the right indent marker from the 6 mark to the 5.5 mark on the Ruler (halfway between the 5 and 6 marks). The paragraph is now indented from the rest of the letter by 0.5 inch on each side.

## Setting alignment

You can also control the *alignment* of paragraphs, which is the way the paragraph text fits against its indents. Paragraphs usually appear *left aligned*; that is, the left edge of the text lines up evenly, and the right edge is uneven. A *right-aligned* paragraph lines up the right edge of text evenly and leaves the left edge uneven. A *center-aligned* paragraph centers each line of text with uneven edges on both sides. And *full justification* (called simply "justified" in Word) fits the words in each line so that both the left and right edges of the line are even against the indents, like the paragraphs in this book.

To set justification for a paragraph, select the paragraph, and then click on any one of the alignment buttons in the Ruler.

**PRACTICE**

### Changing justification

*Try changing the justification of different paragraphs, starting with the paragraph that was selected in the last practice session:*

1. Click the justified-alignment button in the Ruler (the right-most of the four alignment buttons, which are just left of the center of the Ruler). The paragraph text is lined up evenly against both left and right indents.

2. Select a text block beginning in the middle of "Helltax!" and extending down to the middle of the word "Film." (Even though both paragraphs aren't fully contained in the text block, they're both fully selected for paragraph formatting.)

3. Click on the centered-alignment button in the Ruler (the second button from the left of the four alignment buttons, showing centered lines of text). The two paragraphs appear centered on the page.

That's it—you've finished formatting your letter! It should now look like the document in Figure 2-9.

## SAVING A DOCUMENT

It's sometimes tempting to print and close a document when you're finished without ever saving it on disk. However, it's not always wise. You might read your printout and find uncorrected mistakes. Or you might want to send an identical letter to a different person. If you saved the document, you can reopen it, revise it, and print it out again. If you didn't save it, you'll have to type it all over from scratch. Make it a practice to always save a document before printing it; you can delete the file later if you don't need it.

Saving a document at regular intervals as you work is also wise. That way, if the power goes off and your document disappears from the screen, when the power comes back on you can simply reopen the document and regain most of your work. A rule of thumb is to save your document every 15 minutes so that the most you can lose is 15 minutes' worth of work.

9/9/92

Mr. Orloff Petruchio
General Manager
Typecast, Inc.
4526 Ardentia Lane
Heater, CA 93265

Dear Mr. Petruchio:

I just received the first shipment of 10,000 videotape packages you printed for us. We have a problem. The first paragraph on the back of the package should read:

**HELLTAX!**

A HORROR FILM FOR THE ENTIRE FAMILY...

When IRS auditor Nicholas Axolotl is possessed by demons, a week of terror begins for the hapless Trunhill family. As blood oozes from stones, each family member must endure merciless and probing questions from disembodied voices about recent spending habits. Realistic portrayals of disallowed deductions and dire fiscal consequences will raise hairs on the back of every viewing adult while putting the kids to sleep. A perfect film for families with overactive children. Rated PG-13.

You mistakenly printed "A perfect film for families with radioactive children" in the last sentence. This severely limits the market for this movie, so we must have the entire run reprinted with corrections at your expense. I've tried to contact you by phone, but have had no luck. Your secretary tells me you're negotiating contracts at the Fresno Film Festival. Please call me immediately. We *must* fix this problem now.

Yours sincerely,


Pieter Geestliefde
Marketing Director
Goretax Films
Oakland, CA 94601

**FIGURE 2-9.** *The finished business letter includes character and paragraph formatting that emphasizes parts of the letter.*

## Using the Save Command

Choose the Save command from the File menu to save a document. You can tell if a document hasn't ever been saved by looking at the title bar of the document window: It's untitled if it's unsaved. When you save a document, you give it a name that then appears in the title bar.

Word has two simple rules about filenames: A filename can be no longer than 31 characters, and you can use any characters except the colon (:). One suggestion: Try to choose a filename that reminds you of the contents of your document.

### PRACTICE

### Saving a letter

*To save your sample letter, take the following steps:*

1. Choose the Save command from the File menu. A Save dialog box, shown in Figure 2-10, appears.

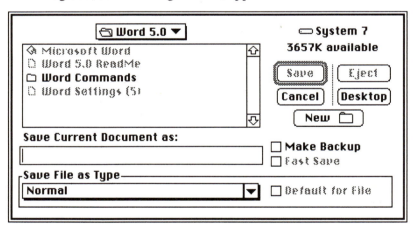

**FIGURE 2-10.** *The Save dialog box.*

2. Type *Petruchio*, a filename that reminds you of the letter's recipient, in the Save Current Document As text box.

3. Click on the Save button or press Return. The dialog box closes and is replaced with a Summary Info dialog box.

4. Create a blank summary for your document by clicking on the OK button. The dialog box closes, and Word saves your document on disk, in the same folder in which Word is located, under the filename "Petruchio." (You'll learn more about document summaries and saving documents to other folders in Chapter 8, "Saving, Opening, and Printing a Document.")

## Using the Save As Command

The Save dialog box appears only the first time you save a document using the Save command. Each time you use Save after that, Word automatically saves your document to the same file, erasing the previous version of the document.

If you want to save a new version of your document without erasing the previous version, choose  the Save As command from the File menu to save your document with a new filename. The Save dialog box opens, and you can then enter a new filename. Word saves your document in a new file, so your old version is intact in its old file. You'll notice a change: The title bar of the document window shows the new filename, and each time you use the Save command for this document, Word saves the revision with the new filename.

# PRINTING A DOCUMENT

The last step in creating a document is printing. The process of printing is slightly different for each different kind of printer you can connect to a Macintosh, but the overall process is the same. Try printing your business letter.

## PRACTICE
### Printing

*Before you begin printing, take the following steps:*

1. Be sure your printer is turned on.

2. Be sure your printer is *on line*, ready to accept information from your computer. (On some printers, a light labeled *select* or *ready* will be lit if your printer is on line.)

3. Be sure the paper is in the proper position for printing. If your printer uses loose sheets of paper, check the supply of paper in the paper tray. If your printer accepts pinfeed paper (fanfold paper with small perforations along the edges), check that the paper in the printer is aligned so that the print head will begin printing at the very top of the page.

*When your printer is ready, you can print your document. Try it now on the letter you created.*

1. Choose the Print command from the File menu. The Print dialog box appears.

2. Click on the Print button to close the dialog box and begin printing. A message box appears, indicating that your document is being printed; the bottom line of the Word window displays the number of pages in your document; and your printer begins to print.

*Your printout will look like Figure 2-9 if you have a LaserWriter or similar printer. If you have a dot-matrix printer such as an ImageWriter, the line breaks may be a little different and the characters not as smoothly formed, but the document should look much the same.*

## CLOSING AND OPENING DOCUMENTS

When you're finished with one document, you can close it to remove its document window from the screen. You can then start another document, beginning a with a new blank document window, or open a previously saved document for revision.

### Closing a Document

You close a document by clicking on the close box of its document window or by choosing the Close command from the File menu. If you have unsaved work in the document, Word asks you if you want to save it before closing.

## PRACTICE

### Closing a document

*Try closing your business letter:*

1. Choose the Close command from the File menu. If you've made changes or printed since you last saved, a dialog box appears, asking whether you want to save changes.

2. Click on the Yes button to save changes and close; click on the No button to close without saving changes. (Click on the Cancel button if you change your mind and don't want to close the document.) When the document closes, the document window disappears.

## Beginning a New Document

Opening a new blank document is simple: Choose the New command from the File menu. An untitled document window appears, in which you can start work on your new document.

## Opening a Previously Saved Document

To work on a previously saved document, choose the Open command from the File menu to activate the Open dialog box, and then choose a document from the list of filenames.

## PRACTICE

### Opening a document

*Try opening the business letter you just saved:*

1. Choose the Open command from the File menu. The Open dialog box, shown in Figure 2-11, appears.

2. Double-click on the filename "Petruchio" in the scrolling list. The dialog box closes, and the business letter appears in a new document window with the title "Petruchio."

If you want to reopen a document you recently closed, you can probably find its filename near the bottom of the File menu, where Word keeps the names of

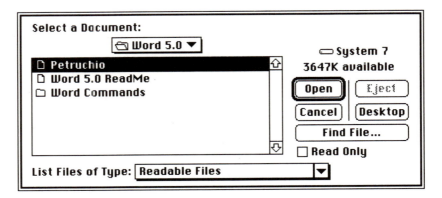

**FIGURE 2-11.** *The Open dialog box.*

the last four documents you closed. Look there now—you should see the name "Petruchio" near the bottom of the File menu. You can open any of the listed documents by simply choosing its name—a quick and convenient technique for opening a recently closed document.

One handy tip to use with a newly opened document: The insertion point always appears at the very beginning of the document. If you want to go back to the spot where you last worked in the document, press the 0 key on the numeric keypad. It moves the insertion point back to your previous location.

Note that it's possible to have more than one open document on the screen at the same time; if you do, the document windows overlap each other. You can activate a document window by clicking on it, or by choosing its name from the Window menu.

## Quitting Word

When you finish using Word, you quit by choosing the Quit command from the File menu. Ever vigilant, Word displays a dialog box if you have unsaved work that asks if you want to save changes. Click on the Yes button to save changes and then quit, click on the No button to quit without saving changes, or click on the Cancel button to go back to running Word.

Congratulations! You're now an accomplished Word user. At least, you're accomplished enough to create and print most standard simple documents. You'll find that Word has many more features to make your work easier and to produce even more impressive documents. But that's the subject for another section of this book—the next one, in fact.

# SECTION II

# For Everyday Work

# Chapter 3

# Formatting and Entering Characters

A Macintosh running Microsoft Word 5 offers a variety of options that are only a distant dream to typewriter users: characters so large that each one fills a page; characters so small that you need a magnifying glass to read them clearly; typefaces that run the gamut from bold and blocky to flowing and cursive; special characters such as ≠ and ®; and characters such as ü and é used for spelling words in languages other than English.

This chapter answers questions about getting the most from all of these character options: What are fonts, and how do I choose one that's appropriate? How do I set the size of the characters? How do I emphasize certain characters and set them apart from surrounding text? What techniques can I use to format characters? And how do I enter special characters?

# CHARACTER FORMATTING

*Character formatting* controls the appearance of characters in your document. Word offers three overall ways to format characters:

- Changing *fonts* (the typefaces used to display and print text)
- Setting *character size* (the height and width of the characters)
- Applying *type styles* (formats such as an underlining or boldface emphasis)

## Changing Fonts

What is a font? As defined in the Macintosh world, it's a family of characters that have the same design. For example, the characters you're reading now in this paragraph all belong to the same font (technically called a *typeface*), even though some of the characters are in italic. A stylistic unity ties all the characters together—they have a similar weight and flow when read.

Each Macintosh font has a *character set*—that is, a collection of characters that you can produce by pressing keys. Most fonts have a standard set of characters: uppercase and lowercase letters of the alphabet, the ten numerals, and special symbols such as • and %. Some special fonts, however, don't use a standard character set, but produce nonstandard characters when you press the keys. For example, some fonts produce Cyrillic characters (used for Russian and other Slavic languages) instead of producing letters of the Roman alphabet. Your Mac probably has at least one special font, Symbol, which produces Greek characters, math symbols, and other symbols such as hearts, clubs, spades, and diamonds.

## PRACTICE

### Playing with fonts

*Now try some of the different fonts available to you:*

1. Start with a new document. If you haven't yet started Word, start it now and it will automatically open a new document for you. If you're already working with Word, choose the New command from the File menu.

2. Type a few words of text and press Return. The text should appear in the *default font,* the font Word automatically sets when it opens a new document. The default font is normally the New York font.

3. Choose Helvetica from the Font list box in the Ribbon, and then type a few more words of text and press Return. The text using the new font should look different from the text using the previous font.

4. Choose Symbol from the Font list box in the Ribbon, type a few words of text, and press Return. It should look like Greek to you, because it is!

5. Experiment by choosing the other available fonts and typing text. You should see the full variety of typefaces available to you within Word. You can see examples of common fonts in Figure 3-1.

## Font Availability

If you go from one Macintosh to another and run Word on each, you'll probably find a different set of fonts available on each computer. That's because Word uses whatever fonts are installed on the Mac—that is, whatever fonts are stored in the System Folder on the Mac's hard disk. You can add or remove fonts to or from your Mac by dragging them in and out of the System Folder. The Chicago, Courier, Geneva, Helvetica, Monaco, New York, Symbol, and Times fonts are standard with System 7 software (the newest release of the software that runs your Mac), so you can expect to find at least these fonts when you check the fonts available within Word.

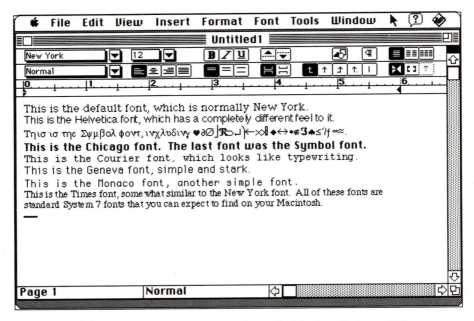

**FIGURE 3-1.** *The standard fonts available on the Macintosh give a different appearance to characters.*

If you want to use more fonts with Word, you can buy Mac-compatible fonts at most computer stores and add them to your System Folder. You'll find information about the process in the documentation that came with your Mac or with your system software.

## Fonts in Printout

The Mac offers two types of fonts: *bitmap fonts* and *outline fonts*. If you have a large collection of fonts, you might notice that a few of them don't look very good when printed on paper. Without getting into gory details, outline fonts look much better than bitmap fonts when printed. An outline font looks smooth and refined on the printed page, whereas a bitmap font looks every bit as jagged and dotty when printed as it does on the screen. Outline fonts have an additional advantage: No matter how large or small you make them, they'll still look smooth. Bitmap fonts often look even more jagged if you increase or decrease their standard size.

How do you tell which fonts will look good on paper? To begin with, any TrueType font (Apple's type of outline font) will look good when printed. The fonts included with System 7 are TrueType fonts, so your Mac's standard fonts should print well. To see whether a font is a TrueType font, select the font from the Font list box in the Ribbon, and then open the Size list box in the Ribbon. A TrueType font will have a wide range of sizes available from 7 points up to 72 points; a bitmap font will usually have no more than seven or eight sizes.

A TrueType font looks good both on the screen and on paper. Other types of outline fonts, such as PostScript, BitStream, and other commercial types of outline fonts, look as jagged on the screen as a bitmap font does, but print as smoothly as TrueType. These fonts are called *printer outline fonts*. There's no simple way to tell whether a font is a bitmap or a printer outline font from within Word. The best way to tell is to print the font. If a font looks rough on paper, it's a simple bitmap font with no printer outline equivalent. If it looks smooth on paper, it's a printer outline font. Another way to check printer outline fonts is to read your printer manual (if you have a letter-quality printer such as a laser printer). The manual will list which outline fonts your printer can print. Examples of printer outline fonts are Palatino and Bookman.

## PRACTICE

### Characters: Printed vs. on-screen

*Look at the difference in smoothness between the document on the screen and the document printed on paper:*

1. Make sure your printer is turned on and ready to print.

2. Choose the Print command from the File menu to open the Print dialog box for your printer.

3. If the Print dialog box offers a choice of print quality options, click on the Best radio button if it isn't already selected.

4. Click on the Print button to start printing. When the printout is finished, compare it to the document on the screen. The printed characters should look smoother than the screen

characters, especially if you use a laser printer or an ink-jet printer, unless the characters are bitmap characters. Figure 3-2 shows an example of a printer outline font.

5. Close the document without saving it when you're done.

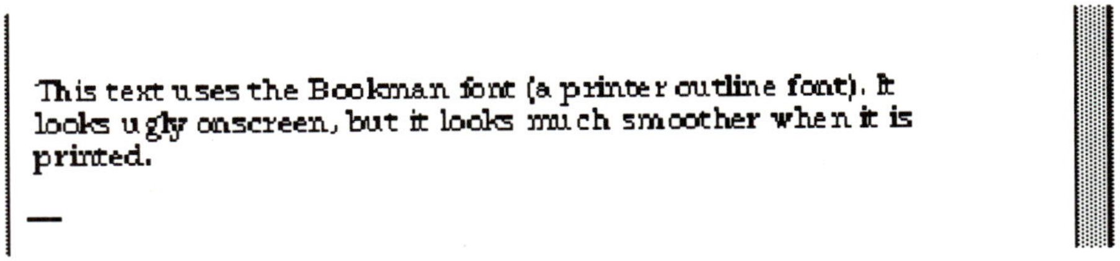

This text uses the Bookman font (a printer outline font). It looks ugly onscreen, but it looks much smoother when it is printed.

FIGURE 3-2. *These on-screen characters will look much smoother when they are output on a laser printer.*

## Setting a Point Size

To change the size of characters, you change their *point size*. Point size is so called because it's measured in *points,* traditional typesetting units of measurement equal to approximately $\frac{1}{72}$ inch. A character set's point size is its height from the bottom of a descender (such as the hook on a ''j'') to the top of a capital letter. A 13-point character is taller (and correspondingly wider) than its 10-point counterpart.

Do some point sizes look better when printed than others? If you're using an outline font such as New York or Helvetica, all point sizes will look well formed and smooth. If you're using a bitmap font without a PostScript or similar printer outline font for your printer, all sizes will look a little rough. Some point sizes, in fact, will look extremely distorted both on screen and when printed.

How do you tell which point sizes are best? If you choose a bitmap font and then look in the Font menu at the available sizes, you will see some sizes displayed in outline characters. As a rule of thumb, use the point sizes displayed in outline characters whenever possible, unless you know for sure that the font is a TrueType font or a printer outline font. In that case, even sizes that look bad on screen look good when printed.

## PRACTICE

### Using multiple point sizes

*Try entering text in different point sizes:*

1. Choose the New command from the File menu to open a new document.

2. Select the New York font from the Font list box in the Ribbon if it isn't already selected. Select 12 from the Size list box in the Ribbon if it isn't already selected.

3. Type a few words on a single line without pressing Return.

4. Choose 14 from the Size list box in the Ribbon and type a few more words, again without pressing Return. The text should appear in 14-point characters, which are larger than 12-point characters.

5. Choose 36 from the Size list box in the Ribbon and type a few more words. The text appears in much larger characters.

6. Experiment with other point sizes, and then close the document without saving when you're finished with it.

Notice that as you type text in large point sizes Word changes the line spacing to accommodate the larger characters (as shown in Figure 3-3). Word does this even when you type multiple point sizes in one line.

## Applying Type Styles

Changing font and point size are the first two kinds of character formatting you can perform; the third is applying *type styles* to add emphasis to text. A type style alters existing characters (whose basic shapes are set by font and point size) to set text apart from surrounding text. Italic text, for example, is a type style that slants characters to the right so they stand out from ordinary text around them. Other type styles include bold, four kinds of underlining, strikethrough, outline, shadow, small caps, all caps, hidden text, and colored text. (Table 3-1 on pages 62–63 displays each of these type styles and describes how to turn them on and off.)

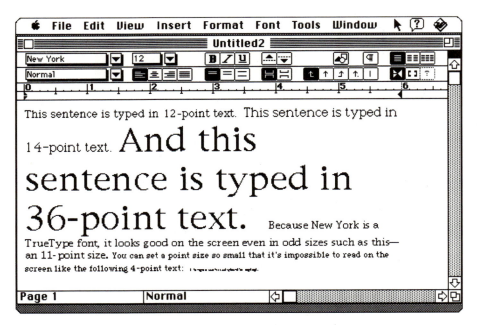

**FIGURE 3-3.** *Changing point sizes changes the line spacing of the text you've entered.*

When you format characters, you can choose only a single font and a single point size at one time, but you can combine type styles that modify the font and size for different effects. You can, for example, use bold, italic, outline, and shadow type styles all together, although the results may look quite baroque.

A few type styles can't be combined. You can use only one kind of underline type style at a time—choosing one underline type style turns off any other underline type style. Likewise, you can't use superscript and subscript type styles simultaneously—choosing one turns off the other.

## Applying Character Formatting

Whenever you apply character formatting, you have two choices about when you apply the formatting: You can apply it before you type, or you can apply it after you type. In this chapter, you've applied character formatting before typing. For example, you chose a new font, typed text in that font, chose another font, and then typed text in that font. In the last chapter, you applied formatting after you typed: You selected a text block and then chose character formatting to apply the formatting to the text block.

When is it best to apply formatting? It depends on your writing habits. If you want to apply formatting as the spirit moves you while writing—adding italic to emphasize a word, for example—apply before you type: Turn on italic, type, and then turn off italic. If you like to go back through text and polish its appearance, apply after you type: Select the text you want, and then apply the formatting.

When you apply character formatting, you can use any of the following methods:

- Using Ribbon controls
- Choosing commands from the Format or Font menu
- Choosing options from the Format Character dialog box
- Using keyboard shortcuts

## The Ribbon

Using the Ribbon (shown in Figure 3-4) is the simplest way to apply character formatting. You can choose a new font from the Font list box on its left; choose a new point size from the Size list box next to the Font list box; or turn on (or off) bold, italic, underline, superscript, or subscript type styles by clicking on the appropriate button in the middle of the Ribbon.

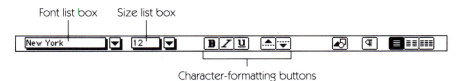

**FIGURE 3-4.** *Ribbon controls are the quickest way to apply character formatting.*

The Ribbon controls are easy to use. The bold, italic, and underline buttons turn the corresponding type style on or off each time you click on them. The button is highlighted when a type style is on, white when it's off. The

Font and Size list boxes are also easy to use: Click on the small arrow to the right of a list box to open a menu showing available options, drag down to highlight the choice you want, and then release. You can also click on the main part of the Font or Size list box (which turns it black), type in the font or the point size you want, and then press Return.

The Ribbon is easy to use, but it doesn't give you access to every possible character-formatting option. For example, you can't use the Ribbon to set alternative forms of underlining or to apply other forms of emphasis such as colored or hidden text.

## The Format menu

Choosing character-formatting commands from the Format menu (as shown in Figure 3-5) or the Font menu is another way to quickly format characters. You'll find a limited set of type style commands (Bold, Italic, and Underline) at the bottom of the Format menu—choose a type style command once to turn on the type style, and choose it once again to turn off the type style. (A type style has a checkmark in front of it when the type style is on.) You'll also

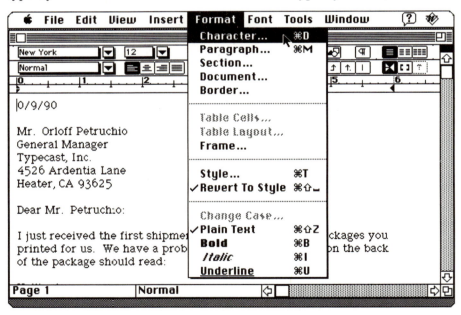

**FIGURE 3-5.** *The Format menu.*

58

find a Plain Text command. If you choose Plain Text, you turn off all other type styles that are set, which gives you plain text.

The Change Case command isn't really a character-formatting command because it doesn't really change character appearance. Instead, it changes lowercase characters to uppercase and vice versa. To use the Change Case command, first select a block of text. Next choose the Change Case command to open the Change Case dialog box shown in Figure 3-6. The Change Case dialog box has five options:

- UPPERCASE, which turns every letter in the text block into an uppercase letter.

- lowercase, which turns all letters in the text block into lowercase letters.

- Title Case, which capitalizes the first letter of every word in the text block and turns all other letters into lowercase letters.

- Sentence case., which capitalizes the first letter of the text block.

- tOGGLE cASE, which turns every lowercase letter in the text block into an uppercase letter and every uppercase letter into a lowercase letter.

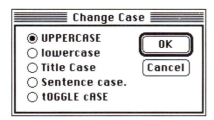

**FIGURE 3-6.** *The Change Case dialog box.*

# Practice

## Changing case

*Try changing the case of letters:*

1. Choose the New command from the File menu to open a new document.

2. Type *this is a line of unimposing text*, with no capital letters and no punctuation.

3. Select all the text as a text block.

4. Choose the Change Case command from the Format menu to open the Change Case dialog box.

5. Click on the Sentence case. button, and then click on the OK button to close the dialog box. The text block changes to "This is a line of unimposing text."

6. Reselect the text.

7. Choose the Change Case command from the Format menu to reopen the Change Case dialog box.

8. Click on the UPPERCASE button, and then click on the OK button to close the dialog box. The text block changes to "THIS IS A LINE OF UNIMPOSING TEXT."

9. Close the document without saving it.

## The Font menu

The Font menu offers you every font available on your Macintosh. It also shows the most common point sizes used for fonts, outlining the sizes that look the best, just as the Size list box does in the Ribbon. To choose a new font or a new point size, simply choose the font or point size you want. Word puts a check mark in front of your choice.

In between point sizes and font names is a set of four commands that give you more character-formatting abilities. The Up and Down commands increase or decrease the current point size by a single point, and are useful for fine-tuning your character size. Choose the Other command to open the Character dialog box, where you can set very specific point sizes. And choose the Default Font command to open the Preferences box, where you can set the font and point size that Word automatically uses when you open a new document.

## The Character dialog box

The Character dialog box (shown in Figure 3-7) offers the most complete set of character-formatting options anywhere in Word. You can open it in three

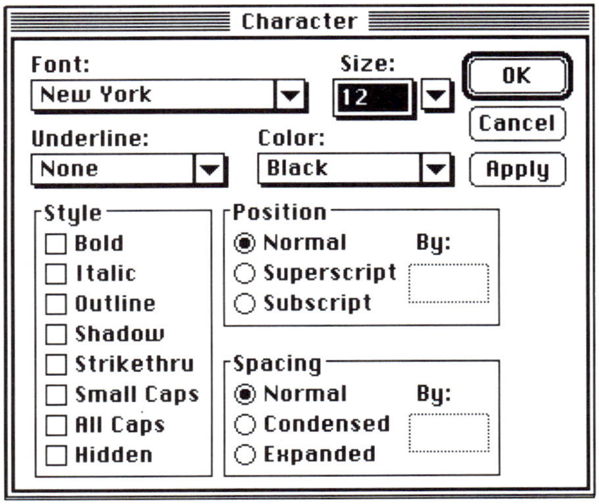

**FIGURE 3-7.** *The Character dialog box.*

ways. The quickest is to put the pointer anywhere in the Ribbon between controls (the blank space between the Underline button and the Superscript button, for example) and double-click. You can also open it by choosing the Character command from the Format menu or by choosing the Other command from the Font menu.

Using the Character dialog box, you can choose a new font from the Font list box (it works like the Font list box in the Ribbon except that you can't type in a font name). You can type in or choose a new point size from the Size list box. You can turn on any of four types of underlining by choosing the appropriate type from the Underline list box, choose any of eight different colors by choosing a color from the Color list box, or turn on any type style listed in the Style area by clicking on its check box. You can also set the position of superscripts and subscripts and change the amount of spacing between characters, but these are advanced functions you probably won't need for simple documents. Table 3-1 lists all the type styles available in the Character dialog box and shows you alternative ways to turn them on and off. (''NA'' indicates that the type style can't be accessed in the manner described by the column head.)

## Keyboard shortcuts

As you can see from Table 3-1, almost every type style you can apply in the Character dialog box you can also apply with a keyboard shortcut. Pressing the key combination toggles the type style on and off.

Keyboard shortcuts take a little time to memorize, but they are well worth the effort because they let you change type styles quickly without removing your hands from the keyboard. Besides, they aren't that hard to memorize. Most keyboard shortcuts require a combination of Shift, Command, and a letter key. That letter is usually the first letter of the type style. For example, Shift-Command-B turns bold on and off, and Shift-Command-I turns italic on and off. And if you need a quick reminder, you can find some keyboard shortcuts listed to the right of each type style command in the Format menu.

| Type Style | Ribbon | Keyboard Shortcut | Format Menu Command |
|---|---|---|---|
| Bold | B button | Shift-Command-B[1] | Bold |
| Italic | I button | Shift-Command-I[2] | Italic |
| Underline | U button | Shift-Command-U[3] | Underline |
| Word Underline | NA | Shift-Command-] | NA |
| Double Underline | NA | Shift-Command-[ | NA |
| Dotted Underline | NA | Shift-Command-\ | NA |
| Strikethrough | NA | Shift-Command-/ | NA |
| Outline | NA | Shift-Command-D | NA |
| Shadow | NA | Shift-Command-W | NA |
| Small Caps | NA | Shift-Command-H | NA |
| All Caps | NA | Shift-Command-K | NA |
| Hidden Text | NA | Shift-Command-V | NA |
| Colors | NA | None | NA |

[1] A simpler shortcut is Command-B.    [2] A simpler shortcut is Command-I.    [3] A simpler shortcut is Command-U.

**TABLE 3-1.** *Available type styles in Word.*

**PRACTICE**

### Using keyboard shortcuts

*Try using a keyboard shortcut to turn type styles on and off:*

1. Choose the New command from the File menu to open a new document.

2. Type *I want to type in* (with a space at the end).

3. Press Shift-Command-I to turn on italic.

4. Type *italic* (with a space at the end).

5. Press Shift-Command-I to turn off italic.

| Character Dialog Box Option | Explanation |
|---|---|
| Bold check box | Makes each character heavier |
| Italic check box | Slants each character to the right |
| Single in Underline list box | Underlines everything you type, including spaces |
| Word in Underline list box | Underlines words you type, but *not* spaces |
| Double in Underline list box | Double-underlines everything you type, including spaces |
| Dotted in Underline list box | Underlines with dots everything you type, including spaces |
| Strikethru check box | Places a dash through the middle of each character, including spaces |
| Outline check box | Creates a hollow outline of each character |
| Shadow check box | Creates a drop shadow beneath an outline of each character |
| Small Caps check box | Turns lowercase letters into small uppercase letters |
| All Caps check box | Turns lowercase letters into uppercase letters |
| Hidden check box | Hides all characters |
| The desired color from the Color list box | Turns the characters the color you choose (if you have a color monitor or printer) |

6. Type *without removing my hands from the keyboard.* You should see the sentence "I want to type in *italic* without removing my hands from the keyboard."

7. Close the document without saving it.

# ENTERING CHARACTERS

Entering standard characters in a document is easy enough, a matter of pressing the appropriate key and of occasionally pressing the Shift key for capital letters or common symbols. For most documents, that's all you'll need. From time to time, however, you may need to add special characters for occasions such as establishing a trademark (®), computing the circumference of a circle using π, or just putting in your 2¢ worth. You might also need to enter foreign words that require special characters or marks.

How do you enter special symbols? Choose the Symbol command from the Insert menu to open the Symbol window, where you can click on the symbol you want to insert. You can also enter other special characters by using other character commands found in the Insert menu, including one command that inserts a page break and another that inserts the current date.

## Special Characters

As you may recall, each font has its own character set, a collection of characters that you produce by pressing keys. The character set also includes a set of special symbols that you can type with key combinations (usually involving the Option key) or insert with the Symbol window. These symbols, like the usual letters and numerals found in a font, are usually standard from font to font. For example, you'll find the bullet (•) and pi (π) characters in almost every font. However, there *are* exceptions: Some fonts have a completely different set of symbols, and may in fact have a completely different set of standard characters as well (as does the Symbol font, for example). The easiest way to see what a font offers in its character set is to use the Symbol window.

### The Symbol window

To open the Symbol window (shown in Figure 3-8), choose the Symbol command from the Insert menu. The Symbol window displays the full character set of the current font, shown in the current point size. If you can't see the full character set, you can use the vertical and horizontal scroll bars, dragging up and down or left and right to reveal the rest of the character set.

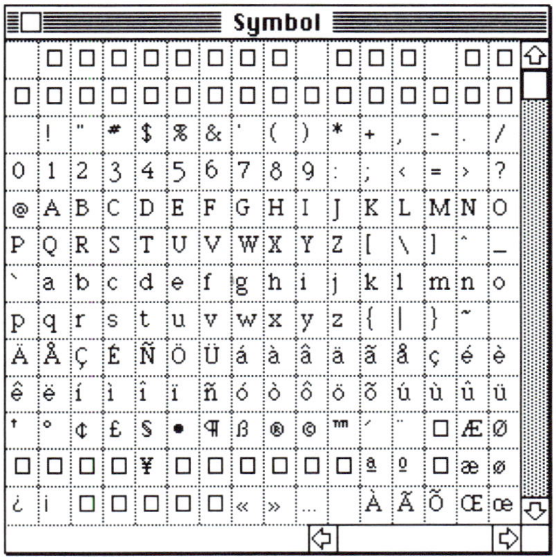

**FIGURE 3-8**. *The Symbol window shows the full character set of the current font.*

If you see a symbol you want to insert, simply click on it; Word inserts the symbol into your document at the insertion point's current location. If you want to insert characters from a different font or in a different point size, you can use the Font menu to choose a new font or point size, and then continue using the Symbol window.

## PRACTICE

### Using the Symbol window

*Try entering some special characters:*

1. Choose the New command from the File menu to open a new document.

2. Type *Squidees.*

3. Choose the Symbol command from the Insert menu to open the Symbol window. The Symbol window shows all the characters available in your current font (which is normally the New York font).

4. Click on the ™ symbol (it's to the right of the © symbol). Word inserts a ™ symbol after "Squidees."

5. Close the Symbols window.

6. Type *! You'll* . (Be sure to end with a space.)

7. Choose the Symbol command from the Insert menu to open the Symbol window.

8. Choose Symbol from the Font menu to change to the Symbol font. The Symbol window now shows all the characters available in the Symbol font.

9. Find and click on the heart symbol (♥) to insert a heart, and then close the Symbol window.

10. Choose New York from the Font menu to change back to the New York font.

11. Type *them!* You should see "Squidees™! You'll ♥ them!"

Whenever you open the Symbol window, you'll probably notice that it contains a lot of square boxes. These represent nonprinting characters. Even though you can sometimes click on one of these characters to enter a square into your document, when you print the document, you will probably get a space or another character in place of the square.

 *If you're a speed typist and you don't want to stop to use the Symbol window for special characters, you'll find that you can enter almost every character in a font's character set by using a key combination. For example, Option-2 inserts the ™ symbol into your document. The Key Caps program, included with your Mac's system software, shows you which key combinations produce what characters. You'll find instructions for the Key Caps program in the manuals that came with your Mac.*

## Invisible characters

Invisible characters are another type of special character—those characters that you enter normally with the keyboard, but that don't usually leave a mark in the text window. Standard invisible characters are the space, the tab, and the paragraph mark, which you enter with the space bar, the Tab key, and the Return key. These characters all produce an effect on the screen—they enter a space, jump further along a line, or start a new paragraph—but they don't leave a visible character on the screen.

Invisible characters (which you shouldn't confuse with hidden characters—those with the hidden-text type style applied to them) are characters just as letters and numerals are, even though you can't see them. You can select, delete, and even format invisible characters, although you won't see the formatting changes. To help you work with invisible characters, you can view them by choosing the Show command from the View menu, or—even simpler—by clicking on the show/hide paragraph button in the Ribbon. Word then uses special symbols to show hidden characters, as shown in Figure 3-9.

Notice that a space in the text appears as a raised dot between other characters, that a tab appears as a right-pointing arrow, and that a paragraph mark appears as a traditional proofreader's paragraph mark. Notice also that there

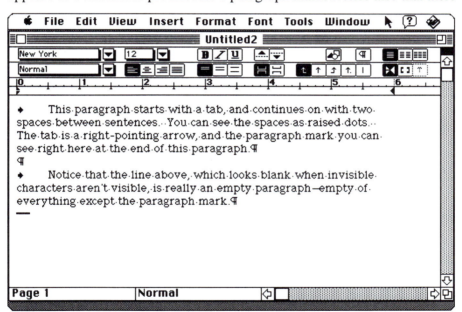

**FIGURE 3-9.** *Word uses special symbols to show invisible characters.*

is *always* a paragraph mark at the end of every document, even if you didn't press Return there. Word always begins a new document with a single paragraph mark that remains at the very end of anything you enter. A paragraph mark must appear at the end of each document; you can't delete this mark.

If you no longer want to see the invisible characters, choose the Hide ¶ command from the View menu, or click once more on the show/hide paragraph button in the Ribbon.

## Page Breaks

When you enter a long document in Word, Word normally shows it on the screen as one single long page that grows as necessary. To see the contents of the document, you scroll up and down through the long page. Your printer doesn't use a long page, however; it requires the document to be broken up into separate pages—a process called *pagination.*

To paginate, Word figures out how much text it can fit on each printed page, and marks where each new page starts—a location called a *page break*—with a horizontal dotted line across the width of the document window (as shown in Figure 3-10). As you add and delete text, Word constantly refigures the pagination to fit your text to the printed pages, and moves the page-break line to show you the current pagination. These page breaks are called *automatic page breaks* because Word places them automatically as you type a document.

You might, on occasion, have text within a document that you want to appear at the top of a page. Automatic page breaks don't usually appear exactly where you want them, so you must place a *manual page break* just before the text to make sure that it appears at the top of the page. To do so, move the insertion point just in front of the text, and then choose the Page Break command from the Insert menu (or press Shift-Enter as a keyboard shortcut). Word inserts a manual page break there, which is, like the automatic page break, shown by a horizontal dotted line across the screen—but the dots in a manual page-break line are closer together than those in an automatic page-break line, so you can tell the two apart.

The manual page break is a special character and can be selected and deleted exactly like any other character.

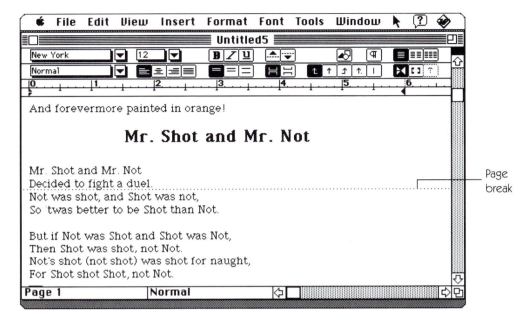

**FIGURE 3-10.** *Word adds page breaks to your document, marking each break with a dotted line.*

## Current Date

Many common documents such as business letters have the day's date included so that the reader knows when they were printed and sent. It's easy enough to type in the date, but Word offers an even more convenient option: the date character.

To insert the date character, you choose the Date command from the Insert menu. Word inserts a special character at the insertion point that displays the current date. (Word gets the date from the Mac's internal clock.) The date character makes sure that the date remains current. If you open the document the next day, the date is updated accordingly. When you print the document, no matter how much later, Word prints the current date—so you never have to update the date.

If you try to select the date, you'll find that it seems a bit different from other text: You can only select the full date as a single character. You can't

select individual numerals or slashes within the date. If you click on the show/
hide paragraph button in the Ribbon to see invisible characters, you'll see a
dotted box around the date, which shows that it's a single special character (as
shown in Figure 3-11). If you select the date character, you can format it just as
you can regular characters. You can also delete it if you want.

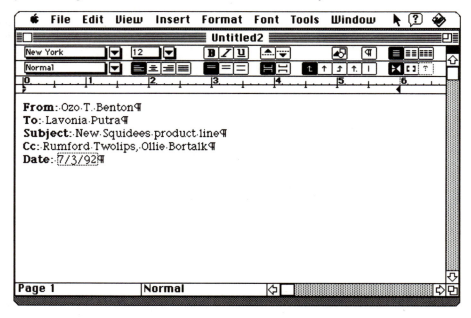

**FIGURE 3-11.** *A date character is a special character that always shows the
current date.*

With that, we reach the end of this chapter on working with characters—
entering them and formatting them to make them look the way you want them
to. In the next chapter, you learn how to work with paragraphs.

# Chapter 4

# Text-Editing Techniques

It's a rare document that springs forth from its writer's fingers and leaps directly onto the printed page. Most are subject to misgivings, second thoughts, third thoughts, and much tinkering before they finally emerge from the printer's maw. When you sit down to polish your documents, the last thing you want is the additional distraction of having to wrestle with your Macintosh to make changes. You should be able to edit without effort or pause.

How can you keep your editing simple and fast? By getting to the text you want to change as quickly as possible and by immediately selecting the text to be changed. This chapter shows you how to move the insertion point exactly where you want it in long documents by using keyboard shortcuts and convenient mouse techniques. You'll see how to select text with and without the mouse and also learn how to shuffle blocks of text around in a document without using the Cut, Copy, and Paste commands in the Edit menu. And finally, you'll learn about the Find and Replace commands, which find and replace text scattered throughout a document.

## PRACTICE

### Creating a practice document

*Before you do anything else in this chapter, you need to create a long document for scrolling and editing. Don't worry, though—you'll only have to type a single paragraph. With some help from the Copy and Paste commands, you can duplicate the paragraph in Figure 4-1 (a fine example of technobabble) to easily create a long document. You can also*

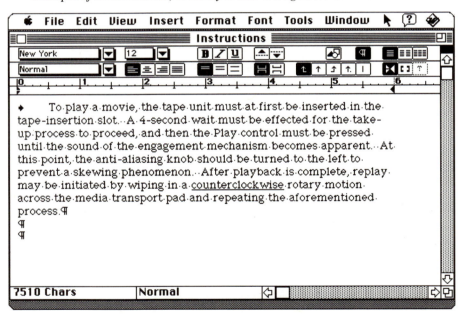

**FIGURE 4-1.** *Enter this sample paragraph.*

*use a very useful tool—the Renumber command in the Tools menu—to number your paragraphs so that you know where you are as you scroll through the document. Take the following steps:*

1. Type the paragraph shown in Figure 4-1. Use the underline type style to emphasize the expression ''counterclockwise.'' The invisible characters (visible here) show you where to press Tab and Return. (A ➜ character represents a tab, a ¶ character represents a return.) Be sure to press Return twice at the end of the paragraph—once to finish the paragraph, and a second time to create a blank line following the paragraph.

2. Select the first two paragraphs—the full paragraph and the blank line following it.

3. Choose the Copy command from the Edit menu to transfer a copy of the text block to the Clipboard.

4. Move the insertion point to the end of the document.

5. Choose the Paste command from the Edit menu 13 times to insert 13 copies of the paragraph into the document (or press Command-V as a keyboard shortcut for the Paste command). You should end up with 14 full paragraphs, each separated from the next one by a blank line. The final document should be three pages long.

6. Move the insertion point to the beginning of the document.

7. Choose the Renumber command from the Tools menu to open the Renumber dialog box, and then click on the OK button to start numbering. Microsoft Word numbers the paragraphs consecutively from 1 to 14.

8. Save the document under the name ''Instructions.''

*You now have a three-page document filled with unclear technical instructions, eminently suitable for editing in practice sessions. You also had a chance to use the Renumber command for its simplest use: numbering paragraphs. If you're interested in using it to number outlines or to number with something besides standard numerals, refer to your Word manual for further information.*

## MOVING THE INSERTION POINT

In previous chapters, you learned how to move the insertion point by pointing and clicking with the mouse. You also learned how to move it a character or a line at a time by pressing the cursor keys or the 2, 4, 6, and 8 keys on the numeric keypad. If you like to keep your hands on the keyboard as you edit, you'll be interested to know that you can also use keyboard combinations to move the insertion point through larger sections of text—a word, sentence, paragraph, screen of text, or even the entire document—all without taking your hands off the keyboard.

Table 4-1 shows the keys and key combinations that move the insertion point. Try using them to move through your sample document:

| Insertion-Point Movement | Key or Key Combination |
| --- | --- |
| Single character forward | Right-arrow cursor key or keypad 6 |
| Single character backward | Left-arrow cursor key or keypad 4 |
| Single line up | Up-arrow cursor key or keypad 8 |
| Single line down | Down-arrow cursor key or keypad 2 |
| Beginning of the current line | Keypad 7 |
| End of the current line | Keypad 1 |
| Beginning of the previous word | Command–left-arrow cursor key or Command-keypad 4 |
| Beginning of the next word | Command–right-arrow cursor key or Command-keypad 6 |
| Beginning of the previous sentence | Command-keypad 7 |
| Beginning of the next sentence | Command-keypad 1 |
| Beginning of the previous paragraph | Command-keypad 8 or Option-Command-Y |
| Beginning of the next paragraph | Command-keypad 2 or Option-Command-B |
| Top of the window | Home key (only on an extended keyboard) or Command-keypad 5 |
| Bottom of the window | End key (only on an extended keyboard) |
| Up one screen | Page Up key (only on an extended keyboard) or keypad 9 |

**TABLE 4-1.** *Keys and key combinations that move the insertion point.* *(continued)*

**TABLE 4-1.** *continued*

| Insertion-Point Movement | Key or Key Combination |
| --- | --- |
| Down one screen | Page Down key (only on an extended keyboard) or keypad 3 |
| Beginning of the document | Command-Home (only on an extended keyboard) or Command-keypad 9 |
| End of the document | Command-End (only on an extended keyboard) or Command-keypad 3 |

Use these keys and key combinations to move the insertion point to a new location. For example, if you type a sentence and then notice that you forgot to capitalize the first letter, you can press Command-keypad 7 to move the insertion point back to the beginning of the sentence to correct your mistake. Or if you need to change something at the beginning of the document, you can press Command-keypad 9.

## Returning to a Previous Location

As you edit, you might need to jump to a distant point in the document, work on that section, and then return to your previous location. Word remembers your last three insertion-point locations. To return to a previous location, press either keypad 0 or Option-Command-Z. Each time you press one of these key combinations, the insertion point jumps back one location. The fourth press of keypad 0 or the Option-Command-Z combination returns the insertion point to your original location.

A good rule of thumb for jumping back is to press keypad 0 until you find the previous location you want or until you return to your original location. If you don't find the location you want after cycling through the previous locations, you'll need to scroll to find the location.

## Jumping to a Specific Page

In particularly long documents, you might want to jump to a specific page. To do so, watch the page-number area at the bottom of the window as you drag the scroll box downward or upward; the page-number area changes to show you the page numbers of the pages you're scrolling through. When you see the number of the page you want, release the scroll box; Word displays the portion of that page appearing at the location you scrolled to. (But remember to click somewhere in the text to move the insertion point to your new location.)

A more precise way to jump to a specific page is to choose the Go To command from the Edit menu and enter your page selection in the Go To dialog box, shown in Figure 4-2. Type the page number you want to move to in the Page Number text box, and then click on the OK button. Word scrolls the text to the top of that page and places the insertion point there.

**FIGURE 4-2.** *Use the Go To dialog box to jump to a specific page.*

# Practice

## Jumping through a document

*Now that you have a fine, long document for editing, try your hand at jumping through it to look at your handiwork:*

1. Press Command-keypad 9 to jump to the beginning of the document if the insertion point isn't already located there.

2. Press Command-keypad 6 several times to jump forward through the text a word at a time, and Command-keypad 4 to jump backward a word at a time.

3. Press Command-keypad 1 to jump forward through the text a sentence at a time, and Command-keypad 7 to jump backward a sentence at a time.

4. Press Command-keypad 2 to jump forward through the text a paragraph at a time, and Command-keypad 8 to jump backward a paragraph at a time.

5. Choose the Go To command from the Utilities menu to open the Go To dialog box, type 2, and then press Return to jump to the beginning of page 2 of your document.

6. Press keypad 0 to jump to your previous editing location.

7. Press the keypad 3 (or the Page Down key) to jump forward by a screen.

8. Press Command-keypad 9 to move back to the beginning of your document.

## SELECTING TEXT

To edit text, you have to select it as a text block. You learned in Chapter 2, "Creating a Business Letter," how to select text by clicking and dragging the pointer across text. You also learned how to select text by holding down Shift and moving the insertion point using the cursor or cursor-movement keys. If you want to select text even faster, Word offers some special selection techniques using either the mouse or the keyboard.

### Selecting Text with the Mouse

You can use the mouse to quickly select the parts of a document that you're most likely to edit at one time: a single letter, a word, a sentence, a line, a paragraph, or the entire document. The different techniques involve single-clicking, double-clicking, and triple-clicking on text elements. Some techniques work with an area of the text window called the *selection bar*. The selection bar is the thin, vertical, blank area of the document window immediately to the left of the text. When you move the pointer into the selection bar, the I-beam turns into a right-pointing arrow. Figure 4-3 shows the pointer resting in the selection bar.

To select a specific block of text, you can use one of the following techniques:

- To select a word: Double-click on the word.

- To select a sentence: Hold down the Command key and click on any word in the sentence.

- To select a line: Click on the selection bar immediately to the left of the line.

- To select a paragraph: Triple-click on the paragraph text *or* double-click on the selection bar immediately to the left of the paragraph.

77

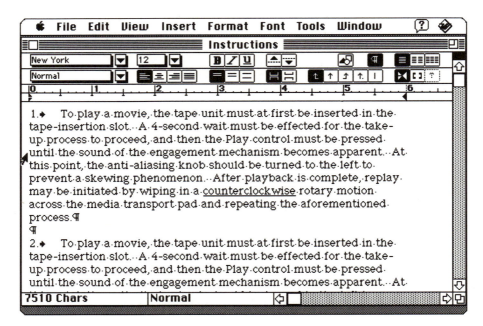

**FIGURE 4-3.** *The I-beam pointer becomes a right-pointing arrow when it is in the selection bar.*

■ To select the entire document: Triple-click on the selection bar *or* hold down the Command key and single-click anywhere in the selection bar.

## Selecting Text with the Keyboard

To select text using keyboard combinations, simply hold down the Shift key as you use the key combinations from Table 4-1 to move the insertion point. For example, you can select a word you just typed by pressing Shift–Command–left-arrow cursor key. Or you can press Command-keypad 9 to move the insertion point to the beginning of the document and then press Shift-Command-keypad 3 to move the insertion point to the end of the document, selecting the entire document. An even easier way to select the entire document is to use the keyboard combination Option-Command-M.

**PRACTICE**

### Selecting text in a document

*Try the following mouse and keyboard selection techniques on the first paragraph of the document:*

1. Double-click on the middle of the word "tape" in the first line. Word selects the entire word and the space following it.

2. Click on the selection bar immediately to the left of the number "1." Word selects the entire first line of the paragraph.

3. Triple-click anywhere in the first paragraph. Word selects the entire first paragraph.

4. Triple-click on the selection bar. Word selects the entire document.

5. Click on the word "tape" to move the insertion point there. Press Shift-Command-keypad 6 to select the entire word. (Command-keypad 6 moves the insertion point to the next word. Shift extends the selection.

6. Press Shift-Command-keypad 6 again to add the following word to the selected text block. To continue adding words to the text block, continue pressing Shift-Command-keypad 6.

7. Press Command-keypad 9 to move the insertion point back to the top of the document and deselect the text block.

## SPECIAL EDITING TECHNIQUES

As you know, Word offers keyboard shortcuts for common editing commands. Word also offers a special technique that lets you move blocks of text with the mouse and another that deletes a word of text in a single stroke.

### Using Cut, Copy, Paste, and Undo

Cut, Copy, Paste, and Undo are the four most commonly used commands in Word's Edit menu. Each has a convenient keyboard shortcut, so you can "choose" a command without using the mouse: Choose the Cut command by pressing Command-X; choose the Copy command by pressing Command-C; choose the Paste command by pressing Command-V; and choose the Undo command, which reverses your last editing action, by pressing Command-Z. If you have an extended keyboard, you can cut by pressing F2, copy by pressing F3, paste by pressing F4, and undo by pressing F1.

## Drag-and-Drop Editing

An even quicker way to move a block of text from one spot to another is drag-and-drop editing, a mouse technique. To use the technique, you first select a block of text and then move the pointer over the text block while holding down the mouse button. A small rectangle appears at the base of the pointer to show that you're ready to drag a block of text. As you drag the pointer around the screen, a dotted-line insertion point follows the tip of the pointer, as shown in Figure 4-4. When you have moved the insertion point to the spot where you want to place the text block, release the mouse button. Word moves the selected text block to the new location.

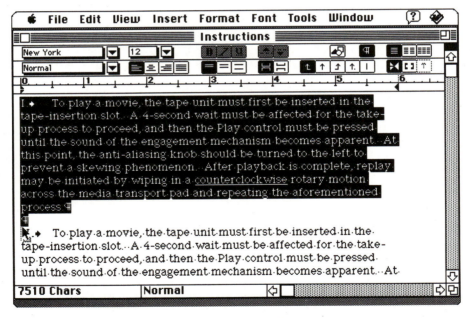

**FIGURE 4-4.** *The pointer includes a small rectangle at its base and drags a dotted-line insertion point on the screen during drag-and-drop editing.*

You can also use drag-and-drop editing to copy a text block from one location to the next. If you hold down the Command key as you drag a text block, Word puts a copy of the text block in the new location.

Drag-and-drop editing differs from editing with the Cut and Copy commands in one significant way: Dragging and dropping doesn't touch the contents of the Clipboard. Each time you use the Cut or Copy command to move a block of text, the text is inserted in the Clipboard and the previous contents of the Clipboard are erased. If you're storing something in the Clipboard— for example, a graphic or a block of text—that you don't want to lose, use the drag-and-drop technique to move or copy text instead of the Cut or Copy command.

Note that if you can't get drag-and-drop editing to work, it's probably turned off in the Preferences window. You can turn it on by choosing the Preferences command from the Tools menu and then clicking on Drag-and-Drop Text Editing in the Preferences window.

## Practice

### Using drag-and-drop editing

*Try using drag-and-drop editing to move the first paragraph of the document to a spot below the second paragraph.*

1. Double-click on the word "tape" to select it, and then press Command-C to copy it to the Clipboard. (This isn't a necessary step for using drag-and-drop editing, but it does put "tape" in the Clipboard to demonstrate that dragging and dropping doesn't touch the contents of the Clipboard.)

2. Select the entire first paragraph and the blank-line paragraph following it.

3. Move the pointer over the first paragaraph and hold down the mouse button. A small rectangle appears at the base of the pointer, and a dotted-line insertion point appears at the tip of the pointer.

4. Drag the dotted-line insertion point down to the spot that precedes the *3* at the beginning of the third paragraph of text, and then release the mouse button. Paragraph 1 disappears

from the beginning of the document and reappears between paragraphs 2 and 3.

5. Choose the Show Clipboard command from the Window menu to open the Clipboard window. It shows ''tape,'' the original contents before you used drag-and-drop editing. Close the Clipboard window.

## Deleting Text One Word at a Time

As you enter text in a document, you can fix most typing errors by pressing the Delete key and deleting one character at a time until you eliminate the error. Some errors, however, stretch out across the screen and take a long time to delete this way. An easier way to delete long stretches of text is to use the Option-Command-Delete key combination. Each time you press this key combination, Word deletes an entire word and the following space to the left of the insertion point. You can delete words to the right of the insertion point by pressing Option-Command-G.

## FINDING TEXT

There are times when you want to find a specific word or phrase for correction but can't remember where the word or phrase occurs in the document. For example, you may realize that somewhere within a 20-page document you misspelled the name ''Yma Sumac'' as ''Amy Camus.'' You can, of course, search through the document yourself, scrolling page by page with an observant eye. It's much easier, though, to use the Find command.

Choosing the Find command from the Edit menu opens the Find window shown in Figure 4-5, in which you can enter the word or phrase you want to find. Click on the Find Next button, and Word searches diligently through the characters in the document until it finds that text. Word then selects the text it found and scrolls your viewpoint to the location of the word or phrase. If Word can't find the word or phrase, you'll see a dialog box telling you that Word reached the end of the document.

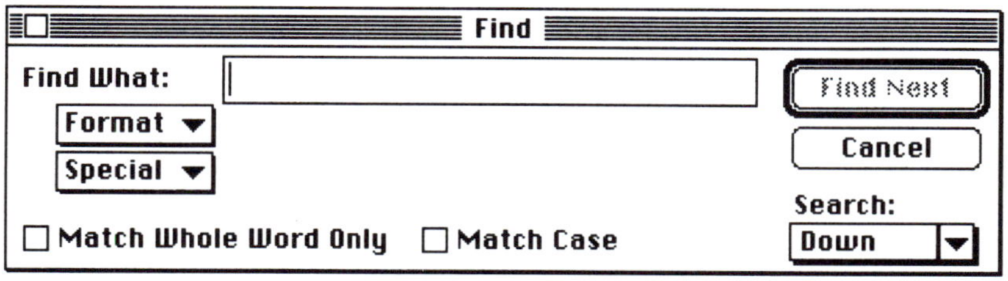

**FIGURE 4-5.** *The Find window asks you for the text you want to find.*

To use the Find window, type the text you want to find in the text box labeled *Find What*. You can type up to 255 characters. (Word scrolls the text as you type, so you aren't limited by the size of the box.) You can also select a text block that contains the text you want and then use the Copy and Paste commands to paste it into the Find What text box.

The Search list box in the bottom right corner of the Find window offers you four search alternatives: Down, Up, All, and Selection. Down searches from the current insertion-point location to the bottom of the document; Up searches from the insertion point to the top of the document; All searches the entire document; and Selection searches only the text block you have selected in a document. (To use the Selection option, you must select a text block before you open the Find dialog box.) The default setting is Down, or if you have a text block selected, the default is Selection. If you want to use a different alternative, choose one from the Search list box before you start the search.

After you've entered your search characters and set the search alternative you want, click on the Find Next button. Word searches using the search alternative you set. If Word finds an occurrence of your search text, it selects the text and scrolls to text's location. You can continue to click on the Find Next button to move to further occurrences of the search text.

If you're searching to the beginning or end of the document and Word doesn't find the text, it opens a dialog box asking whether you want to continue searching from the other end of the document. If you click on the Yes button, Word continues searching until it either finds your search text or reaches the end of the document again. If you click on the No button, Word ends the search.

When you search for text with the Find command, the Find window remains open so that you can continue searching. The window may block the text you need to see. If so, you can drag it to a new location to reveal the text.

## PRACTICE

### Searching through a document

*Try searching for the word "play" in your document:*

1. Move the insertion point to the beginning of the document to begin the search there.

2. Choose the Find command from the Edit menu to open the Find dialog box.

3. Type *play* in the Find What text box.

4. Click on the Find Next button to begin the search. Word finds the first instance of the word "play" and selects it in the document, as shown in Figure 4-6.

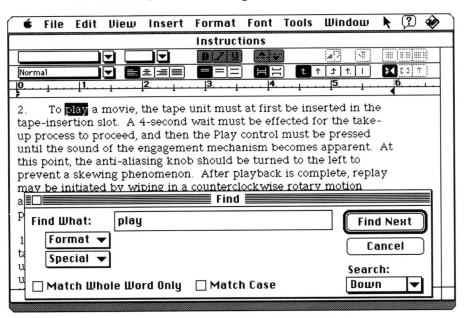

**FIGURE 4-6.** *When Word finds search text, it selects that text in the document.*

84

5. Click on the Find Next button to continue searching. Word searches from the location of the selected word and selects ''Play'' in the middle of the second sentence.

7. Click on the Find Next button once more. Word selects the next occurrence of the word ''play,'' which is the first half of the word ''playback.''

8. Click on the Find Next button again. Word moves on to select ''play'' in the second part of the word ''replay.''

## Searching for Whole Words

In the preceding practice session, Word selected ''play'' even though it was part of the word ''replay.'' The Find command doesn't normally distinguish between whole words and parts of words—it simply looks for the search characters wherever they occur. To look for a whole word only (that is, a string of characters with a space or punctuation mark at each end), select the Match Whole Word Only option in the Find window and then search.

### PRACTICE

#### Searching for a whole word

*Try searching for "play" as a whole word:*

1. Click on the Match Whole Word Only check box. (The check box contains an X when the option is selected.)

2. Click on the Find Next button to begin the search. Word finds ''play'' at the beginning of the next paragraph and selects it.

3. Click on the Find Next button to continue. Word finds ''Play'' in the middle of the next sentence and selects it.

4. Click on the Find Next button again to continue searching. Word skips over ''playback'' and ''replay'' to select ''play'' at the beginning of the next paragraph.

## Matching Case

It's sometimes important to distinguish between a capitalized word and the same word in lowercase. To ask Word to match the case of the characters in the Find What text box, select the Match Case option and then search.

## PRACTICE

### Matching case in a search

*In the last practice session, Word found whole-word occurrences of "play," but didn't distinguish between "play" and "Play." Select the Match Case option to find only the lowercase "play":*

1. Click on the Match Case check box to select that option.

2. Click on the Find Next button to continue searching. Word skips over the words "Play," "playback," and "replay" to select "play" at the beginning of the next paragraph. It is now looking for "play" only as a whole word in lowercase characters.

3. Continue clicking on the Find Next button until you reach the end of the document. Word continues to select "play" as it finds it. When you reach the end of the document, a new dialog box opens, telling you that Word reached the end of the document. Click on the OK button.

4. Close the Find window and return the insertion point to the beginning of the document.

## Searching for Unspecified Characters

To search for a string of text without specifying the exact characters to search for, use *wildcard* characters in the Find What text box. A wildcard holds a place in a string but doesn't specify any particular character. Type a question mark in the Find What text box to specify an indeterminate character. For example, to find all four-letter words that begin with "fl," you type *fl??* in the Find What text box. Word then looks for "fl" followed by any two characters and selects all four characters if it finds them. Typing *fl??* finds and selects "flag," "flit," or "flop," but not "floor" (because it has too many letters, assuming you've selected Match Whole Word Only) or "fly" (because it has too few letters, again assuming you've selected Match Whole Word Only).

Using wildcard characters works best when the Match Whole Word Only option is selected. If the option isn't selected, Word finds your search string in words of any length, even if the string appears as part of another word.

## Searching for Formats

There are times when you want to search for a format instead of text, or for text formatted with a certain emphasis. For example, you might want to find all the boldface words in a document, or every occurrence of the word "effluvium" that appears in boldface (but not those that occur in plain text or italic). The Find window offers a Format list box that lets you specify formats for a search. When you open it, it offers you four options: Clear, Character, Paragraph, and Styles.

Choosing Character, Paragraph, or Styles opens (respectively) the Character, Paragraph, or Styles dialog box, where you can choose character formatting, paragraph formatting, or styles (which you'll learn about in a later chapter) for searching. (The Clear option is for searching for unformatted text.) For now, we'll concentrate only on character formatting.

When you open the Character dialog box for a search, it looks exactly as it does when you open it for character formatting, but none of its options are selected (as shown in Figure 4-7). You select the formats you want to search for by clicking on option buttons or using other controls, just as you do to set character formats. When you're finished, click on the OK button to return to the Find window. Word displays the formats for which you want to search to the right of the Format list box.

If you select a format without specifying any search text, Word finds every occurrence of the format when it searches. If you use both search text and a format, Word finds only the search text formatted in the format you've selected. If you decide that you don't want to search for formats, choose Clear from the Format list box.

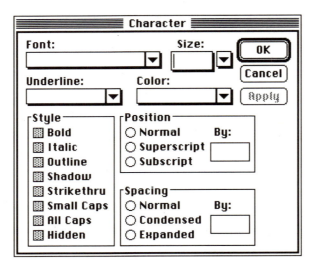

**FIGURE 4-7**. *When you open the Character dialog box for a search, none of its options are selected.*

## PRACTICE

### Searching for formats

*Try searching for underlined text in your document:*

1. Choose the Find command from the Edit menu to open the Find window.

2. Press Delete to remove all text from the Find What text box.

3. Choose Character from the Format list box to open the Character dialog box.

4. Choose "Single" from the Underline list box and click on the OK button to close the dialog box. Word shows the word "Underline" next to the Format list box to show that the search will look for underlined text.

5. Click on the Find Next button to start the search. Word selects the word "counterclockwise," the first occurrence of underlined text (shown in Figure 4-8).

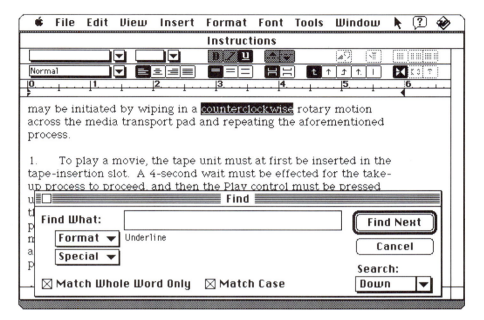

**FIGURE 4-8.** *When underlined character formatting is selected, Word searches for underlined text.*

6. Close the Find window.

## Searching for Special Characters

You might want to search for special characters that are hard to enter in the Find What text box, such as tabs and paragraph marks. To search for one of these special characters, you must enter a code for the character, which is a caret (^) followed by a single letter. The following codes are used to search for the special characters you learned to use in previous chapters:

- ^w—a blank space
- ^t—a tab
- ^p—a paragraph mark

For example, if you enter *^tThree*, Word searches for a tab followed by the word ''Three.''

Because Word interprets question marks and carets as wildcard characters or code starters, you use special codes to search for literal occurrences of these characters, as follows:

- ^?—a question mark

- ^^—a caret

These codes aren't that easy to remember, so Word makes it easier by providing a Special list box in the Find window. When you open the Special list box, you'll find a full list of special characters for which you can search. When you choose any one of these characters from the list, Word inserts the appropriate code for that character in the Find What text box. For example, if you choose Paragraph Mark from the Special list box, Word inserts ^p in the Find What text box.

## CHANGING TEXT

The purpose of most searches is to locate a word or phrase and replace it with different text. For example, you may want to replace every occurrence of the word "fabulous" with the word "marvelous." You can do this by choosing the Replace command from the Edit menu to open the Replace window, as shown in Figure 4-9. The Replace window offers all the features of the Find

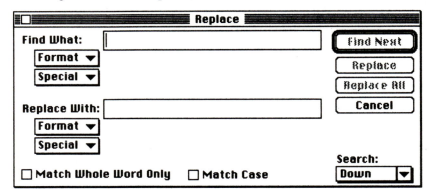

**FIGURE 4-9.** *Use the Replace window to replace a word or phrase with other text or to replace a type of formatting with another type of formatting.*

window but adds a Replace With area that includes a text box, a Format list box, and a Special list box. It also adds two buttons on the right side: Replace and Replace All.

The Find What area, the Match Whole Word Only and Match Case check boxes, and the Search list box all function in the same way as they did in the Find window: You enter the text you want to find in the Find What text box and then select the search options you want Word to use.

Type the replacement text into the Replace With text box. You can also use the Format and Special list boxes below to replace a text format with a new format or to add special characters to the replacement string.

After you enter a search string or format (or combination of the two) in the Find What area and enter a replacement string or format (or combination of the two) in the Replace With area, you can start to replace. First use the Search list box to select the search area you want. If you want to replace every occurrence of your search string or format in the search area, click on the Replace All button. If you want to verify each change (a good idea in some cases), click on the Find Next button. Word selects the first occurrence of the search text or search format, and you can decide how to proceed from there.

If you choose to replace the text, click on the Replace button. Word replaces the selected text and moves on to the next occurrence. If you choose not to replace the text, click on Find Next, and Word moves on to the next occurrence without replacing the text. When you've finished replacing text, close the Replace window. If you're not satisfied with the changes, you can undo them by choosing the Undo Replacement command from the Edit menu.

Note that when you use the Replace command, Word follows whatever initial and full capitalization is present in the search text unless the Match Case option is selected. For example, if you're changing the word "cat" to "dog" throughout a document, Word replaces "cat" with "dog," "Cat" with "Dog," and "CAT" with "DOG." If the Match Case option is selected, Word uses only the capitalization in the Find What and Replace With text boxes for its searches and changes. Continuing the previous example, "cat," "Cat," and "CAT" would all be replaced with "dog" when Match Case is selected.

## PRACTICE

### Replacing text

*Try replacing the word "play" in your document with the word "view" as follows:*

1. Move the insertion point to the top of the document, and then choose the Replace command from the Edit menu to open the Replace window.

2. Enter *play* in the Find What text box and *view* in the Replace With text box.

3. Choose Clear from the Find What Format list box to clear out any formatting, and then check to be sure that both the Match Whole Word Only and Match Case options are deselected.

4. Click on the Find Next button to begin the search. Word shows you each proposed change. It selects "play" in the first sentence.

5. Click on the Replace button. Word changes "play" to "view" in the document and then continues, selecting "Play" in the second sentence.

6. Click on the Replace button again. Word changes "Play" to "View" and then continues, selecting "play" in "playback."

7. Click on the Find Next button to reject this change. Word continues, selecting "play" from "replay."

8. Click on the Find Next button to reject this change. Word continues, selecting "play" in the second paragraph.

9. Select the Match Whole Word Only option so that Word won't change the words "playback" and "replay" to "viewback" and "review."

10. Click on the Replace All button. Word replaces every occurrence of "play" in the document with "view," and displays a dialog box asking whether you want to continue changing

from the beginning of the document. Click on the No button. Word closes the dialog box and reports the number of changes in the Page-Number area of the document window.

11. Close the Replace window and scroll through the document to view Word's changes.

## PRACTICE

### Replacing formatted text

*Now try replacing underlined text in the document with italicized text:*

1. Move to the top of the document and choose the Replace command from the Edit menu to open the Replace window.

2. Delete all text from the Find What text box and the Replace With text box.

3. Choose Character from the Format list box in the Find What area to open the Character dialog box.

4. Choose Single from the Underline list box, and then click on the OK button to close the dialog box. Word shows ''Underline'' to the right of the Find What Format list box.

5. Choose Character from the Format list box in the Replace With area to open the Character dialog box.

6. Click on the Italic option to select it, and then click on the OK button to close the dialog box. Word shows ''Italic'' to the right of the Replace With Format list box.

7. Click on the Replace All button to replace all underlined text with italic text. An End Of Document Reached dialog box appears. Click on the OK button to close this dialog box.

8. Close the Replace window and scroll through your document. All the occurrences of the word ''counterclockwise'' throughout the document should now be in italic.

You've now learned some quick and easy ways to edit your text. In the next chapter, you'll learn how to format paragraphs to make your edited text look even better.

# Chapter 5

# Working with Paragraphs

Paragraph formatting, more than any other type of formatting, controls your document's overall appearance. By shaping the text in paragraphs, you control the balance of your document, adding weight in some locations with dense text and lightening other locations with the white space created by open lines and wide margins.

This chapter answers questions you may have about paragraph formatting: How do you shape paragraphs using indents and text alignment? How do you control the line spacing so that you can fill more space with less text? (Handy for term papers!) How do you put borders around paragraphs for emphasis? And just what do those mysterious paragraph marks do, anyway?

## PARAGRAPH MARKS

Let's start with the mystery of the paragraph mark. You learned in Chapter 2, "Creating a Business Letter," that each time you press Return, Word enters a paragraph mark (an invisible character) at the end of one paragraph and starts a new paragraph. The paragraph mark separates paragraphs, but it does much more: It also stores the paragraph formatting specifications—indents, alignment, line spacing, border type, and other information.

Think of each paragraph mark as a "text mold" for the paragraph preceding it. Any text you type in that paragraph conforms to the paragraph mark's formatting. For example, if you enter text in a paragraph whose paragraph mark is set to be left aligned and double spaced, Word aligns each new line with the left margin and inserts a blank line after each line of text.

Word starts every new document with a paragraph mark that's set for default formatting. When you press Return at the end of the first paragraph, Word duplicates the paragraph mark (including its formatting) and leaves the duplicate at the end of the paragraph you just entered. As you continue entering paragraphs and pressing Return, Word continues duplicating the paragraph mark and its formatting. This is how the program carries paragraph formatting from one paragraph to the next as you enter new text.

You've probably noticed that a paragraph mark always appears at the end of the document, even if you try to delete everything from the document. The mark is there because Word needs at least one paragraph mark in which to store the paragraph formatting. You can never delete this final paragraph mark—but you can change its formatting.

## CHANGING PARAGRAPH FORMATS

Whenever you change a paragraph format such as alignment or line spacing, Word changes the formatting stored in the paragraph marks of any paragraphs you have selected. As you recall, all it takes to select a paragraph for paragraph formatting is to put the insertion point anywhere in the paragraph (which means that a paragraph is always selected for formatting as you type it). A paragraph is also selected for paragraph formatting if any small part of it—even a single character—is selected as part of a text block.

Word offers several types of paragraph formatting. The most important—those we'll look at in this chapter—are

- Indents (the width of the paragraph, determined by the location of its left and right sides)

- Alignment (how the text fills the paragraph indents—all even against one side, or spread equally between the sides)

- Line spacing (the amount of space between lines of text in the paragraph)

- Borders (lines around the exterior of the paragraph that set it apart from other text)

## Paragraph-Formatting Methods

You can apply paragraph formatting in several different ways, depending on which is most convenient for you. Word offers the following tools:

- The Ruler

- The Paragraph dialog box (which you can open by choosing the Paragraph command from the Format menu or by double-clicking on any of the indent markers in the Ruler)

- Keyboard shortcuts

The following sections describe each tool and how to use it.

### The Ruler

The Ruler, shown in Figure 5-1, lets you use the mouse to quickly change paragraph formatting. Although Word normally shows a Ruler in each document window, you can hide the Ruler if you want to by choosing the Ruler command from the View menu. (Choose it again to display the Ruler again.) By hiding the Ruler, you can see more of the text in your document. Note that you can also hide the Ribbon by choosing the Ribbon command from the View menu to free up even more display space for text.

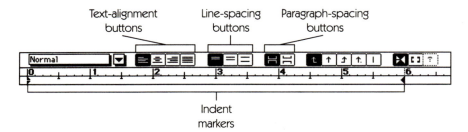

**FIGURE 5-1**. *The parts of the Ruler.*

As shown in Figure 5-1, the Ruler's three center buttons set line spacing. The four buttons to the left of center set text alignment, and the two buttons to the right of center close or open a line space before each paragraph. You move the wedges at the left and right ends of the measure, located below the buttons, to set paragraph indents.

You'll learn about the other parts of the Ruler, such as the Style Name list box and the buttons for setting tab stops, in following chapters.

## The Paragraph dialog box

Choosing the Paragraph command from the Format menu opens the Paragraph dialog box, shown in Figure 5-2, and displays the Ruler if it isn't already visible. You can also double-click on most parts of the Ruler to open the Paragraph dialog box: the indent markers, the line-spacing buttons, the text-alignment buttons, and the paragraph-spacing buttons.

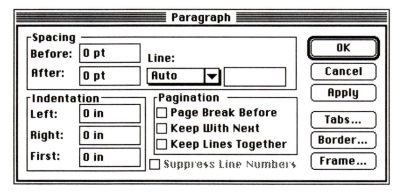

**FIGURE 5-2**. *The Paragraph dialog box offers controls that shape paragraphs within a document.*

98

Once it is open, you can use the Paragraph dialog box to change the appearance of selected paragraphs. The Spacing area in the upper left corner has controls that set the spacing between lines of text and space before and after each paragraph. The Indentation area in the lower left corner controls paragraph indents, and the Pagination area to its right controls how page breaks split (or don't split) paragraphs.

The three buttons in the bottom right corner of the dialog box open three dialog boxes:

- The Tabs dialog box, in which you can set tab stops within the selected text

- The Border dialog box, in which you can add borders to the selected text

- The Frame dialog box, in which you can position the selected text at a fixed location on a page (an advanced feature).

You'll learn to use the Border dialog box in this chapter and the Tabs dialog box in the next chapter.

### Keyboard shortcuts

As usual, keyboard shortcuts can help you format directly from the keyboard. The shortcuts, listed throughout this chapter, require you to press a combination of Shift-Command plus a letter key.

## SETTING PARAGRAPH INDENTS

You can set any of three kinds of indents for a paragraph: left, right, and first-line, all shown in Figure 5-3. Word measures each of these indents from the left and right *margins* of the document. Margins are normally 1.25 inches from the left and right edges of the page, and 1 inch from the top and bottom edges. Although the figure shows margins as dotted lines, they are invisible on the screen and on the page. Think of margins as guidelines for the paragraph indents—you can set the indents to the inside or the outside of the margins, although most indents are set inside the margins. (You'll learn more about margins and how to change them if necessary in Chapter 12, ''Margins and Document Formatting.'')

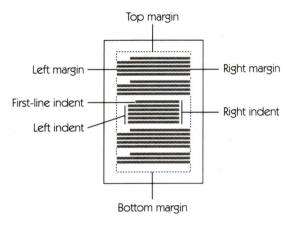

**FIGURE 5-3**. *Word offers three types of paragraph indents, all measured from the page margins around the edges of the printed page.*

The measure on the Ruler shows distance from the left margin of the page. The 0 mark is located directly on the left margin, and all the other measurements are measured from that point. When an indent is set at 0, it falls exactly on the left margin—normally 1.25 inches from the left edge of the paper. If an indent is set to 1 inch, it falls 1 inch to the right of the left margin—a total of 2.25 inches from the left edge of the page.

A quick summary of the three types of indents:

- The first-line indent sets the left edge of the first line of the paragraph. It doesn't affect any of the subsequent lines in the paragraph.

- The left indent sets the left edge of all the lines of the paragraph except the first line.

- The right indent sets the right edge of all the lines of the paragraph, including the first line.

Why does Word allow you to set a separate first-line indent? Because you can set it to automatically indent the first line of each paragraph without your having to press Tab or the space bar. In fact, you should always use a first-line indent setting instead of using a tab or spaces to create indented para-

100

graph lines. Using the first-line indent makes it much easier to control the paragraphs' appearance: You simply select the paragraphs and drag the first-line indent marker.

Note one measurement quirk about setting the right indent: On the Ruler, the right indent is measured from the left margin. It is usually set at 6 inches, which is a total of 7.25 inches from the left page edge—or, on standard paper, 1.25 inches from the right edge, which is directly on the right margin. (If you look closely at the 6-inch mark on the Ruler, you'll see a short vertical dotted line there to show the location of the right margin.) In the Paragraph dialog box, on the other hand, the right indent is measured from the right margin instead of the left margin. Although the right indent normally shows up at 6 inches on the Ruler, the Paragraph dialog box shows it set at 0 inches: 0 inches from the right margin, which is 1.25 inches from the right edge of the page. If this sounds confusing, stick to using the Ruler, where you can clearly see the right indent location.

## Setting Indents Using the Ruler

To set indents using the Ruler, use the mouse to drag the appropriate indent marker to the position you want on the measure. Figure 5-4 labels the three indent markers. As you drag any one of the indent markers, the Page-Number area at the bottom of the document window displays the marker's location in inches from the left margin.

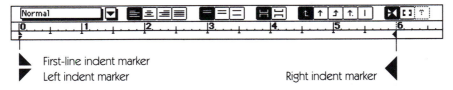

**FIGURE 5-4.** *Use the three indent markers on the Ruler to control a paragraph's indents.*

Note that when you drag the left indent marker, the first-line indent marker moves with it, keeping the first-line indent set relative to the left indent. You can easily move the first-line indent marker by itself to change the first line's indention, but to move the left indent marker by itself, you must hold down the Shift key as you drag the left indent marker.

## Setting Indents Using the Paragraph Dialog Box

To set indents using the Paragraph dialog box, choose the Paragraph command from the Format menu. When the dialog box appears, click in the appropriate Indentation text box: *Left* for the left indent, *Right* for the right indent, or *First* for the first-line indent. Enter the indent setting you want in inches, and then press Return to close the dialog box and apply the indent. Remember that the Right indent is measured from the right margin, and note that the First indent is measured from the location of the left indent.

## Setting Indents Using Keyboard Shortcuts

Four keyboard shortcuts let you change indents, but not with the finesse of the Ruler or the Paragraph dialog box:

- Shift-Command-N moves the left and first-line indents to the right by 0.5 inch (a process called *nesting*).

- Shift-Command-M moves the left indent to the left by 0.5 inch and moves the first-line indent so that it is even with the left indent.

- Shift-Command-F moves the first-line indent 0.5 inch to the right of the left indent.

- Shift-Command-T creates a "hanging indent" by moving the left indent to the right by 0.5 inch.

## PRACTICE

### Setting indents

*Try setting indents as you re-create the paragraphs shown in Figure 5-5. For the time being, ignore the line spacing and text alignment you see there—you'll set them later.*

1. Choose the New command from the Edit menu to open a new document.

2. Before you type the first paragraph, set the first-line indent to 0.5 inch by dragging the first-line indent marker to the 0.5-inch mark on the measure, creating a first-line indention.

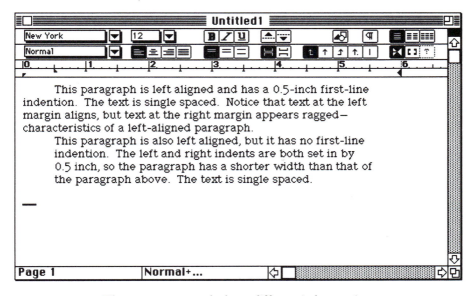

**FIGURE 5-5.** *These two paragraphs have different indent settings.*

3. Type the first paragraph, and press Return after you finish.

4. Type the second paragraph, stopping before you press Return. Notice that the indention you created in the first paragraph is duplicated in this paragraph.

5. Choose the Paragraph command from the Format menu to open the Paragraph dialog box.

6. Change the 0 to *.5* in the Left text box, the 0 to *.5* in the Right text box, and the .5 to *0* in the First text box.

7. Press Return to close the dialog box and apply the new indents. The text moves in 0.5 inch on both sides, and the first-line indention disappears.

8. Press Return to end the paragraph.

## SETTING PARAGRAPH ALIGNMENT

Setting indents sets the left and right boundaries of a paragraph; setting alignment determines how text fits into those boundaries. Word offers four types of alignment: left, right, centered, and justified.

- In *left alignment,* all text aligns with the left indent, leaving a ragged right edge.

- In *right alignment,* all text aligns with the right indent, leaving a ragged left edge.

- In *centered alignment,* each line of text centers exactly between the left and right indents, leaving both edges ragged.

- In *justified alignment,* all text aligns with both the left and right indents (except the last line of the paragraph, which might be shorter than the other lines and would therefore align only with the left indent) to create smooth edges. Word adjusts the blank space between words to create full justification.

You can apply each type of alignment by using either the Ruler or keyboard shortcuts.

## Setting Alignment Using the Ruler

To align paragraphs using the Ruler, simply select the paragraphs and click on the appropriate alignment button. All the text in the selected paragraphs is aligned using the alignment you choose.

## Setting Alignment Using Keyboard Shortcuts

The following keyboard shortcuts align selected paragraphs:

- Shift-Command-L applies left alignment.

- Shift-Command-R applies right alignment.

- Shift-Command-C applies centered alignment.

- Shift-Command-J applies justified alignment.

 **Practice**

### Setting alignment

*You've already entered two paragraphs that use left alignment. Now try your hand at centered and justified alignment, entering the new text in Figure 5-6.*

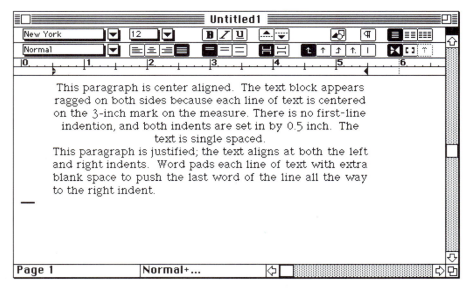

**FIGURE 5-6.** *These two paragraphs have different alignments.*

1. Type the first new paragraph of text, stopping before you press Return.

2. Click on the Ruler's center-alignment button to center each line of text in the paragraph.

3. Press Return to begin a new paragraph, and then type the second new paragraph of text, again stopping before you press Return.

4. Press Shift-Command-J to apply justified alignment. The text in the paragraph aligns with both the left and right indents.

## SETTING LINE SPACING

*Line space* is the amount of space between lines of text in a paragraph. You can give the text in your document a feeling of density or lightness, depending on how you set line spacing. Word measures line space in points, the same unit of measurement it uses to measure the height of fonts. It measures line space from the bottom of one line of text to the bottom of the line below it. The bottom of a text line is determined by the lowest point of a font's *descenders*, as shown in Figure 5-7. Descenders are "tails" on characters such as "j" and "p."

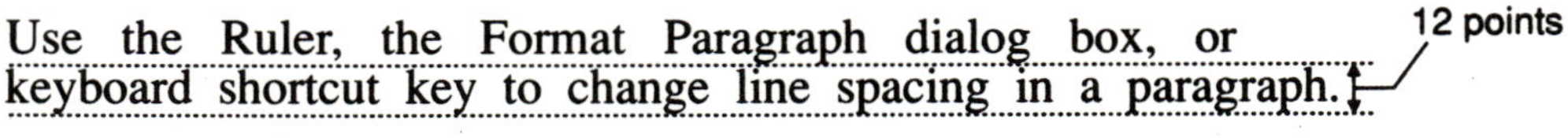

Use the Ruler, the Format Paragraph dialog box, or       12 points
keyboard shortcut key to change line spacing in a paragraph.

**FIGURE 5-7.** *Word measures line space from the bottom of one line to the bottom of the following line.*

Word normally uses *"auto" line spacing*—that is, line spacing that automatically adds 3 points to the largest font size in any line. If all the text is in a 12-point font, Word sets line spacing at 15 points. If the text is in a 9-point font, Word sets line spacing at 12 points. And if the text is in a mixture of 12- and 18-point fonts, Word sets line spacing at 21 points (3 points larger than the larger font). Because auto line spacing is flexible to match varying font sizes, you might have a single paragraph with many different line spacings if you've used many different font sizes within the paragraph.

You can also set *exact line spacing* or *minimum line spacing*. Exact line spacing puts a set number of points between lines no matter what the font size, so that fonts too large for the spacing are chopped off at the top. Exact spacing isn't often useful—who likes chopped-off characters?—so you'll most likely use minimum line spacing, which lets you set the minimum number of points between lines but which will expand to accommodate large fonts. Line spacing is set with either the Ruler or the Paragraph dialog box.

## Setting Line Spacing Using the Ruler

The Ruler displays three buttons you can use to set line spacing:

- Single-spacing button—instructs Word to set single line spacing

- One-and-one-half-spacing button—instructs Word to set one-and-one-half line spacing, which is a minimum spacing of 18 points

- Double-spacing button—instructs Word to set double line spacing, which is a minimum spacing of 24 points

To set line spacing, select the desired paragraphs and click on the appropriate line-spacing button in the Ruler. Figure 5-8 labels the line-spacing buttons.

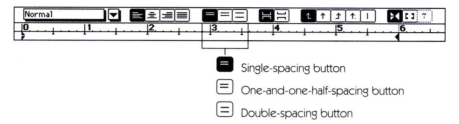

FIGURE 5-8. *The line-spacing buttons in the Ruler set line spacing in selected paragraphs.*

Notice that the one-and-one-half-spacing button and the double-spacing button are set for line-spacing sizes that work best with a 12-point font size. If you use a larger font size, such as 24-point, these line-spacing settings have no effect because the large font size forces spacing to 24 points. Or if you use a much smaller type size, such as 9-point, these settings will seem much larger than double spacing or one-and-one-half spacing. To get more precise line settings for other font sizes, use the Paragraph dialog box.

## Setting Line Spacing Using the Paragraph Dialog Box

To set line spacing using the Paragraph dialog box, choose the Paragraph command from the Format menu to open the dialog box. Use the list box in the right half of the Spacing area, which is labeled *Line.* The list box allows you three choices:

- *Auto,* which automatically sets line spacing according to font size
- *At Least,* which tells Word to use minimum line spacing
- *Exactly,* which tells Word to use exact line spacing

If you set either At Least or Exactly, you must fill in the text box to the right of the Line list box with the number of points you want for line spacing.

As a rule of thumb, to get double spacing for the font size used in the paragraph, choose At Least in the list box and then enter a point value in the text box that's twice as large as your font size. For example, set At Least to 18 if you want double line spacing for a paragraph of 9-point text. For one-and-one-half spacing, enter a point value one and one half times as large as the font size you are using.

## Setting Line Spacing Using Keyboard Shortcuts

Word offers one keyboard shortcut for setting line spacing: Shift-Command-Y, which sets 24-point minimum line spacing (which is double line spacing for 12-point text).

**PRACTICE**

### Setting line spacing

*Try changing the spacing of the last paragraph you typed:*

1. Select the last paragraph of the sample document.

2. Open the Paragraph dialog box by choosing the Paragraph command from the Format menu.

3. Choose At Least from the list box, type *36* in the text box, and press Return to apply the 36-point minimum line spacing. All the lines in the paragraph are separated by 36 points from line bottom to line bottom, which is triple spacing for the 12-point text in the paragraph.

4. Click on the double-spacing button in the Ruler. The line spacing reduces to 24 points (double spacing for 12-point text) as shown in Figure 5-9.

## Inserting Space Before and After Each Paragraph

In addition to controlling the amount of space between lines, Word controls the amount of space between paragraphs to help set paragraphs apart. Two buttons in the Ruler, shown in Figure 5-10, let you add space or not add space before a paragraph. Click on the open-line button to add 12 points of line space (one blank line) before each selected paragraph, and click on the close-line button to format the paragraph without an extra 12 points of line space before each selected paragraph.

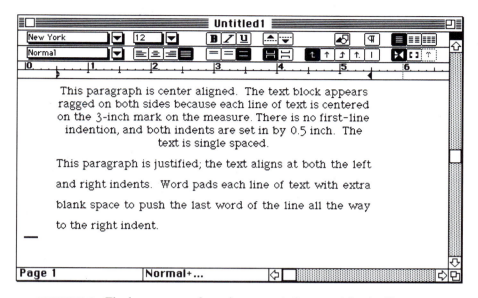

**FIGURE 5-9.** *The last paragraph on the screen is formatted for double spacing.*

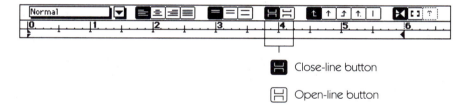

**FIGURE 5-10.** *The paragraph-spacing buttons in the Ruler set paragraph spacing for selected paragraphs.*

You can also control spacing between paragraphs using the Spacing area of the Paragraph dialog box. Entering a point value in the Before text box instructs Word to add that much line space *before* each selected paragraph. Entering a point value in the After text box instructs Word to add that much line space *after* each selected paragraph.

Word offers one keyboard shortcut for setting paragraph spacing: Shift-Command-O, which adds 12 points of line space before each selected paragraph. Pressing Shift-Command-O again removes the 12 points of line space.

### PRACTICE

### Adding single lines

*Now try adding a single line before each paragraph in your document:*

1. Select the entire document by pressing Option-Command-M.

2. Click on the open-line button in the Ruler. An extra 12 points of space precedes each paragraph in the document.

*If you want open space between paragraphs, it's a good idea to use paragraph formatting instead of pressing Return an extra time between paragraphs. The practice sessions up to this point have had you press Return to add space between paragraphs; in your own documents, use the open-line button in the Ruler instead. Not only is it easier, but it makes it much simpler for you to get rid of the space between paragraphs later: You simply select the paragraphs and turn off the open space.*

## ADDING PARAGRAPH BORDERS

If you really want to set a paragraph or group of paragraphs apart from surrounding text, you can use paragraph formatting to add a border around the paragraphs. Word offers a full variety of borders that you can set around paragraphs, from a single thin line to double lines and shadowed backdrops. We don't need to learn about all of them here; using Word's preset borders should take care of most of your border needs. (You'll find more about borders in the Word manual if you're interested in further refinements.)

To add paragraph borders, first select as a text block the paragraph or paragraphs you want bordered. Choose the Paragraph command from the Format menu to open the Paragraph dialog box, and then click on the Border button to open the Border dialog box, shown in Figure 5-11.

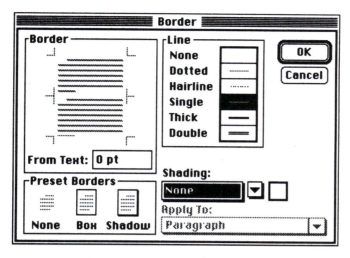

**FIGURE 5-11.** *Use the Border dialog box to set a border around selected paragraphs.*

## Border Options

The Border dialog box offers a variety of border options that allow you to enclose a paragraph partially or in full and to add background shading. We're interested in two areas: the Line area, which sets the type of line (or lines) that Word uses to border a paragraph, and the Preset Borders area, which uses the line type you choose to enclose the paragraphs.

## Choosing a Line Type and a Preset Border

To place a border around paragraphs, first choose a line type, and then choose a preset border. Word offers a full set of border line types, as shown in the document in Figure 5-12. You can choose any one of the border line types by clicking on the one you want in the Line area. The available line types are (from top to bottom) none, dotted line, hairline, single line, thick line, and double line. Notice in the figure that the hairline border is a very thin border, a line as thin as the printer can print. Although it appears as a 1-pixel-wide line on the screen, it appears as a much thinner line in a laser-printer printout.

Once you've chosen a line type, you can choose a preset border that uses that line type. You have three choices in the Preset Borders area: *None,* which turns off all borders; *Box,* which puts a box around the paragraph using the selected line style; and *Shadow,* which does the same as Box but adds a drop shadow that shows on the right and bottom edges of the border. You can see a drop-shadow border around the last paragraph in Figure 5-12.

This is paragraph one.  It has a dotted border.

This is paragraph two.  It has a hairline border.

This is paragraph three.  It has a single border.

This is paragraph four.  It has a thick border.

This is paragraph five.  It has a double-line border with a drop shadow.

**FIGURE 5-12.** *These printouts show the variety of border line types..*

## Practice

### Adding a border

*Try adding a double-line border to the last paragraph of the document you're working on:*

1. Move the insertion point into the last paragraph.

2. Choose the Paragraph command from the Format menu to open the Paragraph dialog box.

3. Click on the Border button to open the Border dialog box.

4. Click on the Double line style in the Line area to set a double line.

5. Click on the Box icon in the Preset Borders area to create a plain box. A double-line box appears in the Border area to show what you've created.

6. Click on the OK button to close the Border dialog box, and then click on the OK button to close the Paragraph dialog box. Word adds a double-line border around the paragraph you selected, as shown in Figure 5-13.

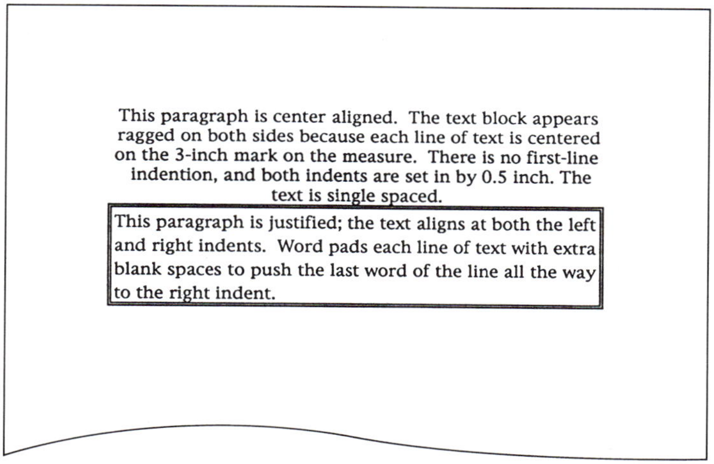

This paragraph is center aligned. The text block appears ragged on both sides because each line of text is centered on the 3-inch mark on the measure. There is no first-line indention, and both indents are set in by 0.5 inch. The text is single spaced.

This paragraph is justified; the text aligns at both the left and right indents. Word pads each line of text with extra blank spaces to push the last word of the line all the way to the right indent.

**FIGURE 5-13.** *A double-line border surrounds the last paragraph.*

# SPLITTING AND COMBINING PARAGRAPHS

The fact that a paragraph's formatting information is stored in its paragraph mark leads to some interesting questions when you start editing text: What happens to the paragraph's text if you cut the paragraph mark out of the paragraph? What happens to the text if you split a paragraph in two? Or if you paste a paragraph mark with different paragraph formatting into the middle of a paragraph?

## Splitting a Paragraph

The simplest way to split a paragraph is to move the insertion point to the location where you want the split and then press Return. The paragraph mark you insert splits the paragraph into two new paragraphs. Both have the same paragraph formatting because Word copies the formatting information from the paragraph mark at the end of the original paragraph to the inserted paragraph mark.

You can also split a paragraph by pasting a new paragraph (with its own paragraph mark) somewhere within it. The split paragraph text that appears before the inserted paragraph takes on the paragraph formatting of the inserted paragraph; the text that appears after the inserted paragraph retains its original formatting. For example, if you paste a single-spaced paragraph into the middle of a double-spaced paragraph, the text in front of the pasted paragraph becomes single spaced (it's now part of the single-spaced paragraph), and the text after the pasted paragraph remains double spaced. If you think about it, it's logical: The text is formatted using the closest following paragraph mark.

### PRACTICE

### Splitting a paragraph

*Do the following steps on your current document to see how this works:*

1. Select a text block in the last paragraph (the bordered paragraph) that extends to the end of the paragraph. This block contains the paragraph mark (at the end of the paragraph) that contains centered and bordered paragraph formatting.

2. Select the Copy command from the Edit menu (alternatively, press Command-C) to copy the text block into the Clipboard.

3. Move the insertion point to the middle of the first paragraph, and choose the Paste command from the Edit menu (or press Command-V) to paste the text block into the middle of the first paragraph.

*The first paragraph splits into two paragraphs. The first of the split paragraphs is centered and bordered because it ends with the paragraph mark copied from a centered and bordered paragraph. The second of the split paragraphs retains its original paragraph formatting because it ends with the original paragraph mark.*

## Combining Paragraphs

To combine two paragraphs, delete the paragraph mark at the end of the first paragraph. Word combines the text from the first paragraph with the text in the second paragraph. If the two paragraphs have different paragraph formatting, the formatting of the first paragraph is lost (along with its paragraph mark). To prevent this from happening accidentally, Word won't let you use the Delete key when the cursor is positioned between two paragraphs with different formatting.

If you do want to remove a paragraph mark from between two differently formatted paragraphs, select the paragraph mark and choose the Cut command from the Edit menu or press the Delete key to remove the paragraph mark. (You might need to make the paragraph mark visible first by clicking on the show/hide paragraph button in the Ribbon.)

### PRACTICE

**Combining paragraphs**

*Try combining the paragraphs of the sample document as follows:*

1. Place the insertion point at the end of the first paragraph and double-click. Word selects the paragraph mark at the end of the paragraph.

2. Press the Delete key. The two paragraphs combine, and the formatting of the first paragraph changes to match that of the second: left-aligned, left and right indents set to 0.5 inch, and no first-line indention.

3. Close the document without saving it.

You've now learned how to format paragraphs to control the appearance of text in a document. In the next chapter you'll learn about an aspect of paragraph formatting not covered in this chapter: setting tabs.

# Chapter 6

# Aligning Text with Tabs

Tab stops have traditionally helped typists line up columns of text by setting position markers across the width of a page. A press of the Tab key moved the typewriter carriage to the next tab stop, where the typist would resume typing. Microsoft Word offers more advanced tabbing capability. With Word tabs, you can not only set position markers across a page but also align text by its right or left edge, center text, and align numbers by their decimal points. You can also fill in the spaces between columns with dotted-line, dashed-line, or solid-line leaders. Once columns of text are in place, changing the tab stops moves the columns to their new tab positions on the page.

This chapter should answer some questions you may have about tabs: What exactly happens when you press the Tab key? How do you set tab stops? How do you change existing tab stops? How can you use tab leaders to good advantage? And how do you line up columns of text with tabs?

To help you get some practice with tabs, you'll re-create the document shown in Figure 6-1, a menu for Señor Fujiyama's Japanese-Mexican restaurant. The practice sessions show you how to use tabs to align the columns of items and prices, to create the leaders that connect the items and prices, and to align the parts of the menu heading.

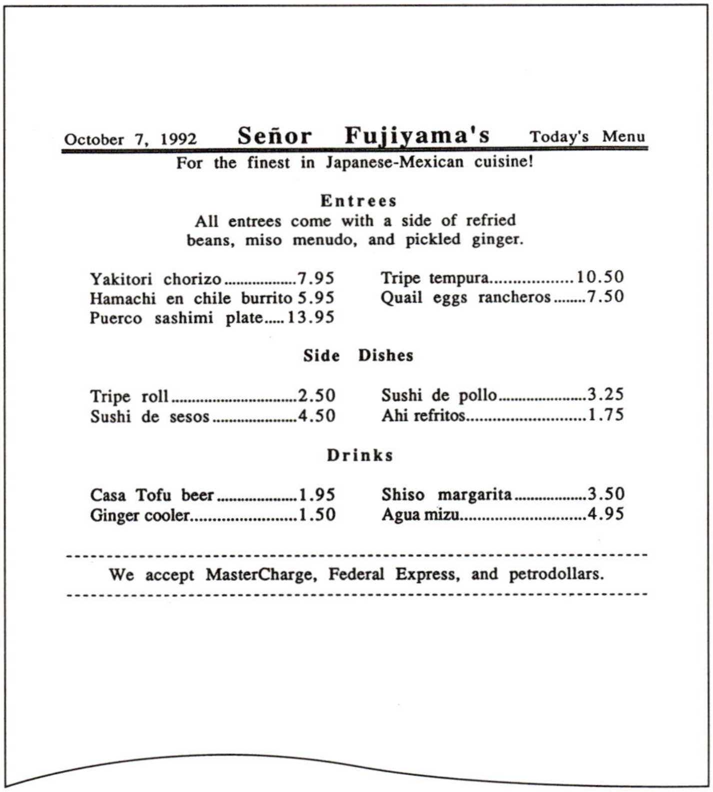

October 7, 1992     **Señor    Fujiyama's**     Today's Menu
For the finest in Japanese-Mexican cuisine!

**Entrees**
All entrees come with a side of refried
beans, miso menudo, and pickled ginger.

| | |
|---|---|
| Yakitori chorizo.................7.95 | Tripe tempura...................10.50 |
| Hamachi en chile burrito 5.95 | Quail eggs rancheros........7.50 |
| Puerco sashimi plate.....13.95 | |

**Side   Dishes**

| | |
|---|---|
| Tripe roll...............................2.50 | Sushi de pollo.....................3.25 |
| Sushi de sesos.......................4.50 | Ahi refritos...........................1.75 |

**Drinks**

| | |
|---|---|
| Casa Tofu beer.....................1.95 | Shiso margarita...................3.50 |
| Ginger cooler..........................1.50 | Agua mizu.............................4.95 |

-----------------------------------------------------
We accept MasterCharge, Federal Express, and petrodollars.
-----------------------------------------------------

**FIGURE 6-1.** *This restaurant menu uses tabs to align columns and to position information within lines.*

# TAB STOPS

As you learned in previous chapters, pressing the Tab key moves the insertion point to the right. The stopping point is called a *tab stop*. Tab stops are position markers; when you press the Tab key, the insertion point moves to the right along the current line to the next tab stop. If no tab stop remains on the line, the insertion point moves to the next line and stops at the first tab stop on that line.

Each tab stop performs three functions:

■ It marks a location where the insertion point stops after you press the Tab key.

■ It controls the alignment of the text you type after you press the Tab key.

■ It can add a dotted-line, dashed-line, or solid-line leader in the space between tabbed columns.

Because tab stop settings are a type of paragraph formatting, each paragraph has its own set of tab stops. Any tab stops you set are stored in the paragraph mark and duplicated in the next paragraph when you press Return.

In previous chapters you used the Tab key to jump to Word's *default tab stops*. If you don't set tab stops, Word sets default tab stops every half inch along the Ruler's measure. Tab stops are marked with small horizontal lines, as shown in Figure 6-2.

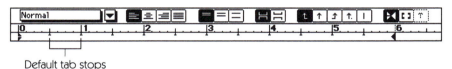

Default tab stops

**FIGURE 6-2.** *Default tab stops appear every half inch along the Ruler's measure.*

Setting a tab stop is a simple matter of inserting a tab-stop marker on the measure. Word offers four types of tab stops: left-align, center-align, right-align, and decimal-align. In addition, it offers a fifth, similar, control: the bar marker. Figure 6-3 shows the buttons for the bar marker and each type of tab stop.

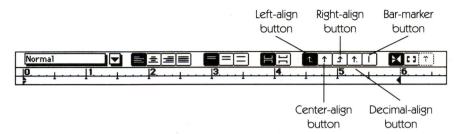

**FIGURE 6-3.** *The bar-marker button and the four tab-stop buttons in the Ruler.*

Each type of tab stop controls the alignment of the text you type after you press the Tab key. The bar marker, which isn't a tab stop but is set like one, doesn't align text but adds a vertical bar at the tab location. You set it just as you do a tab stop. Figure 6-4 shows how the four types of tab stops align text. Each tab stop is set in the middle of the page, at the 3-inch mark on the measure.

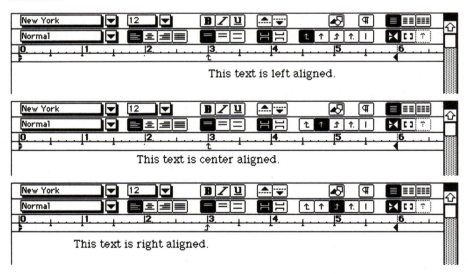

*(continued)*

**FIGURE 6-4.** *The left-align tab stop aligns text by its left edge. The center-align tab stop centers each line of text. The right-align tab stop aligns text by its right edge. The decimal-align tab stop aligns numbers by their decimal points. The bar marker adds a vertical bar at the specified location.*

FIGURE 6-4. *continued*

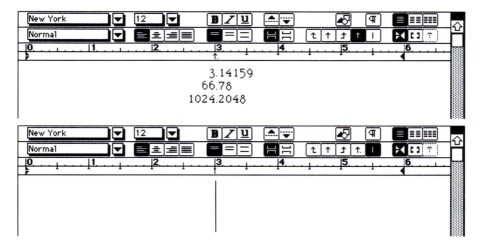

## SETTING TAB STOPS

To set a tab stop, select a paragraph or group of paragraphs as you would for paragraph formatting. You can then position the desired tab-stops on the Ruler's measure (by dragging a tab-stop button), or you can enter tab-stop locations in the Tabs dialog box. You can open the Tabs dialog box either by clicking on the Tabs button at the bottom right corner of the Paragraph dialog box or by double-clicking on a tab-stop button in the Ruler. Whenever you set a tab stop, all the default tab stops to the left of the new tab stop are removed. The exception is the bar marker; when you set a bar marker, all the default tab stops remain.

### Setting Tab Stops Using the Ruler

To set a tab stop using the Ruler, click on one of the tab-stop buttons. Then click on the desired tab-stop location on the measure. The selected tab stop appears in that position. If you prefer, you can also drag a tab-stop marker to the desired position on the measure.

### PRACTICE
#### Setting tab stops with the Ruler

*Try setting a tab stop for the first paragraph of Señor Fujiyama's menu:*

1. If you haven't already, start Word and open a new document.

2. Click on the center-align tab-stop button.

3. Click on a spot just below the 3-inch mark on the measure.
   A center-align tab stop appears there.

## Setting Tab Stops Using the Tabs Dialog Box

To use the Tabs dialog box to set tab stops, first open the Paragraph dialog box by choosing the Paragraph command from the Format menu. Then click on the Tabs button to open the Tabs dialog box, shown in Figure 6-5. Or, for faster access, simply double-click on a tab-stop button in the Ruler to open the Tabs dialog box.

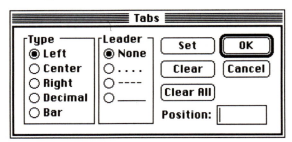

**FIGURE 6-5.** *You can enter tab-stop positions in the Tabs dialog box.*

To set a tab stop using the Tabs dialog box, first click on one of the tab-stop buttons in the Type area, and then drag the desired tab-stop marker from the tab-stop button (in the Ruler of the document window) onto the measure. The Position text box in the Tabs dialog box displays the current position of the tab-stop marker. You can also type the desired position for the tab stop (in inches) in the Position text box, and then click on the Set button to set that tab stop. Note that you can't place tabs closer to each other than 0.0625 inch ($\frac{1}{16}$ inch) and probably wouldn't want to. When you've finished setting tab stops, click on the OK button or press Return to close the Tabs dialog box and apply your tab stops to the selected paragraphs. Then click on the OK button to close the Paragraph dialog box, if necessary.

### PRACTICE

#### Setting tabs with the Tabs dialog box

*Use the Tabs dialog box to set a second tab stop for the first paragraph of the menu as follows:*

1. Double-click on a tab-stop button in the Ruler to open the Tabs dialog box.

2. Click on the measure to insert a tab stop. (The position of the tab stop is not important now.)

3. Click on the Right button in the Type area of the Tabs dialog box to turn your inserted tab stop into a right tab stop.

4. Type the value 6 in the Position text box to set the tab stop at the 6-inch mark on the measure.

5. Click on the Set button to set the tab stop. A right-align tab-stop symbol appears on the right indent marker for the paragraph.

6. Click on the OK button to close the Tabs dialog box.

## Typing Text at a Tab Stop

Once you set tab stops, you can press the Tab key to move the insertion point to the next tab stop and enter text that is aligned according to the nature of the tab stop.

### PRACTICE

#### Typing text at a tab stop

*Try your two tab stops by entering the first few paragraphs of the menu:*

1. Type *October 7, 1992* and press the Tab key to jump to the center tab stop.

2. Change the font's point size to 18 and set bold text formatting.

3. Type *Señor Fujiyama's.* (To enter the ''ñ,'' press Option-N, and then type *n*.) The name centers at the tab stop.

4. Press the Tab key to jump to the next tab stop.

5. Reduce the font's point size to 12 and turn off bold formatting.

6. Type the phrase *Today's Menu,* and then press Return to start a new paragraph. The phrase appears flush against the right tab stop (and the right indent). The top line of Figure 6-6 shows the results.

7. To emphasize the text you entered, double-underline the text in the paragraph. First select the entire first paragraph, then open the Character dialog box. Choose Double from the Underline list box, and press Return to apply the underlining.

8. Move the insertion point to the end of the document and change the paragraph alignment to centered.

9. Type *For the finest in Japanese-Mexican cuisine!* and press Return twice.

10. Turn on bold character formatting, type *Entrees*, and then press Return.

11. Turn off bold character formatting. Use the Paragraph dialog box to set the left indent to 1.25 inches and the right indent to 1.25 inches. (Because the right indent marker is underneath the right tab stop, it is easier to move the right indent by using the Paragraph dialog box than by dragging the right indent marker in the Ruler.) Press Return.

12. Type *All entrees come with a side of refried beans, miso menudo, and pickled ginger.*

13. Press Return twice. Figure 6-6 shows the results. (Tab and paragraph marks are visible to indicate where to press Tab and Return.)

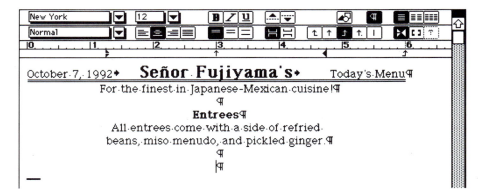

**FIGURE 6-6.** *The centered and right-aligned phrases of the first line are positioned by tab stops. Notice the tab-stop markers along the measure of the Ruler.*

*Notice that the tab stops you set in the first paragraph allowed you to left-align, right-align, and center various blocks of text in that paragraph.*

## ADDING TAB LEADERS

A tab leader is a useful device for leading the eye across tab space. In Señor Fujiyama's menu, you see dotted tab leaders used to connect the menu entries with their prices in the next column.

To add a leader to a tab, you use the Tabs dialog box. The Ruler is always visible when the Tabs dialog box is open, so you can see the tab stops for the currently selected paragraph as they're set along the measure. Note that if you select several paragraphs that have different indents or tab stops, the bottom strip of the Ruler's measure appears gray. The tab stops and indents that appear in the gray strip are those of the first paragraph in the text block. Changing margins or tab stops in the Ruler affects *all* the selected paragraphs, not just the first paragraph.

To add a leader to a tab stop, first double-click on a tab marker on the measure. The Tabs dialog box opens and shows the type of tab stop, the leader it uses (which is probably ''None''), and its position (in inches) on the measure. To change the leader setting from None to a visible leader, click on the dotted-line, dashed-line, or solid-line button in the Leader area of the Tabs dialog box. You can then click on another tab stop and change its leader. Click on the OK button to close the dialog box and apply the new leader settings.

## Practice

### Setting tabs and leaders

*One section of the sample menu displays food prices. Try setting the tabs and leaders for that section:*

1. Move the insertion point to the end of the document, reset the indents to 0 and 6 inches, set the paragraph alignment to left, and clear all tab stops from the Ruler. (To clear them, open the Tabs dialog box, click on the Clear All button, and then click on the OK button to close the dialog box.)

2. Set a left tab at 0.25 inch on the measure.

3. Set a decimal tab at 2.5 inches on the measure.

4. Set a left tab at 3.25 inches on the measure.

5. Set a decimal tab at 5.5 inches on the measure.

6. Open the Tabs dialog box.

7. Click on the 2.5-inch tab marker on the measure and then click on the dotted-line button in the Leader area of the Tabs dialog box.

8. Click on the 5.5-inch tab marker on the measure and then click on the dotted-line button.

9. Click on the OK button to close the dialog box and apply the tab settings.

10. Press the Tab key and then type the first line of the menu, pressing the Tab key between each menu item and its price: *Yakitori chorizo*, Tab, *7.95*, Tab, *Tripe tempura*, Tab, *10.50*.

11. Press Return to begin a new paragraph, and then enter the next two lines of the menu using the same technique. (Copy the text from Figure 6-7.) Press Return twice at the end of the "Entrees" section.

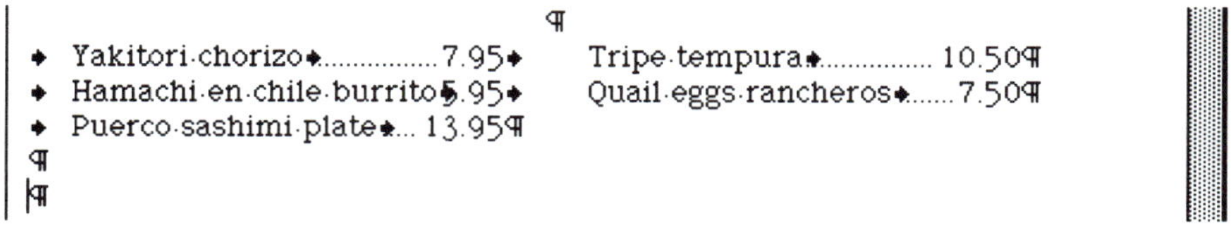

```
 ◆  Yakitori·chorizo◆...............7.95◆      Tripe·tempura◆............... 10.50¶
 ◆  Hamachi·en·chile·burrito5.95◆      Quail·eggs·rancheros◆.......7.50¶
 ◆  Puerco·sashimi·plate◆... 13.95¶
 ¶
|¶
```

**FIGURE 6-7.** *Menu items and prices are connected by tab leaders.*

*Notice that each time you press the Tab key to jump to a tab stop that has a leader, a dotted line stretches from the previous insertion point to the new location.*

## CHANGING TAB STOPS

You can easily change tab stops after you've inserted them. As you change tab stops, you change the position of the text aligned with them. This is a convenient tool: You can change the location of columns of text you've entered by moving tab stops to new positions. You can also change text alignment at a tab stop by changing the *type* of the tab stop, and you can change the type of leader preceding a tab stop by choosing a different leader. You can entirely remove a tab stop if necessary. Any text aligned with that tab stop then moves to the right, to the next tab stop.

### Removing a Tab Stop

To remove a tab stop using the Ruler, drag the tab-stop marker from the measure in the Ruler to any position below the measure and release the mouse button. The tab-stop marker disappears. To remove a tab stop using the Tabs dialog box, click on the tab-stop marker on the measure and then click on the Clear button in the Tabs dialog box. To remove all the tab stops from the Ruler, click on the Clear All button in the Tabs dialog box.

### Changing a Tab-Stop Position

To change a tab-stop position using the Ruler, simply drag the tab-stop marker from one position on the measure to another; any text aligned with that tab stop moves with the tab-stop marker to its new position. To change a tab-stop position using the Tabs dialog box, double-click on the tab-stop marker on the measure, and then type a new value (in inches) in the Position text box in the lower right corner of the dialog box. Click on the Set button; Word moves the tab stop to the position you entered.

### PRACTICE
#### Moving tab stops

*Try moving a tab stop in the last three paragraphs you entered:*

1. Select as a block the three lines of menu items beginning with "Yakitori," "Hamachi," and "Puerco."

2. Move the left tab-stop marker at 0.25 inches on the measure to 0.5 inches. All the text in the first column moves with the mark.

3. Return the tab-stop marker to 0.25 inches. All the text moves back to its original position.

*Notice that changing the tab stops moved columns of text only in the paragraphs you selected.*

## Changing Tab-Stop Alignment

To change the text alignment of a tab stop using the Ruler, first remove the tab-stop marker from the measure and then replace it with a different type of tab-stop marker. To change text alignment using the Tabs dialog box, double-click on the desired tab-stop marker on the measure, click on a different button in the Type area of the Tabs dialog box, and then click on the Set button. As soon as you change the alignment, all the text aligned at that tab stop changes its alignment to match the selected tab-stop type.

## Changing a Tab-Stop Leader

To change a tab-stop leader, you must use the Tabs dialog box. Double-click on the desired tab-stop marker on the measure, click on a leader option in the Leader area of the Tabs dialog box, and then click on the Set button. If you click on the None button, you remove the leader completely. After you change a tab-stop leader, all the leaders that are assigned to that tab stop change to the new type of leader.

## PRACTICE

### Using tab leaders

*To complete the sample menu, enter the next two sections of text as you did the first section and then finish by using a new tabbing technique.*

1. Move the insertion point to the end of the document.

2. Turn on bold character formatting and change the paragraph alignment to centered.

3. Type *Side Dishes* and press Return twice.

4. Turn off bold character formatting and change the paragraph alignment to left. Type the next two lines of text, pressing Tab where you see the tab marks in Figure 6-8.

5. Press Return twice to finish the ''Side Dishes'' section.

6. Enter the next section, ''Drinks,'' as you entered the previous section. When you finish, press Return twice.

7. Clear all tab stops from the Ruler, and then drag a right-align tab marker to the 6-inch mark so that it is directly on the right margin marker.

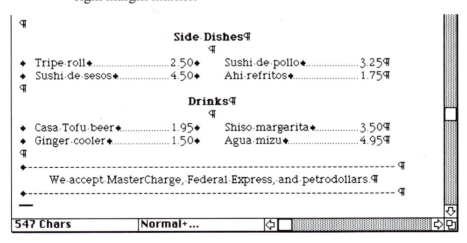

**FIGURE 6-8.** *The last section of the sample menu uses tab leaders to create two lines of dashes.*

129

8. Use the Tabs dialog box to turn on the dashed-line tab leader for the tab stop you inserted, and then click on the OK button to close the dialog box.

9. Press Tab. A dashed line appears across the width of the page.

10. Press Return to begin a new paragraph, and then set the paragraph alignment to centered.

11. Type the last sentence and press Return.

12. Press Tab to create a dashed line that runs across the width of the page.

*You finished Señor Fujiyama's menu by using a tab stop as a convenient way to add a dashed line across the width of the page.*

Now that you've learned how to handle tabs, you should know most of what you need to know about paragraph formatting. In Chapter 7, ''Using Writing Tools,'' you'll learn how Word can help you with spelling, grammar, hyphenation, checking the size of your document, and finding an alternative word.

# Chapter 7

# Using Writing Tools

Writing is a process of momentum. A quick stop to fumble for the right word or to calculate a number can easily become a long stop as you try to recapture your thoughts and continue the flow of writing. Microsoft Word offers several tools that can keep you writing without serious interruption.

In this chapter, you'll learn to use each of these tools to your advantage:

- The Thesaurus, which provides a wide selection of words at the tips of your fingers

- The Calculate command, which instructs Word to perform calculations on numbers in a text block so that you don't need to stop writing to use a calculator

- The Glossary, which lets you create a collection of frequently used phrases, paragraphs, headings, graphics, and other document elements that you can insert with a minimum of typing

- The spelling checker, which scours your document for misspelled words

- The grammar checker, which checks sentences for grammatical errors and weak writing style

- The Sort command, which automatically puts lines of text in alphabetical order

## CHECKING THE TOOLS

Before you start working with the practice sessions in this chapter, first check to make sure that your version of Word has all of the tools we work with here. To check, use the Mac Finder to look in the folder that stores Word 5.0 on your hard disk. Within that folder is another folder labeled *Word Commands,* where you'll find icons for the many of the tools Word offers when you run it.

**PRACTICE**

### Checking your setup

*Check now to see whether your Word Commands folder contains the files you'll need to use the tools described in this chapter.*

1. If you haven't done so already, turn on your computer.

2. Open the folder in which you store Word (probably labeled *Word 5.0* or something similar).

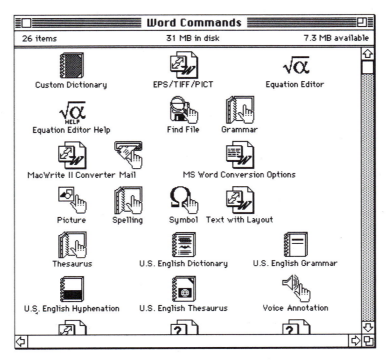

**FIGURE 7-1.** *Word stores some of its writing tools in the Word Commands folder.*

3. Find and open the folder labeled *Word Commands*. Figure 7-1 shows the contents of a typical Word Commands folder.

4. Check to make sure you see files labeled *Spelling, Grammar,* and *Thesaurus* in the folder.

*If you can't find these three files in the folder, the spelling checker, the grammar checker, and the Thesaurus won't work within Word. You'll need to reinstall Word to use these commands.*

Figure 7-2 shows a memo that you'll re-create as you use the practice sessions in this chapter. As you take on the role of conductor of the Beautiful Music Symphonette of Glamour Valley, you'll find that this memo not only motivates your employees to increase their productivity but also gives you the opportunity to use Word's writing tools.

## Beautiful Music Symphonette of Glamour Valley

### Music That Won't Surprise You

To: All Employees
From: Maestro Edouard Amadeus Thompson
Re: Monthly productivity awards

I want to take this opportunity as conductor and commander of the Beautiful Music Symphonette of Glamour Valley to tell you the results of this month's productivity survey. The string division has topped the other divisions by playing the most notes per player this concert month, followed by the woodwinds, brasses, and (ahem!) percussion. The table below shows our most productive players with their weekly note tallies:

| Week | Bo Longo | Raoul Romero | Tanya Pitchov |
|------|----------|--------------|---------------|
| One | 62,709 | 55,465 | 64,012 |
| Two | 54,809 | 49,441 | 75,545 |
| Three | 57,669 | 58,710 | 81,003 |
| Four | 62,466 | 60,989 | 1,079 |
| Totals: | 237,653 | 224,605 | 221,639 |

Violist Bo wins a recording of the complete set of the waltzes of Johann Strauss, Jr., as transcribed for flute and harp by Emil Waldteufel—a full 32-compact-disk set donated by the Beautiful Music Symphonette of Glamour Valley Docent Society. Harpist Raoul, a grizzled veteran of the Sugarplum Variations, wins the fully annotated scores of Leroy Anderson's Christmas works—the famous "Winter Wonder" and "Sleighride of Joy" masses—donated by the Beautiful Music Symphonette of Glamour Valley Junior Auxiliary. Flutist Tanya is, alas, in the hospital recuperating from cruelly chapped lips after her solo performance of *Satyagraha* for the Beautiful Music Symphonette of Glamour Valley Musician's Relief Fund. We know she'll be back in the running soon.

Good health, Tanya, and thank you one and all for a productive month!

Maestro Edouard Amadeus Thompson

P.S. The brass division might have a better notes-per-player-per-week rating if the trombone section stopped reading automobile magazines during long rests.

**FIGURE 7-2.** *You will use the Thesaurus, the Glossary, the Calculate command, and the spelling checker to create this document.*

## Using the Thesaurus

The Thesaurus is a tool to help you find the word that's on the tip of your tongue—or to help you find fresh alternatives to overused words. If you're an old hand with a thesaurus in book form, you'll find that Word's Thesaurus, an online source of words, minimizes interruptions while you write—you won't need to stop writing in order to open a book, look up a word in the index, and turn to the word's location.

If you've never used a thesaurus, Word's Thesaurus will show you the value of a thesaurus for finding synonyms or for finding a word when you know the meaning but not the word. It's a simple matter of selecting a word in your document, choosing the Thesaurus command from the Tools menu, and then choosing from the synonyms Word offers.

## Finding synonyms

To find a synonym for a word in your document, you can select the entire word or merely put the insertion point within or next to the word. You then choose the Thesaurus command from the Tools menu, which opens the Thesaurus dialog box shown in Figure 7-3. Your word is displayed at the top of the dialog box in the Replace area and is also inserted in the With text box.

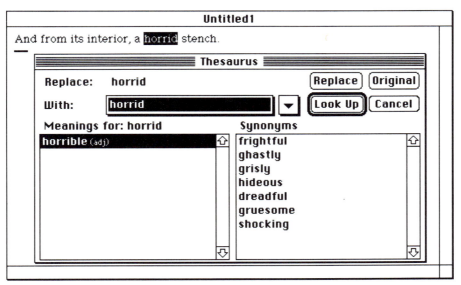

**FIGURE 7-3**. *The Thesaurus dialog box shows synonyms for the word displayed in the With text box.*

The Synonyms list box in the bottom right corner of the dialog box shows synonyms for the word. If you see a synonym you like, click on it to put it in the With text box. You can then click on the Replace button, which replaces the selected word in your document with the contents of the With text box and closes the Thesaurus dialog box.

If, after you've opened the Thesaurus dialog box, you'd like to see synonyms for a different word, you can type a new word into the With text box and then click on the Look Up button—Word brings up new synonyms to fit the new word. If you see a word in the Synonyms list box that you'd like to explore further, you can double-click on it to put it in the With text box and have Word look up new synonyms for that word.

It's often fun to explore words, double-clicking on any word that interests you to see still more words. Word remembers all the words you look up. To see them, click and hold on the down arrow next to the With text box. It opens a list to show you—in chronological order—all the words you've looked up since you opened the Thesaurus dialog box. To return to an area of interest, choose any one of them. Or you can click on the Original button in the upper right corner of the dialog box to return to the word you started with.

## The Meanings For list box

The lower left list box in the Thesaurus dialog box is the Meanings For list box, which helps you handle words that have multiple meanings. For example, many nouns are also verbs. The synonym list for a noun is quite different from that for a verb, even if the word is the same; a boss in the office (with synonyms such as manager, chief, tyrant, and so on) is quite different from to boss, a verb (with synonyms such as command, order, and dictate).

Whenever you look up a word with multiple meanings, the Meanings For list box shows all meanings. When you click on any one of them, the Synonyms list box to the right changes to show the synonyms for that shade of meaning.

## Antonyms and related words

For some words, the Thesaurus will supply antonyms (words of opposite meaning) as well as synonyms. When it does, the word ''Antonyms'' appears in the Meanings For list box. Click on Antonyms to see antonyms for the selected word. You might also see the term "Related Words" in the Meanings For list box. If you click on it, Word shows a list of words that are related to the selected word but aren't necessarily synonyms or antonyms.

## Closing the Thesaurus

When you're finished using the Thesaurus, you can close its dialog box either by clicking on the Replace button, which substitutes whatever's in the With text box for the selected word in your document, or by clicking on the Cancel button, which closes the dialog box without replacing text.

 **PRACTICE**

### Using the Thesaurus

*The first part of the sample memo, shown in Figure 7-4 as you'll first enter it, provides a good place to try out the Thesaurus. As you write the memo, you want to describe your authority as conductor in no uncertain terms. For some reason, though, the phrase "conductor and dictator" seems too harsh. The Thesaurus offers some alternatives.*

**FIGURE 7-4.** *Type the first part of the sample memo as shown here.*

1. Start Word if you haven't started it yet.

2. If you don't have a new document open, choose the New command from the File menu.

3. Set the paragraph alignment to centered, set the font's point size to 18, and turn on bold text formatting.

4. Type the first two lines of the memo, pressing Return at the end of each line.

5. Reduce the font's point size to 12 points, and then press Return to create a blank line.

6. Type *Music That Won't Surprise You* and press Return twice.

7. Change paragraph alignment to left, and turn off bold text formatting.

8. Type the next three lines of the memo, and press Return twice at the end of the third line.

9. Begin typing the first paragraph of the body of the memo as it appears in Figure 7-4. Stop typing at the end of "dictator."

10. Choose the Thesaurus command from the Tools menu. The Thesaurus dialog box opens, showing a list of synonyms for "dictator" as shown in Figure 7-5.

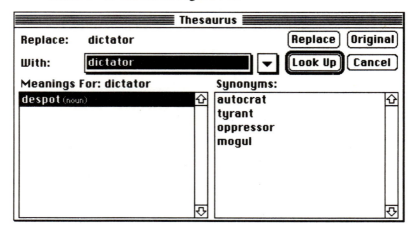

**FIGURE 7-5.** *The Thesaurus dialog box shows a list of synonyms for the word "dictator."*

11. After looking at the synonyms, you choose "mogul" as the one most apt for your description. Click on it; Word puts it in the With text box.

12. Click on the Replace button; Word closes the Thesaurus dialog box and replaces the word "dictator" with the word "mogul."

13. Finish typing the paragraph (click the mouse button first to deselect the word "mogul," and be sure to misspell the word "survay"—you'll correct it later) and then press Return twice at the end of the paragraph.

## USING THE CALCULATE COMMAND

Some documents contain lists of numbers that need to be added or other arithmetic that needs to be performed, forcing you to stop writing to pull out a calculator and determine the result before you can go back to writing. The Calculate command in the Tools menu can save you the trouble of reentering all those numbers. You simply select a block of text and choose the Calculate command from the Tools menu. Word performs any simple mathematical operations contained in the text block, displays the result at the bottom of the document window, and places the result in the Clipboard.

### Selecting Text for Calculation

You can select a block of text for calculation using normal selection techniques, which select text in rows. There are instances, however, especially with numbers, when you want to select a column of text for addition (such as the columns of note tallies in the sample memo). If you use normal selection techniques, you can't separate one column from the next because Word selects an entire row before it moves down to select another row. To select a column by itself without selecting text to either side, you use a special selection technique called *column selection.*

To use column selection, hold down the Option key and drag the pointer from one corner of the column to its diagonally opposite corner. The selection rectangle stretches only as wide as the pointer moves so that you don't select parts of rows that extend outside the column. Release the mouse button when you have selected the column.

You can also use extended selection with this technique: Move the pointer to one corner of the column, and click the mouse button to place the insertion point there. Move the pointer to the opposite corner of the column, hold down Shift-Option, and click the mouse button. Word selects the entire column.

## Calculating

Choose the Calculate command from the Tools menu to begin calculating within a text block. The order in which Word encounters numbers and mathematical operators in the text determines the result.

### Mathematical operators

A *mathematical operator* is a symbol that tells Word to perform a particular mathematical operation. Word recognizes five types of operators that add, subtract, multiply, divide, and set percentages:

- ■ + (or no symbol) for addition
- ■ − (or enclosing parentheses) for subtraction
- ■ * for multiplication
- ■ / for division
- ■ % for percentage (the same as dividing the number by 100)

When you type expressions for calculation, place operators—except the percent sign and parentheses—directly to the left of a number. Place a percent sign directly to the right of a number. If you use parentheses instead of a minus sign, enclose the number you want to subtract in parentheses. A few examples: */45* means to divide by 45, **34%* means to multiply by 34 percent, *(72)* means to subtract 72, and *4* by itself means to add 4.

### Order of calculation

Word calculates by reading the selected text block from left to right, top to bottom (as you read a page), and by performing operations in the order in which it encounters them. It ignores any text between numbers and operators.

For example, if you select a text block that reads ''34 shoulder pads at *$5.00 each multiplied by *15%,'' Word calculates *34 * 5.00 * 15%*, which is 34 multiplied by 5.00 multiplied by 15 percent, which equals 25.50.

## Decimal places

After Word calculates, it returns a result that contains a number of decimal places equal to the maximum number of decimal places in the text block. For example, the operation *9 * 0.3333333* returns the value *2.9999997*. Word uses seven decimal places because 0.3333333 contains seven decimal places.

## Pasting the Result

After Word calculates, it places the result in the Clipboard and temporarily displays the result in the Page-Number area at the lower left corner of the document window. To paste the result in the document, place the insertion point where you want the result and choose the Paste command from the Edit menu (or press Command-V).

## PRACTICE

### A calculation example

*The memo contains four columns of numbers, shown in Figure 7-6. The bottom three numbers are the total number of notes played by three musicians in the orchestra. Type this part of the memo, and use the Calculate command to total the numbers as outlined on the following page.*

| Week◆ | Bo·Longo◆ | Raoul·Romero◆ | Tanya·Pitchov¶ |
|--------|-----------|----------------|-----------------|
| One◆ | 62,709◆ | 55,465◆ | 64,012¶ |
| Two◆ | 54,809◆ | 49,441◆ | 75,545¶ |
| Three◆ | 57,669◆ | 58,710◆ | 81,003¶ |
| Four◆ | 62,446◆ | 60,989◆ | 1,079¶ |
| Totals◆ | 237,633◆ | 224,605◆ | 221,639¶ |

**FIGURE 7-6**. *Use the Calculate command to calculate the sums of these columns of numbers.*

1. Set up the heading-line paragraph by placing center-align tab stops at 1.75, 3.50, and 5.25 inches.

2. Turn on underline and bold text formatting, and then enter the first line shown in Figure 7-6. (The tab characters are visible to show you where to press the Tab key.) Press Return at the end of the line.

3. Remove the tabs on the Ruler, and insert new decimal-aligned tab stops at 2, 3.75, and 5.50 inches.

4. Turn underline and bold text formatting off and type the next four lines, referring to Figure 7-6 to see where to press Tab. Be sure to press Return at the end of the last line of figures.

5. Turn bold text formatting on and type *Totals:*. Turn bold text formatting off and then press the Tab key.

6. To select the first column of numbers, move the pointer to the beginning of the number *62,709*, hold down the Option key, drag the pointer to the end of the number *62,466*, and then release the mouse button and the Option key.

7. Choose the Calculate command from the Tools menu to add the column numbers. The result appears in the lower left corner of the document window and is also placed in the Clipboard.

8. Move the insertion point back to the end of the line you last typed, and choose the Paste command from the Edit menu to insert the result below the column of numbers.

9. Press the Tab key to move to the next column.

10. Select the column of numbers under the name "Raoul Romero," as you did in the preceding column, and then choose the Calculate command from the Tools menu (or press Command-=) to add the numbers.

11. Move the insertion point back to the end of the document, and choose the Paste command from the Edit menu to paste the result at the bottom of the second column.

12. Press the Tab key to move to the final column of numbers. Select the column, calculate its sum, and paste the result as you did previously. Press Return twice at the end of the line to prepare for entering the rest of the document.

## THE GLOSSARY

You might find, as you type your way through many documents, that you use common phrases, sentences, or document parts repeatedly. Lawyers, for example, might have stock contract paragraphs that they insert in most contracts. Corporate letter writers might use company names or disclaimers in the majority of the letters they write. If you find yourself typing the same text repeatedly, you should use the Glossary to store the repeated text (or text with graphics). You can then insert the whole thing at any time with a few simple keystrokes.

### Creating a Glossary Entry

Think of the Glossary as a collection of commonly used elements, each stored as an entry. You can add entries, delete entries, or change their contents. To create a glossary entry, you first enter the text and graphics you want in a document. (You'll see how to add graphics to a Word document in Chapter 10.) Once entered, the entry is selected as a block. You can select all text, all graphics, or a mixture of both; the Glossary stores the entire contents of the block, preserving all graphics and character formatting.

With a text block selected, choose the Glossary command from the Edit menu to open the Glossary window, shown in Figure 7-7. The entry list box in the main part of the window shows glossary entries that come with Word. It also shows *New* selected at the top of the list to show that the Glossary is ready to accept a new entry.

To give your entry a name and make it a part of the glossary, type a name in the Name text box. Brevity counts. The shorter your entry name, the easier it will be to type when you want to recall the entry. Of course, being too brief can cause problems: A name such as ''j'' or ''4'' often doesn't remind you of the entry contents. A key word in a phrase, a short word describing a picture, the initials of a name, or the title work well as entry names.

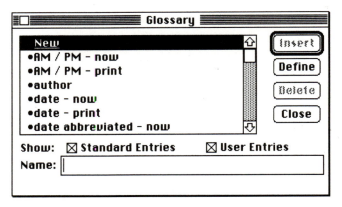

**FIGURE 7-7.** *The Glossary window contains a list of glossary entries.*

After you type the name you want, click on the Define button to add the entry to the Glossary. The entry name appears in the entry list box, and the bottom line of the Glossary window shows the contents of the entry. Because it is only a single line, this description area doesn't show any selected graphics or text formatting. The line displays only the beginning of the selected text and shows each graphic as a small empty box.

When you're finished working with the Glossary window, click on the Cancel button to close the window and return to your document.

## Practice

### Defining a glossary entry

*The phrase "Beautiful Music Symphonette of Glamour Valley" occurs often in the rest of the memo. Define it as a glossary entry:*

1. Select *Beautiful Music Symphonette of Glamour Valley* as a text block in the first full paragraph of the memo.

2. Choose the Glossary command from the Edit menu to open the Glossary window. *New,* at the top of the entry list, is highlighted.

3. Type *bms* (the initials of the Beautiful Music Symphonette) in the Name text box.

4. Click on the Define button to add the entry to the entry list. The name appears in the entry list, and the contents of the entry appear in the bottom line of the window.

5. Click on the Close button to close the window.

## Inserting a Glossary Entry in a Document

You can insert a glossary entry in a document in either of two ways:

- Press Command-Delete. The Page-Number area turns black, indicating that you can type the name of the glossary entry (or enough of the name to distinguish it from other entries). Press Return after you've typed the name. Word inserts the contents of the glossary entry at the insertion-point location, including any graphics and character formatting that are part of the entry. (Press Esc instead of Return if you decide not to insert the glossary entry.)

- Open the Glossary window by choosing the Glossary command from the Edit menu, click on the glossary entry you want in the entry list, and then click on the Insert button (or simply double-click on the entry name). The window closes and Word inserts the full contents of the glossary entry at the location of the insertion point.

Pressing Command-Delete and typing an entry name in a document is the quickest way to insert a glossary entry. Note that Word ignores uppercase and lowercase characters in a glossary name, so you don't need to use the Shift key as you type the name. If you forget an entry name you need, you can open the Glossary window and read the list of entries. As you select entries in the list, the first part of each entry is displayed at the bottom of the Glossary window.

## Types of Glossary Entries

The Glossary contains two types of entries: *user entries* and *standard entries*. User entries are the custom entries that you and other Word users create in the Glossary; standard entries are the entries that come with Word. To mark the difference in the entry list, Word puts a bullet (•) before each standard entry.

Word lets you choose whether you see both types of entry or only one type in the entry list. The Show line just below the entry list contains two check-box options, Standard Entries and User Entries. You can click on them to turn them on and off. Turn on Standard Entries to see standard entries; turn on User Entries to see user entries. And turn on both options to see all entries.

## Using Standard Entries

Word's standard glossary entries offer you some convenient elements for insertion, some that you can't create in any other way. Most standard entries insert the current time or date with great flexibility. You can, for example, insert the current day of the week, the current hour, just the year, or almost any form of the date and time.

Date and time entries come in two types: *now* and *print*. If you choose *now*, the date or time you insert is the time read from the Mac's clock at the moment of insertion. It doesn't change when you print or reopen the document later. If you choose *print*, the date or time you insert is updated whenever you print or reopen the document.

You'll also find some other convenient entries. The *page-number* entry inserts the page number of the page on which the entry is inserted, and is updated whenever you print or repaginate the document. The *author* entry inserts the current author's name (the one you enter when you first run Word). The *keywords, section, subject, title,* and *version* entries all insert information about the document itself, which you enter when you save the document (as you'll learn in Chapter 8). Experiment by inserting some of these entries; you might find some you want to use regularly.

### PRACTICE

### Inserting glossary entries

*The remaining text of the memo shows "Beautiful Music Symphonette of Glamour Valley" in several places. Use the glossary feature to insert it as follows:*

1. Type the rest of the memo shown in Figure 7-2, at the beginning of this chapter, stopping at the beginning of "Beautiful Music Symphonette of Glamour Valley" in the first paragraph following the "Totals" line.

2. Choose the Glossary command from the Edit menu to open the Glossary window.

3. Double-click on *bms* in the entry list. The Glossary window closes, and Word inserts the entry in your document.

4. Continue typing, stopping at the beginning of ''Beautiful Music.''

5. Press Command-Delete. The Page-Number area turns black.

6. Type *bms*. It appears in the Page-Number area.

7. Press Return. Word inserts *Beautiful Music Symphonette of Glamour Valley*.

8. Type the rest of the memo, using the Glossary command to insert the phrase a final time. (It's not important that you enter this text verbatim, so feel free to abridge it if your fingers begin to rebel.)

## Saving Glossary Entries

Word retains all the glossary entries you create during a Word session. If you close one document and begin a new one, the glossary entries you created in the earlier document are available to you in the new one. When you close Word at the end of your session, Word asks whether you want to save your glossary changes. If you click on the Yes button, Word stores the glossary entries on disk under the filename ''Standard Glossary'' along with Word's own glossary entries. If you click on the No button, Word deletes the glossary entries you created in that session (previously created glossary entries are not deleted). You won't see them the next time you run Word and open the Glossary.

## Deleting and Renaming Glossary Entries

As you add to the entries in the Glossary, you might want to remove some that are no longer useful and rename others that don't work well with their current names. To remove an entry, select its name in the entry list box and click on the Delete button. Word asks whether you want to delete the glossary entry;

click on the Yes button to remove the entry from the list, or on the No button to cancel the deletion.

To rename an entry, select its name from the entry list so it appears in the Name text box, type the new name, and then click on the Define button. The old name disappears from the entry list and the new name replaces it.

## Advanced Glossary Features

Word also offers advanced glossary features that you should be aware of in case you'd like to learn more about them. The following are two useful glossary features:

- *Creating more than one glossary.* You can create specialty glossaries that you open only when working with documents that might use the entries in the glossaries. This feature helps you manage the size of the glossary you work with as you write.

- *Adding a glossary entry to a menu.* You can directly insert a glossary entry by simply choosing a command from a menu.

If you'd like to learn more about either of these features, you can find more information about them in the Glossaries section of the *Microsoft Word User's Guide*.

# CHECKING SPELLING

After you've finished a document, it's a good idea to check for spelling mistakes; if the inexplicable spelling rules of the English language didn't trip you up, then straying fingers on the keyboard probably did. Word's spelling checker can carefully comb through your text for spelling mistakes and typing errors, and alert you to possible misspellings.

## What Does the Spelling Checker Do?

Choosing the Spelling command from the Utilities menu starts Word's spelling checker, which reads through your document (or any portion you have selected), comparing each word to a list of over 100,000 words stored in the main dictionary. If the spelling checker comes across a word it can't find there, it displays the word and asks whether you want to replace it.

You can deal with an unmatched word in several ways. You can replace the word if it's misspelled. If you don't know how to spell a word, you can ask Word to suggest alternative spellings for you to choose from. If the word is spelled correctly but isn't included in Word's dictionary, you can tell Word to move on without changing the word. If you use that word often, you can add it to a custom dictionary (an advanced feature not described in this book). Once you've placed words in the custom dictionary, Word scans both that dictionary and its main dictionary as it runs the rest of the spelling check.

Word's spelling checker does have a limitation: It cannot check for proper usage. If you use a word improperly in a sentence, Word won't notice the problem if the word is in its dictionary. For example, the sentence "It's reel butter" is wrong, but Word won't alert you because "reel" is a word in its dictionary.

## Starting a Spelling Check

Before you start a spelling check, you must decide whether to check the entire document or only a portion of it. If you've already checked a document and then added a new section to it, you can save time by checking only the new or revised section. To check a section of a document, first select the section as a text block. If you want to check a single word, select only that word. To check the entire document, select no text blocks.

To start a spelling check, choose the Spelling command from the Tools menu to open the Spelling window shown in Figure 7-8.

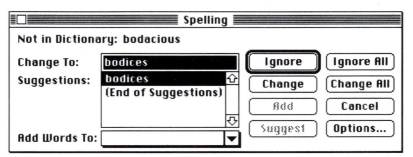

**FIGURE 7-8.** *The Spelling window presents the unrecognized words found in a document and offers suggestions for correcting spelling.*

149

Word immediately starts the spelling check. If you're checking the entire document, Word reads from the insertion-point location to the end of the document, where it pauses and asks whether you want to continue the check from the beginning of the document. If you click on the Yes button, Word reads from the beginning of the document to the insertion-point location, where it then stops. If you are checking a text block, Word reads from the beginning to the end of the block. You can quit the check at any time by clicking on the Cancel button or by pressing Command-. (period).

## Correcting Misspellings

Occasionally Word can match every word in your document to a word in its dictionaries—it finds no misspellings or typing errors. If so, the spelling check ends, and you can go back to work on your document. More often, however, Word finds unmatched words. When it finds one, it stops the check and presents the unmatched word in the Not In Dictionary area at the top of the Spelling window. It also highlights the unmatched word in the document to let you read it in context. If the Spelling window covers the selected text, drag the window to a new location.

To correct a spelling error, you use the Change To text box. If you know how to correct the error yourself, type a correction directly into the Change To text box. If you don't know how to spell the word, look in the Suggestions list below the Change To text box, and click on the suggestion you think is right. Word puts the suggested respelling in the Change To text box.

Note that although Word is normally set to offer suggestions for each unmatched word, you can turn off Suggestions in the Preferences window to speed up the spelling check. When Suggestions are off, you don't normally see any suggested respellings, but you can ask for them if you want by clicking on the Suggest button.

After the correct spelling is in place, you can take two courses of action: Click on the Change button, which tells Word to substitute the correct spelling for the misspelled word in just this one case; or click on the Change All button, which tells Word to substitute the correct spelling for the misspelled word any place that misspelled word shows up in the document.

## When the Spelling Checker Flags Correctly Spelled Words

The spelling checker will sometimes flag words that are spelled correctly but just don't happen to be in Word's spelling dictionary. This will happen often with specialty words such as medical or legal terms, or with names of companies and people. (A main dictionary that included all these words would be too large to use with reasonable speed and would be impossible to keep up to date.) If the spelling checker flags such a word, you can move on without correcting it by clicking on the Ignore button, which makes the spelling checker ignore the word only in this spot, or by clicking on the Ignore All button, which makes the spelling checker ignore the same word any place it appears in the document.

### PRACTICE

#### Running a spelling check

*Try checking the spelling of your sample memo. You know you have one intentionally misspelled word: "survay." You might find others as well.*

1. Move the insertion point to the very beginning of the document.

2. Choose the Spelling command from the Tools menu to open the Spelling window and start the spelling check. The spelling checker first flags the word "Symphonette" as an unmatched word, selecting it in the text and showing it in the Not In Dictionary area of the Spelling window. Word has no suggestions for this word.

3. Because we know that "Symphonette" is spelled correctly, we want to ignore it anywhere it occurs in the document: click on the Ignore All button.

4. The spelling checker goes on to flag each element (one by one) of Edouard Amadeus Thompson's name. Click on Ignore All each time to mark the names as correctly spelled.

5. The spelling checker flags the misspelled word "survay" and suggests "survey" as the correct spelling. (If there are no suggestions, click on the Suggest button.) Click on the Change button to correct "survay," replacing it with "survey."

6. The spelling checker moves on, continuing its check. Click on the Cancel button to stop it and to close the Spelling window.

## Setting Spelling Preferences

To change the way the spelling checker runs, you can set Spelling preferences. Word offers you two ways to do this: Click on the Options button in the Spelling window; or choose the Preferences command from the Tools menu to open the Preferences window, where you can click on the Spelling icon to bring up Spelling preferences. Both methods bring you to the window shown in Figure 7-9.

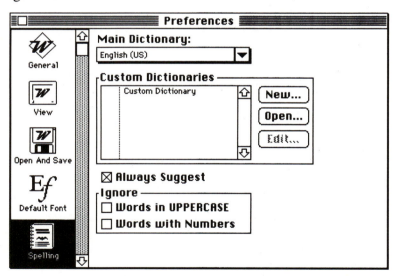

**FIGURE 7-9.** *You can set Spelling preferences in the Spelling section of the Preferences window.*

Two buttons located in an area labeled "Ignore" instruct the spelling checker to ignore certain words:

■ The Words In UPPERCASE check box controls whether the spelling checker should skip over words in all capital letters.

■ The Words With Numbers check box controls whether the spelling checker should skip over "words" containing numerals, such as *1040ai*, *rx411*, and similar strings.

The first option is very useful for ignoring acronyms (words such as ASAP, MIDI, ASCII, and many others); the second option is useful for skipping over model numbers, license numbers, and other "words" that mix letters and numerals. Turn either option on to speed up your spelling checks.

Above the Ignore area is the Always Suggest check box, which, when turned on, tells the spelling checker to always try to suggest spellings whenever it can't find a word in the main dictionary. To considerably speed up the spelling checker, turn this option off by clicking on the check box: You'll no longer have a long pause while Word comes up with suggestions for each flagged word. You can always use the Suggest button in the Spelling window any time you really want suggestions.

## Advanced Spelling Features

The rest of the Spelling preferences deal with an advanced spelling feature: dictionaries. If you do a lot of spelling checking with Word, you'll find them useful. You can

■ *Use non-English dictionaries.* If you have non-English dictionaries available, you can use them to check the spelling for documents written in other languages.

■ *Create your own custom dictionaries.* You can create custom dictionaries filled with your own frequently used words and names that aren't contained in the main dictionary. You can then set the spelling checker to use them (using controls in the Preferences window) whenever appropriate in conjunction with the main dictionary.

If you want to know more about advanced spelling features, read the chapter titled "Proofing a Document" in the *Microsoft Word User's Guide.*

# CHECKING GRAMMAR

If you'd like to check your document for mistakes in grammar and style—split infinitives, run-on sentences, and the like—Word's grammar checker can help you. To do its job, the grammar checker must overcome two major hurdles: First, it must understand the rules of grammar and style, which aren't as concrete as those of spelling; and second, the grammar checker must understand the components of each sentence so that it can apply the rules.

The grammar checker doesn't always clear the hurdles. It often makes suggestions that are wrong, and it can take a long time to check a document. Still, you can make good use of the grammar checker if you fine-tune it to look for specific grammar and style mistakes that you habitually make.

## What Does the Grammar Checker Do?

When you check a document (or part of a document) for grammar, the grammar checker reads through sentences word by word and tries to understand the sentence structure. It checks the structure it finds against a set of rules to see whether the structure is in compliance with the rules of grammar. If the structure isn't in compliance, the grammar checker shows you the sentence and highlights the parts that seem wrong. It tells you which rule the sentence breaks and, if you request it, explains the rule.

If a flagged sentence seems easy to correct, the grammar checker might offer you a corrected version of the sentence, which you can choose to substitute for the original sentence. If the sentence needs extensive work, the grammar checker gives you suggestions for altering the sentence. You can ignore the grammar checker's suggestions at any time and move on to the next suggestion if you want.

When the grammar checker has completed its check, it provides you with a summary that shows how many words, characters, paragraphs, and sentences the document contains. The summary also gives you the average number of sentences per paragraph, words per sentence, and characters per word, followed by readability ratings of the document.

## Starting a Grammar Check

Starting a grammar check is like starting a spelling check. If you want to check only a part of a document, you select that part as a text block. To check the full document, select no text blocks. Choose the Grammar command from the Tools menu to open the Grammar window shown in Figure 7-10.

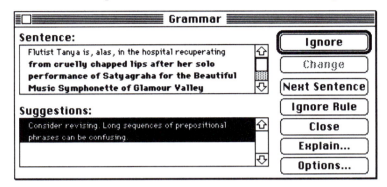

**FIGURE 7-10.** *The Grammar window displays grammatical errors and weak style and suggests possible corrections.*

When the Grammar window opens, Word immediately starts checking grammar. By default, it checks spelling at the same time, and opens the Spelling window if it finds any misspelled words so that you can correct or pass over those words. If the grammar check starts from the middle of a document and then reaches the end of the document, Word pauses to ask whether you'd like to continue the check from the beginning of the document. Click on the OK button to continue checking—Word continues from the beginning and stops at the original starting place in the middle of the document.

To stop a grammar check, click on the Close button in the Grammar window or press Command-. (period).

## Correcting Grammar and Style

When the grammar checker flags a sentence for correction, it displays the sentence in the Sentence text area of the Grammar window. The Suggestions text area below explains how Word thinks the sentence should be corrected. If Word can correct the sentence itself, it offers the Change button, which you can click on to accept Word's change. If the correction is beyond Word's capabilities, the Change button is grayed so that you can't click on it.

If you'd like an explanation for Word's suggestion, click on the Explain button to open the Grammar Explanation window. It contains a full explanation of the rule that Word followed when it flagged the sentence. If you'd like to ignore Word's suggestion, you have three options:

- Click on the Ignore button (or press Return) to ignore this suggestion and move to the next suggestion, possibly within the same sentence.

- Click on the Next Sentence button to move on to the next sentence, even if there are more suggestions Word can make about the current sentence.

- Click on the Ignore Rule button to tell Word to ignore the rule behind the current suggestion for the rest of the search and move on to the next suggestion. This option is particularly useful if Word continually uses the same rule to flag sentences that you don't want to change.

At the end of the grammar check, Word presents a Document Statistics dialog box (shown in Figure 7-11). For an explanation of the statistics, read the chapter titled "Proofing a Document" in the *Microsoft Word User's Guide*.

## Setting Grammar Preferences

The key to making the grammar checker a useful tool is to set the Grammar preferences so that it checks only for the grammar and style rules you're concerned about. The more rules you can turn off, the faster the grammar checks finish, and the fewer suggestions you get that you don't want to accept. To set preferences, either click on the Options button in the Grammar window while a check is in process, or choose the Preferences command from the Tools menu to open the Preferences window. There you click on the Grammar icon to see Grammar preferences (shown in Figure 7-12).

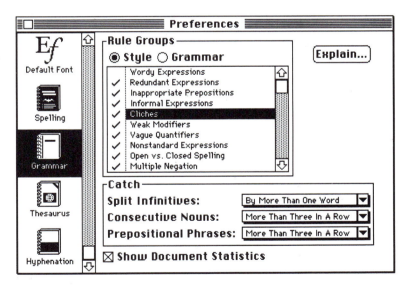

**Document Statistics**

**Counts:**
| | |
|---|---|
| Words | 260 |
| Characters | 1724 |
| Paragraphs | 17 |
| Sentences | 9 |

OK

**Averages:**
| | |
|---|---|
| Sentences per Paragraph | 0 |
| Words per Sentence | 28 |
| Characters per Word | 5 |

**Readability:**
| | |
|---|---|
| Passive Sentences | 0% |
| Flesch Reading Ease | 37.0 |
| Flesch Grade Level | 14.9 |
| Flesch-Kincaid | 13.7 |
| Gunning Fog Index | 13.1 |

**FIGURE 7-11.** *The Document Statistics dialog box shows document statistics compiled during a grammar check.*

**Preferences**

*Ef* Default Font

Spelling

Grammar

Thesaurus

Hyphenation

**Rule Groups**

◉ **Style** ○ **Grammar**

[ Explain... ]

| | |
|---|---|
| | Wordy Expressions |
| ✓ | Redundant Expressions |
| ✓ | Inappropriate Prepositions |
| ✓ | Informal Expressions |
| ✓ | Cliches |
| ✓ | Weak Modifiers |
| ✓ | Vague Quantifiers |
| ✓ | Nonstandard Expressions |
| ✓ | Open vs. Closed Spelling |
| ✓ | Multiple Negation |

**Catch**

**Split Infinitives:** By More Than One Word ▼

**Consecutive Nouns:** More Than Three In A Row ▼

**Prepositional Phrases:** More Than Three In A Row ▼

☒ **Show Document Statistics**

**FIGURE 7-12.** *Set Grammar preferences in the Preferences window.*

157

The top of the Grammar preferences lists the rule groups the grammar checker uses to check grammar and style. You can look at either the style or the grammar rule group by clicking on the appropriate button at the top of the Rule Groups area. To see an explanation of what a rule group does, click on the rule group to select it, and then click on the Explain button. To turn on a rule group, click in the margin to its left; a checkmark appears, showing that the rule group is on. To turn off a rule group, click on the checkmark.

The controls below the Rule Groups area allow you to fine-tune the grammar checker's sensitivity to split infinitives, consecutive nouns, and prepositional phrases. You can also turn off the document statistics. For more information about grammar preferences, read the chapter titled "Proofing a Document" in the *Microsoft Word User's Guide*.

### Grammar Checker Suggestions

As you can see, you have to know something about grammar before you can understand all of the grammar checker's suggestions. Some outside reading may help if you're not a grammarian. *The Elements of Style,* by William Strunk, Jr., and E. B. White, is a short, inexpensive, and entertaining little book that clearly explains the fundamentals of grammar and style. Reading it will not only help you use the grammar checker effectively but will help you write clearly on your own.

## SORTING LISTS

Many documents contain lists of names, series of instructions, or other ordered items. Often the information as you first type it or import it from another source follows no particular order; reading it would be much easier if the list were sorted in alphabetic or numeric order. Sorting is a tedious process perfectly suited to a computer. You can turn the task over to Word by using Word's Sort command.

### Creating Lists

When Word sorts a list, it actually sorts paragraphs. If you're entering a list, it's important that you enter each item as a separate paragraph: Press Return at the end of each item. When you're finished creating the list and you're ready to sort, select all the paragraphs in the list as a single text block.

## Selecting and Sorting Techniques

To sort paragraphs in selected text, simply choose the Sort command from the Tools menu. Word then sorts the records in alphabetic and numeric order. For variations, consider using the following special selection and sorting techniques:

- *Sorting in reverse order.* If you want to sort a list in reverse alphabetic and numeric order, select records just as you would for forward sorting and then hold down the Shift key while you open the Tools menu. You'll find that the Sort command has been replaced with *Sort Descending.* Choose the Sort Descending command to sort the selected records in reverse alphabetic and numeric order.

- *Sorting an entire document.* To sort all the paragraphs in a document, first be sure that no text block is selected. Then choose the Sort or Sort Descending command; Word sorts all the paragraphs in the document.

- *Undoing a sort.* Immediately after you've sorted a list, you can undo the sort by choosing the Undo Sort command from the Edit menu. If you perform any other editing tasks after you sort, the Undo Sort command will not undo your sort.

### PRACTICE
#### Sorting a list

*Try sorting the list of note totals in the middle of the sample memo:*

1. Select as a text block the five paragraphs shown in Figure 7-13A.

2. Choose the Sort command from the Tools menu. Word sorts the lines in alphabetic order, as shown in Figure 7-13B.

3. Hold down the Shift key, open the Tools menu, and choose the Sort Descending command. Word sorts the lines in reverse alphabetic order, as shown in Figure 7-13C.

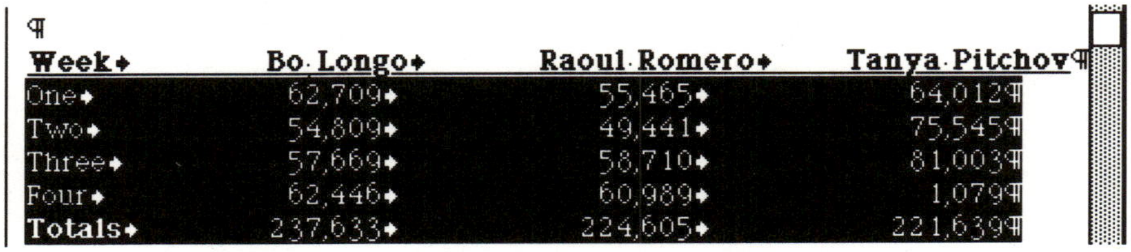

| ¶ |
| :--- |

| Week→ | Bo·Longo→ | Raoul·Romero→ | Tanya·Pitchov¶ |
| :--- | ---: | ---: | ---: |
| One→ | 62,709→ | 55,465→ | 64,012¶ |
| Two→ | 54,809→ | 49,441→ | 75,545¶ |
| Three→ | 57,669→ | 58,710→ | 81,003¶ |
| Four→ | 62,446→ | 60,989→ | 1,079¶ |
| Totals→ | 237,633→ | 224,605→ | 221,639¶ |

A

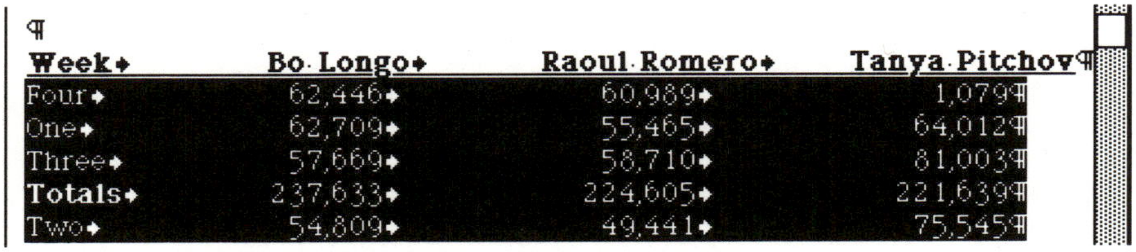

| ¶ |
| :--- |

| Week→ | Bo·Longo→ | Raoul·Romero→ | Tanya·Pitchov¶ |
| :--- | ---: | ---: | ---: |
| Four→ | 62,446→ | 60,989→ | 1,079¶ |
| One→ | 62,709→ | 55,465→ | 64,012¶ |
| Three→ | 57,669→ | 58,710→ | 81,003¶ |
| Totals→ | 237,633→ | 224,605→ | 221,639¶ |
| Two→ | 54,809→ | 49,441→ | 75,545¶ |

B

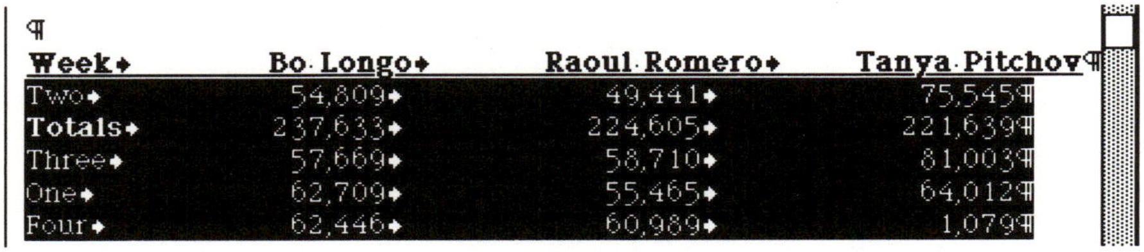

| ¶ |
| :--- |

| Week→ | Bo·Longo→ | Raoul·Romero→ | Tanya·Pitchov¶ |
| :--- | ---: | ---: | ---: |
| Two→ | 54,809→ | 49,441→ | 75,545¶ |
| Totals→ | 237,633→ | 224,605→ | 221,639¶ |
| Three→ | 57,669→ | 58,710→ | 81,003¶ |
| One→ | 62,709→ | 55,465→ | 64,012¶ |
| Four→ | 62,446→ | 60,989→ | 1,079¶ |

C

**FIGURE 7-13.** *(A) Select these five lines (each a full paragraph) for sorting. (B) After an alphabetic sort, the five lines look like this. (C) After a reverse-order sort, the lines look like this.*

## Word's Sort Order

To sort effectively, you should know the character order that Word uses to sort records. When Word sorts in forward alphabetic and numeric order, it follows these rules:

- It sorts full paragraphs by looking at the contents of the paragraph up to the first tab mark.

- It ignores commas, quotation marks, tabs, and diacritical marks such as ^ and ~. For example, the list *"baboon" cormorant abacus* is sorted as *abacus "baboon" cormorant.*

160

- It ignores case when sorting unless it sorts two identical letters, one uppercase and the other lowercase. In that instance, it places the uppercase letter before the lowercase letter. For example, Word places *C* before *c* but after *b*.

- International characters such as *ü* and *ë* fall after their unaccented English equivalents. For example, *ü* comes after *u* but before *v*.

- Word sorts numbers by value instead of alphanumerically. For example, *35* comes before *157* in Word. (In a conventional alphanumeric sort, the *1* at the beginning of *157* would come before the *3* at the beginning of *35*.)

- If you sort numbers that are followed by letters—for example, *25a* and *16c*—Word first sorts the numbers by their value and then sorts the letters alphabetically if any number values match. For example, *25a* comes after *24c* but before *25b*.

Knowing these sorting rules will help you understand how Word sorts your lists. If you're interested in advanced sorting features, you can find out how to sort by parts of a paragraph other than its first section (by address, for example, in paragraphs where the name comes first). You'll find more information in the chapter titled "Sorting" in the *Microsoft Word User's Guide*.

You now know how to work with the Thesaurus, the Glossary, the spelling checker, the grammar checker, and the Calculate and Sort commands to help you write and edit your documents. In the next chapter you'll learn more about saving your documents once you've finished working with them, and reopening them later when you want to work with them again.

# Chapter 8

# Saving, Opening, and Printing a Document

A word processor's big advantage over a typewriter is that after you create and save a document, you can use the document again and again without retyping it. You can open the document at any time to print or to revise or to browse for material to use in a new document. As you work with Microsoft Word, you can accumulate a substantial library of documents.

Saving, opening, and printing a document is usually an uncomplicated process, but you might ask a few questions if you want to save your documents in an orderly fashion on your hard disk: How do I save documents in different folders or on different disks? How can I find a document if I've forgotten its location?

If you want to swap documents with a program other than Word, you might ask: How can I save a document so another program can read it? Can Word read documents created by other programs?

And finally, when you decide to print a document, you might ask these questions: How can I print just a few pages of a document? How can I speed up printing? How can I make the printing look better? How can I select one printer from many connected to my Mac?

This chapter answers those questions, and shows you a few tricks to make saving, opening, and printing your documents easier and more versatile.

## SAVING A DOCUMENT

As you learned in Chapter 2, "Creating a Business Letter," saving a document is an important safeguard. It ensures that all your work won't disappear in a flash of interrupted electrical power. For effective protection, you should save frequently while you work, and you should always save before you turn your computer off. You can open your saved document later to continue your work, or you can recall previously completed documents to reuse them in a slightly altered form (a boon to teachers who use the same multiple-choice tests year after year).

### Using the Save and Save As Commands

You can use either the Save or the Save As command to save documents. You normally use Save, but if you want to duplicate and rename a document, you use Save As. The difference between the two commands is the way they use a document name to save the document. The Save command will ask you for a name only if you use it to save an unnamed document. Once the document is saved, the Save command no longer asks for a name, but saves using the document's given name.

The Save As command, on the other hand, asks you for a document name no matter when you use it. If you use it for a document that already has a name, you can create a new name for the document. When you save a document under a new name, you then have two copies of the document: one under the old name, the second under the new name.

## Entering a Document Name in the Save As Dialog Box

Whenever you choose the Save As command or whenever you choose the Save command to save an unnamed document, Word opens the Save As dialog box shown in Figure 8-1, where you can enter a name for the document. If the document already has a name, Word proposes that name in the Save Current Document As text box; you can replace it with a new name. If the document has no name, the text box is empty, waiting for you to type in a name.

After you enter a document name in the Save Current Document As text box, you click on the Save button to close the dialog box and instruct Word to save the document under the new document name. (The document name is the name you'll see if you look at the document file with the Mac's Finder.) Before it saves, Word checks to see whether another file already has the new name, and if it finds one, it displays a dialog box asking whether you want to replace that file with the recently saved document. If you click on the Replace button, Word erases the old file and replaces it with the new one. If you click on the Cancel button, Word cancels the save.

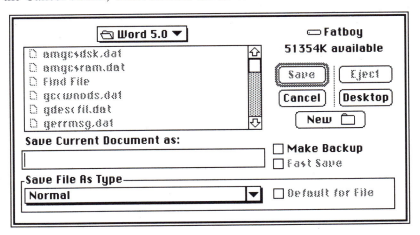

**FIGURE 8-1.** *Use the Save As dialog box to name a document or to save it in any folder on any disk.*

## Creating Folders

You can, of course, save all your documents in a single folder, but a folder can get messy and disorganized if it contains 20, 30, or more documents. In fact, because Word saves documents by default in the folder where you start Word, it's usually Word's own folder that gets cluttered with scattered documents. It's neater to create new folders within Word's folder or in other locations on your disk where you can store different types of documents. Reserving one folder for letters, another for reports, and another for personal work might be one convenient way of organizing documents within folders; only you know what will work for you and your documents.

You'll probably create new folders most often with the Macintosh Finder, where you can choose the New Folder command from the File menu. You can then rename the folder and drag it wherever you want it. You can also create new folders from within Word by clicking on the New button (which shows a folder icon next to the word New) in the Save As dialog box. Word opens a dialog box that asks you for a folder name. Enter a folder name and click on the Create button; Word then creates the new folder and sets up the Save As dialog box so that any documents you save will be saved to the new folder by default.

## Changing Folders

The list box at the top of the Save As dialog box displays the name of the current folder; that is, it shows where any saved files will be stored. If you don't know where the current folder is located on a disk (folders can be contained within folders within folders), move the pointer to the disk/folder list box and hold down the mouse button; the list drops down and shows the hierarchical order of folders at that location. You read the list from top to bottom, from your current folder to the folders that contain it, to the disk that contains all the folders, and finally to the desktop. Figure 8-2 shows an open disk/folder list box. The top name—Circulation Reports—is the current folder, and the name below it—Market Research—is the name of the folder that contains the folder Circulation Reports. The name listed below Market Research is Fat Boy, the name of the disk that contains all the folders, and below that, you see the desktop.

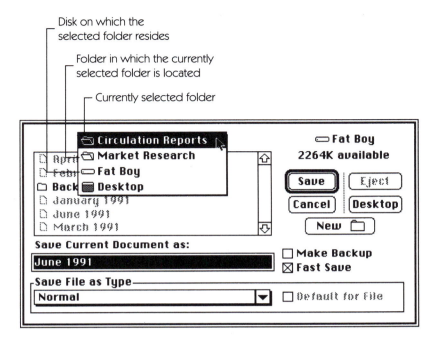

**FIGURE 8-2.** *Open the disk/folder list box, and read it from top to bottom to see the currently selected folder, the folder in which the selected folder is located, and the disk on which the selected folder resides.*

The file list box under the disk/folder list box displays all the document files and folders contained in the current folder. Document filenames are marked with document-file icons that appear gray. You can't open document files from the Save As dialog box; they appear only for reference. Folder names are marked with file-folder icons and appear black. You can double-click on a folder icon to move into that folder. The disk/folder list box then displays the name of the folder you are currently in, and the file list box displays the names of all files and folders contained in that folder.

To move back to a previous folder or out of all folders to the disk or to the desktop, choose a name from the disk/folder list box. The disk/folder list box displays the name of the folder you moved to, and the file list box displays the names of all files and folders contained in that folder.

## Changing Disks

You might not want to save a document on the currently selected disk. For example, after looking at the disk information in the upper right side of the Save As dialog box, which lists the current disk and the amount of free disk space in kilobytes, you might notice that the remaining space is not sufficient to store your document. If so, you can move to another disk by choosing Desktop from the disk/folder list box. The file list box below the disk/folder list box shows all the disks available on the desktop, and you can choose a disk by double-clicking on it. The file list box then shows the contents of that disk.

If you switch to a floppy-disk drive and decide you don't want to use the floppy disk that's currently in the drive, you can eject the disk by clicking on the Eject button. Word ejects the disk, and you can insert another disk. Once the disk is inserted, the dialog box displays the disk's name and its contents.

Note that if you insert an unformatted disk, the Mac displays a dialog box that asks whether you want to initialize the disk. Answer yes by clicking on either the One-Sided button or the Two-Sided button to indicate the type of disk you've inserted. Another dialog box appears, stating that this process will erase everything on the disk; click on the Erase button. Yet another dialog box appears, prompting you to name the disk. After you type a name and click on the OK button, the Mac initializes the disk, and the Save As dialog box displays the new disk's name in the disk/folder list box.

## PRACTICE

### Changing disks

*Try creating a new folder, moving up to the desktop, and then moving back to the folder to save a copy of the test document:*

1. Start Word if you haven't already, and open a new document.

2. Type *This is a test document* to insert some text into your document.

3. Choose the Save command from the File menu. Because this document is unnamed, Word opens the Save As dialog box.

4. Enter the name *Delete Me!* in the Save Current Document As text box. (This name will remind you to get rid of the document when you're done with the exercise.)

5. Click on the New button on the right side of the dialog box. Word opens the dialog box you see in Figure 8-3.

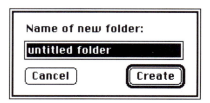

**Name of new folder:**

untitled folder

Cancel          Create

**FIGURE 8-3.** *When you click on the New button in the Save As dialog box, Word asks you to name your new folder.*

6. Enter the folder name *Test Docs* and click on the Create button. Word creates a new folder named ''Test Docs'' within the current folder, and moves to that new folder. Word displays *Test Docs* in the disk/folder list box in the Save As dialog box and shows the contents of the new folder in the file list box: nothing, because you have yet to put anything there.

7. Move the pointer to the disk/folder list box at the top of the file list and drag down. You see the list open to show the hierarchy of folders above the new folder. Pay close attention to where the folder is located: memorize the disk you're on, and the folders in which you're located.

8. Choose Desktop, and then let go of the mouse button. The file list changes to show you the contents of your desktop, which is your hard disk and any other disks you have available to your Macintosh.

9. Double-click on the hard-disk name to see the contents of the hard disk.

10. Double-click on the name of the first folder (probably the Word 5.0 folder) you need to enter to find your new folder. The file list shows the contents of the folder.

11. If your new folder appears in the file list, double-click on its name to move there. If it doesn't appear in the file list, keep moving into folders until you get into your new folder.

12. Click on the Save button to save your test document to your new folder.

13. When Word opens the Summary Info dialog box, click on the OK button to close the dialog box.

## File format

Normally, when you ask Word to save a document, it saves it in Word's own format, which stores all the characters in your document along with formatting information that tells Word where to put italics, indents, and other similar information. Because not all programs can read this format, if you save a Word document in this format and then open the file in another text program, the program is likely to display the file as gibberish—if it can translate it at all. If you want to use a Word document in another text program that can't read Word 5 files, you can make the document compatible with other programs by saving it in a compatible format. The following format options are available in Word:

- *Normal* saves a document in Word 5's own format. It includes characters, graphics, and all the formatting information needed to control the appearance of the document.

- *Text Only* saves a document as characters only, without any formatting. It inserts a single paragraph mark at the end of each paragraph. Almost all programs can read a text-only file, so use this format if you're transferring a document to a text program you think might not be compatible with other file formats.

- *Text Only with Line Breaks* saves a document as characters only, without any formatting. It inserts a single paragraph mark at the end of each line of text in the document instead of only at the end of each paragraph. Many telecommunications programs require a document in this format so that they don't transmit each paragraph as a single long line that runs off the edge of the screen.

- *Microsoft Word 3.x* saves a document in a file format that Word version 3 can read. Because these versions of Word aren't able to format in as many ways as Word 5, some formatting in Word 5 documents might be lost in the transfer to this format.

- *Interchange format (also called RTF, for Rich Text Format)* saves a document in a format that other Microsoft applications can read, including Microsoft Word for MS-DOS and Word for Windows, which run on PC-compatible computers.

- *Stationery* saves a document in the same format as Normal does, but with one difference: It identifies the document as stationery, which means that you can open and alter it, but when you save it, Word requires you to give it a new name so that you won't change the original document. You use Stationery format to create standard documents that you can use to start other documents—for example, a blank letter with the heading and signature areas already typed out.

- *MacWrite* saves a document in a format that the word processor MacWrite can read.

- *MacWrite II 1.x* saves a document in a format that MacWrite II version 1 can read.

- *Word for MS-DOS* saves a document in a format that Word for MS-DOS can read. (Word for MS-DOS is a version of Word that runs on IBM PC–compatible computers.)

- *Word for Windows 1* saves a document in a format that Word for Windows version 1 can read. (Word for Windows is a version of Word that runs under Microsoft Windows, a graphical user interface that runs on IBM PC–compatible computers.)

- *Word for Windows 2.0* saves a document in a format that Word for Windows version 2 can read.

- *WordPerfect 5.0* saves a document in a format that WordPerfect 5.0 can read.

- *WordPerfect 5.1* saves a document in a format that WordPerfect 5.1 can read.

To save a document in a file format other than Normal, choose a new format from the Save File As Type list, and then click on the Save button. Word saves the document in the new format.

After you save a document in a file format other than Normal, it remains in that format only until you choose the Save command again. Choosing the Save command again opens the Save As dialog box, where you'll have to type in the filename and choose the file format again. If you want to set the document so that Save always saves it using an alternative file format, turn on the Default For File option to the right of the Save File As Type list box. After the option is turned on and the document is saved once, Word uses the alternative file format to save the document each time you choose the Save command (although you'll still need to type in the filename).

## Summary Information

Normally, whenever you save a document for the first time, Word opens a Summary Info dialog box (shown in Figure 8-4) where you can fill in information about the document. If you don't save many documents and you keep the documents you do save arranged in an orderly way, summary information is probably not necessary; you can click on the OK button to close the dialog box without adding any information. If you're working on a disk used by many people to store documents or if you save a lot of documents that you think you'll have a hard time finding later, fill in whatever information here that you think will be helpful. Later you can use an advanced Word feature— Find File—to search through the documents on your disk for specific summary information.

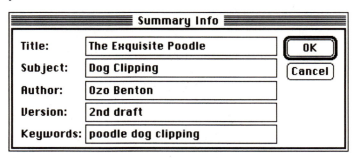

**FIGURE 8-4.** *Word asks for summary information so that you can more easily identify the document later.*

To add summary information or revise existing summary information for a document, choose the Summary Info command from the File menu. Word reopens the Summary Info dialog box so that you can see the current document's information and change it.

# OPENING A DOCUMENT

After you save and close a document, you can open it again using either the Open command, which lets you browse through disks and folders, or the Find File command, an advanced feature that helps you search through a disk for a lost document.

## The Open Command

To open a document, choose the Open command from the Edit menu. The Open dialog box appears, as shown in Figure 8-5.

Most of the features in the Open dialog box are the same as those you used in the Save dialog box. You choose names in the disk/folder list box and the file list box to move from folder to folder and from disk to disk, and you use the Eject button to change floppy disks. The file list box in the Open dialog box shows both files and folders, so you can choose either type. To open a document, either double-click on its name in the file list box or click once on its name to select it and then click on the Open button.

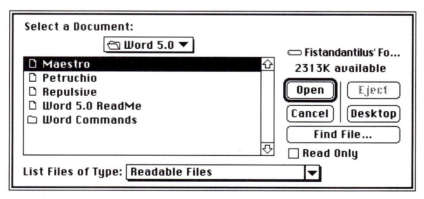

**FIGURE 8-5.** *Use the Open dialog box to choose a document to be opened.*

### Different types of files

Word normally displays all the files that it can read in the file list box. This includes Word version 5 documents, documents created with previous versions of Word, text files created in programs such as TeachText (the simple text program that comes with your Macintosh), and graphics files created by programs such as MacPaint or SuperPaint. It doesn't display files that it can't read, such as spreadsheet files, files containing other programs, and so forth.

You can change the file list to show more or less than this—if you find it convenient—by choosing a new option from the List Files Of Type list box. Beginners should keep the option set to Readable Files. You might find, however, that restricting the kinds of files that appear—for example, to graphics only—can help you more easily sort through a folder that contains many files of mixed types. You'll find more information about the options in the *Microsoft Word User's Guide*.

### Opening other file types

When you open a file that's stored in a format other than Word's Normal format, Word might present a message on the screen informing you that it's translating the document, or it might display the document on the screen and show its file format in the Page-Number area. If Word opens a graphics file, it creates a new document that includes only the graphic, which it positions at the top of the page. If you try to open a document that Word doesn't normally read (which you can do if you set the file list to show all files), you might see a jumble of characters and symbols on the screen or you might get an empty document.

### Using the Read Only option

You might want to open a document for reading only and not take the chance of accidentally making changes. If so, you can turn on the Read Only option in the Open dialog box before you open a document. When the Read Only option is turned on, Word opens the document and lets you make changes but won't let you save those changes to the original file. You can save them under a new filename instead, or you can close the document without saving any changes. This option is very handy if you're using a document as a base for creating another document and don't want to alter your original document.

# Find File

You might have problems finding a document you saved earlier. Perhaps it's stashed inside a folder you've forgotten about or saved under a name that no longer reminds you of the document's contents. If so, you can use Word's Find File feature to locate the document. It first searches through a disk for all document files, regardless of their locations within folders, and then presents the files to you in an easy-to-scan list that shows you the text content of each document.

To use Find File, you can either click on the Find File button in the Open dialog box or choose the Find File command from the File menu. Both actions open the Search dialog box shown in Figure 8-6.

You can use the controls in the Search dialog box to define the particular type of document you're looking for. By filling in one or more of the File Name, Title, Any Text, Subject, Author, Version, Keywords, and Finder Comments text boxes, you can ask Word to search for all the files that match your entries; Word looks through the summary and file information stored for each document. You can also use the Created and Last Saved areas to define a search for documents created or last saved within a specific time range. The

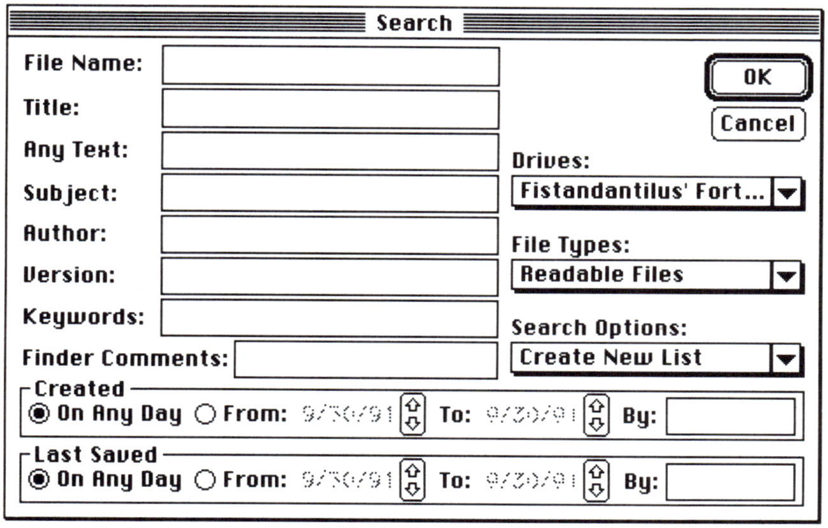

**FIGURE 8-6.** *The Search dialog box helps you define a search for files scattered throughout a disk.*

Drives, File Types, and Search Options list boxes allow you to choose which disk drive you want to search, what file formats you want to search for, and how you want Word to compile its list of files found.

Using the Search dialog box is an advanced Word technique. Beginners need only work with two controls: the Drives list box and the File Types list box. Use the Drives list box to choose the drive through which you want to search for files. You'll find your main hard disk listed here as well as any floppy disks in the Mac and any additional hard disks attached.

After you've set the drive you want to search, tell Word what kind of file format you want to look for by choosing it from the File Types list box. You'll find a big list of different formats; if you don't have a particular format in mind, choose Word Documents to create a list of Word documents.

After your search criteria are set, click on the OK button to begin the search. Word opens the Find File window (shown in Figure 8-7) when the search is complete.

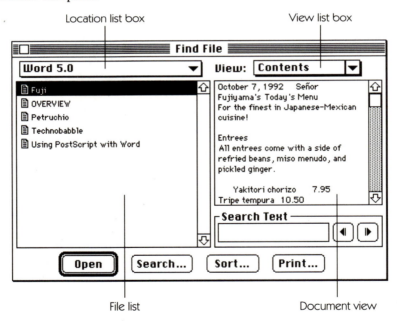

**FIGURE 8-7.** *The Find File window shows the files found by your search.*

The Find File window displays all the files found by the search, regardless of their locations within folders. You'll find them in the file list on the left side. You can scroll through the list to see all the files available, and select any one by clicking on it. To open a selected file, click on the Open button. Or, for faster opening, you can double-click on a file's name.

If you open the location list box at the top left of Find File, it shows you the location of any file you have selected: the disk it's on and the hierarchy of folders that contain it. The document view to the right shows the full text of the document, unformatted and without graphics. You can scroll through it to get a quick idea of a document's contents.

The View list box at the top right of the Find File window controls the document view. In addition to the document's contents, you can also look at a summary of its contents (when it was created, how many characters, and so on), comments attached to its file in Finder, and any summary information you entered for the document.

Find File offers much more than I've described here. You'll find more information about searching for documents in the *Microsoft Word User's Guide*.

## PRACTICE

### Opening a file

*Try opening the document "Petruchio" that you created and saved in Chapter 2 (or any other document, if you've deleted "Petruchio"):*

1. Choose the Open command from the File menu to open the Open dialog box.

2. Click on the Find File button to open the Search dialog box.

3. Choose Word Documents in the File Types list, and then click on the OK button. Word searches for all the Word documents on your hard drive and then opens the Find File window.

4. Scroll through the files in the file list until you see the title "Petruchio," and then click on the name to select it. The document view to the right shows the contents of the letter.

5. Choose Statistics from the View list. The document view changes to show you when the letter was created and how large the file is.

6. Click on the Open button to open the letter and close the window. Leave the document open for the next practice session in this chapter.

# PRINTING A DOCUMENT

After you create and save a document, the big payoff is in turning your printer on and printing the document on paper. In Chapter 2, "Creating a Business Letter," printing was a simple matter of choosing the Print command, clicking on the OK button in the Print dialog box, and waiting for your printer to print the document. This section presents some useful alternatives that make printing more flexible and convenient.

## Using the Chooser

If you have more than one printer connected to your Macintosh, you can choose any of those printers to print your document by using the Chooser program that comes with your Mac. The Chooser presents a list of the printers connected to your Macintosh and lets you choose the one you want to use for printing. The Chooser is especially useful if your Mac is part of a network of computers and printers because it shows all printers available to you on the network. If one printer is busy, you can choose another for printing and then close the Chooser and print.

You can open the Chooser window, shown in Figure 8-8, at any time by choosing the Chooser command from the Apple menu. The printer icons in the printer icon list box show the types of printers that are connected via AppleTalk or the ports on the back of your Mac. Click on any one of the printer icons to select the type of printer you want. If more than one printer of that type is available, the printer name list box at the right side of the Chooser window shows the names of those printers. Click on the name of the printer you want to print on.

If you're not connected to a network and you use the Chooser, it might offer you a choice of ports when you select a printer. These ports tell the Chooser where your printer is connected to your Macintosh: through the

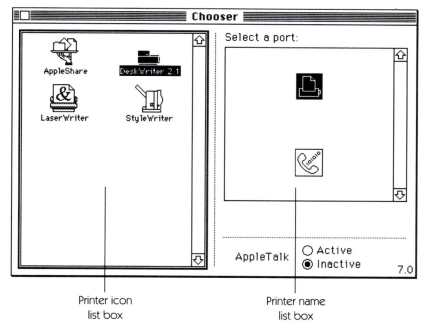

**FIGURE 8-8.** *The Chooser window shows all printers available to your Macintosh.*

printer port (the icon with the printer symbol) or through the serial port (the icon with the telephone). You normally won't have to choose either one, because the port is already set. If your printer won't print, however, you might want to try setting a port in the Chooser: Look at the back of your Mac to see whether your printer is plugged into the printer port or the serial port (they're labeled with the same icons you see in the Chooser window). Then choose the correct port (usually the printer port).

After you've set a new printer, close the Chooser window. Any printing you do now is sent to the selected printer. You won't have to use the Chooser again until you want to switch printers.

## The Print Dialog Box

When you choose the Print command from the File menu to print a document, the Print dialog box you see depends on the type of printer you have set in the Chooser. LaserWriters, DeskWriters, ImageWriters, StyleWriters—each printer you connect to the Mac has its own *printer driver,* a custom piece of software that tells Word how to send the proper information to that specific type of printer and determines the kind of Print dialog box that opens when you choose the Print command.

Figure 8-9 shows you three standard Print dialog boxes for three popular printers used with the Macintosh. If you use a different printer, you might see a completely different dialog box when you print. Although the dialog boxes differ in many ways, they also offer options that are common to most printers. The sections that follow describe some of the common printer options.

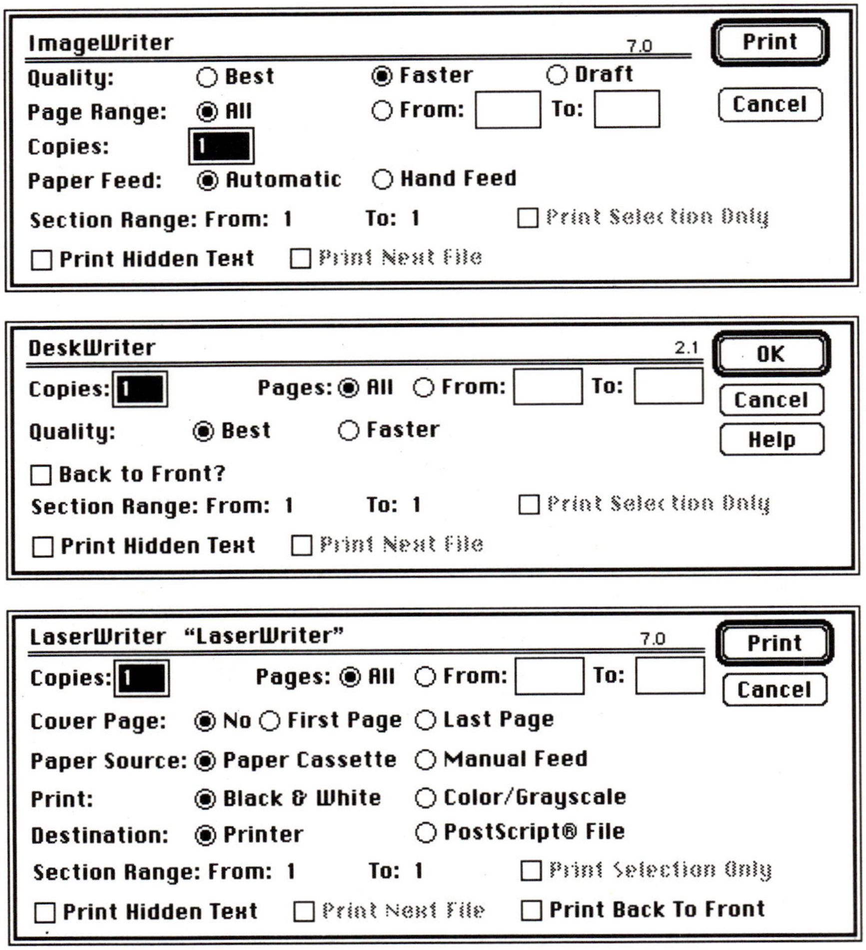

**FIGURE 8-9.** *The ImageWriter, DeskWriter, and LaserWriter Print dialog boxes all offer their own printing options.*

## Printing several copies

To print more than one copy of a document, enter the number of copies you want in the Copies text box.

## Printing a range of pages or selected text

The Pages section (also called Page Range in some dialog boxes) controls the range of pages that Word prints. Clicking on the default button All instructs Word to print all the pages in the document. To print a limited range of pages, click on the From To button, and then enter the beginning page number in the From text box and the ending page number in the To text box. To print a single page, enter the same page number in both the From and To text boxes. To print from any page in the document to the end of the document when you don't know the final page number, leave the To box empty; Word will print to the end of the document and stop.

To print a section of a document that doesn't begin or end neatly at a page break, first select as a text block the section you want to print, and then turn on the Print Selection Only option before you print. Word prints only the section you selected and paginates the printout so that the selected section starts at the top of the first page.

## Printing hidden text

When you learned to format characters in Chapter 3, "Formatting and Entering Characters," you learned to apply the Hidden Text type style to text that you didn't want to appear in a document. Word doesn't normally print hidden text, but it will print it if you turn on the Print Hidden Text option.

## Setting paper feed

Different printers have different paper-feeding capabilities. Some can accept a single hand-fed sheet of paper (useful for letterhead or other special paper) or can print continuously on sheets of fanfold paper fed through the rollers by the printer's tractors. Others can print on hand-fed sheets of paper or on single sheets that feed into its rollers from a paper cassette.

If your printer prints on fanfold paper (as the ImageWriter printer does, for example), you'll see two options in the Print dialog box: *Automatic* and *Hand Feed*. Click on the Automatic button if you're printing on fanfold paper or on the Hand Feed button if you're feeding the printer one sheet at a time. If your printer takes paper from a cassette, as most laser printers do, you'll find two similar options in the LaserWriter dialog box: *Paper Cassette* and *Manual Feed*. Click on the Paper Cassette button if you're printing on paper from the printer's paper cassette or on the Manual Feed button if you're feeding the paper one sheet at a time.

If you choose Hand Feed or Manual Feed, Word stops before printing each page and displays a dialog box that asks whether you want to print the page. You can then insert a sheet of paper by hand and click on the OK button to print the page. You repeat this procedure until you finish printing the document or until you click on the Cancel button in the dialog box.

## Setting print quality

Most Print dialog boxes offer different qualities of printing in a line labeled ''Quality.'' Choose the option that best suits your purposes:

- *Draft* is an option found only for dot-matrix printers such as the ImageWriter printer. It offers a very fast printing speed, but pages printed in draft quality don't include graphics, show only rudimentary type styles, and display only one character size. Draft-quality printing is only a crude approximation of what you see on the Mac screen because it uses the printer's built-in character set instead of actual fonts. Use draft quality when you want to proofread text and don't require exact formatting.

- *Faster* prints slower than Draft and faster than Best. It shows all the graphics and formatting you've added to your document and uses the fonts you see on the Mac screen. The Faster setting is perhaps the most useful print-quality setting for everyday printing on the ImageWriter and other dot-matrix printers. For laser printers and ink-jet printers such as the LaserWriter or the Desk-Writer, the Faster setting is used only for quick printouts because its quality is not high.

- *Best* is the slowest option of all, but it improves the quality of the printed characters by printing them at a higher resolution than other options do. Although Best doesn't show any more formatting or graphics than Faster does, its printout is darker and the characters are better formed. Use Best when you print a document for copying or when you really want to impress the reader.

## Setting a cover page and the page-printing order

Laser printer and ink-jet printer dialog boxes often offer the options *Cover Page* and *Print Back To Front*. The Cover Page option offers a cover page that prints before or after your document prints. The cover page lists the document title, your name, and other information that identifies your document—a very useful feature if you share your printer with other users.

If you click on the No button, Word prints no cover page with your document. If you click on the First Page button, Word prints the cover page before it prints your document. And if you click on the Last Page button, Word prints the cover page after it finishes printing your document.

Word normally prints a document beginning with the first page, working toward the last page. If your LaserWriter is set up to deposit one printed page on top of another with the printed side up, you'll find your document is arranged in a pile that reads from the last page through the first page. To print in the opposite order, turn on the Print Back To Front option; Word then prints in the reverse order so that your pile of printed pages reads from the first page through the last page.

## Printing

To begin printing after you set the printing options you want, simply click on the Print button. Word displays a message telling you that it's printing your document, and the Page-Number area at the bottom of the document window displays the number of the page currently being printed. If you want to stop printing at any time, press Command-. (period). Word stops printing and returns you to the document window.

## PRACTICE

### Printing a document

*Try printing two copies of one page of the document "Petruchio" that you created and saved in Chapter 2:*

1. Open the "Petruchio" document. Or, if you've lost it or haven't created it yet, create a two-page document by simply opening a new document and filling it with random text. (Don't forget the Copy and Paste commands; they'll make your job easy.)

2. Move the insertion point to the center of the letter, and then press Shift-Enter to enter a page break there. This breaks the letter into two pages.

3. Choose the Print command from the File menu to open the Print dialog box for your printer.

4. Type *2* in the Copies text box.

5. In the Pages line (or the Page Range line, depending on how it's labeled in your dialog box), turn on the From To option.

6. Type *1* in the From text box and *1* in the To text box.

7. Click on the Print button to begin printing.

*Word prints two copies of page 1 and displays the page number in the Page-Number area as it prints.*

You now know how to handle finished documents—saving, opening, and printing them using many different options. You've reached the end of this section, which means you should now be an experienced Word user. Congratulations! In the next section, you'll go beyond basics to learn about some of Word's features used to create special documents.

# Section III

# For Special Documents

Chapter 9

# Creating Headers and Footers in Long Documents

Imagine printing out a document of 40 unnumbered and unlabeled pages. As you collect the pages from the printer, you accidentally trip, and the papers cascade onto the floor. Now imagine trying to put them back together in the right order, and you'll see why it's important to have page numbers and other document information printed on each page of a long document. To help you add this information, Microsoft Word offers *headers* and *footers*, two elements that label the top and bottom of each document page.

In this chapter, you'll learn to create headers and footers that include page numbers, the date and the time, and any other text you want. You'll learn to set header and footer positions on a page, suppress them on the first page, and create alternating headers and footers for subsequent pages. You'll also learn how to preview headers and footers before you print your document.

## CREATING A SAMPLE DOCUMENT

To work with headers and footers in the practice sessions for this chapter, you'll first need a multiple-page document. A three-page report should do the trick—it has a first page that requires special treatment and two following pages. The content of the document isn't important, so you can use the Copy and Paste commands to duplicate a single paragraph 10 times to create the body of the document.

### PRACTICE
#### Creating a sample document

*Create a sample three-page report:*

1. Set the paragraph alignment to *centered* and the font's point size to *24*. Turn on bold text formatting, type *Reiteration Report,* and then press Return to begin a new paragraph.

2. Set paragraph formatting to insert a blank line before each paragraph.

3. Change the font's point size to *12* and type *by Randall Redux.* Press Return.

4. Set the paragraph alignment to left aligned and set line spacing to double spaced. Turn off bold text formatting.

5. Type the text of the paragraph shown in Figure 9-1, and press Return at the end of the paragraph.

6. Select the paragraph you typed, and choose the Copy command from the Edit menu.

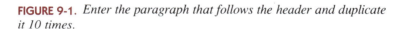

# Reiteration Report¶

### by Randall Redux¶

Researchers in rural regions relate repetitious renderings of regional
revelations… "Rack and ruin!" rant reports… "Rubbish," reply rational
readers… "Rout and remorse" repeat reports… Readers rejected
reports; reports relinquished reliability… Repeated reporting rates
reservations; recent ratings reveal retreating revenue for rumor rags…
Repeating:¶

**FIGURE 9-1.** *Enter the paragraph that follows the header and duplicate it 10 times.*

7. Move the insertion point to the beginning of the blank line following the paragraph.

8. Press Command-V 10 times to paste 10 copies of the paragraph into the document.

The resulting document should be three pages long. In the following practice sessions you'll add headers and footers to this document. The result will be similar to the document shown in Figure 9-2. Notice that although the first page has no information at the top of the page, the following pages do. And notice, too, that pages 2 and 3 have different information at the top of each page because they're facing pages—just as the pages of this book are.

## WHAT ARE HEADERS AND FOOTERS?

A *header* is a banner of text that appears at the top of each page of a printed document. A typical header includes the name of the document, the page number, and other information such as the author's name or the date on which the document was created. A header in Word can be as short or as long as you want. You can apply character formatting and paragraph formatting to a header as you do to the main body of text. You can also add graphics.

A *footer* serves the same purpose as a header but appears at the bottom of each document page. Some documents use footers in place of headers, displaying page numbers and title information at the bottom of each page.

Other documents use footers in addition to headers, displaying document information such as copyright notices or company names. A footer in Word, like a header, can be as long or as short as you want. You can apply character and paragraph formatting and add graphics to a footer. And you can insert both a footer and a header on the same page.

---

## Reiteration Report

### by Randall Redux

Researchers in rural regions relate repetitious renderings of regional revelations. "Rack and ruin!" rant reports. "Rubbish," reply rational readers. "Rout and remorse" repeat reports. Readers rejected ~~reliability.~~ Repeated reporting rates

Researchers in rural regions revelations. "Rack and ruin!" rant reports. "Rubbish," reply rational readers. "Rout and remorse" repeat reports. Readers rejected reports, reports relinquished reliability. Repeated reporting rates

**Redundant Research—Rights Reserved**

---

2                          Reiteration Report          October 27, 1992

reservations; recent ratings reveal retreating revenue for rumor rags. Repeating:

Researchers in rural regions relate repetitious renderings of regional revelations. "Rack and ruin!" rant reports. "Rubbish," reply rational readers. "Rout and remorse" repeat reports. Readers rejected ~~reliability.~~ Repeated reporting rates

revelations. "Rack and ruin!" rant reports. readers. "Rout and remorse" repeat reports. Readers rejected reports, reports relinquished reliability. Repeated reporting rates

**Redundant Research—Rights Reserved**

---

**FIGURE 9-2.** *The finished report's headers and footers identify and number its pages.*                    *(continued)*

**FIGURE 9-2.** *continued*

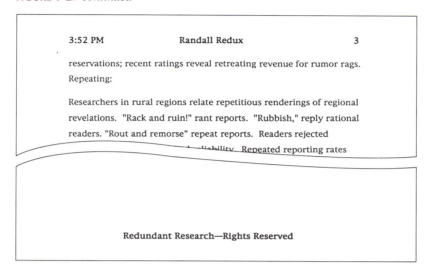

Headers and footers don't normally appear in the main document window on your monitor because they break up the body of your text and make editing difficult. To create and edit headers and footers, you open special windows called the *Header window* (to create a header) and the *Footer window* (to create a footer). Later in this chapter you'll learn how to view headers and footers with the rest of the document.

## CREATING HEADERS AND FOOTERS

To open a Header or Footer window, choose the Header or the Footer command from the View menu. Choosing the Header command opens the Header window, whose title bar displays the name of your document with the tag "Header." Choosing the Footer command opens the Footer window, whose title bar displays the name of your document with the tag "Footer." Both windows contain the same elements, and you work with them in the same way. The only difference is that anything you enter or insert in the Header window appears as a header on the document pages, and anything you enter or insert in the Footer window appears as a footer on the document pages. Figure 9-3 shows a Header window.

The bar at the top of the Header window or the Footer window is the *icon bar*. Clicking on one of the three icons at the left end of the icon bar instructs

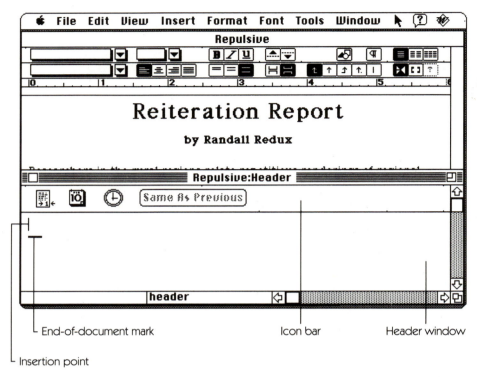

End-of-document mark                    Icon bar          Header window

Insertion point

**FIGURE 9-3.** *Enter the contents of a header in the Header window, which appears in the lower half of the screen.*

Word to insert the current page number, date, or time in the header. To the right of these icons is the Same As Previous button for use in documents containing more than one section. (You'll learn about dividing a document into sections in Chapter 11, "Setting Columns and Document Sections.")

The text area below the icon bar contains an insertion point and an end-of-document mark like those in the main document window. As you type in the text area, you enter text that becomes part of the header, not part of the body of the document.

## Entering Text

You enter text in the Header window or the Footer window in the same way in which you enter text in the main document window. You can apply character and paragraph formatting using the Ruler and the commands in the Format menu. Word presets two tab stops on the Ruler's measure for creating headers and footers. It sets a center-align tab stop in the middle of the measure and a right-align tab stop at the right end of the measure. Use these tab stops to center text or to right-align it at the right margin. If you prefer, you can remove these tab stops and set your own.

## Entering Page Numbers, Date, and Time

Some information you enter in a header or a footer changes from page to page or from one session to the next: the current page number, date, and time. You can click on the icons in the icon bar to insert this information into the header or footer. Move the insertion point to the location in the header or the footer where you want the information to appear, and then click on the appropriate icon. Word inserts the chosen information at the insertion point's location. Clicking on the three icons inserts the following information:

- Clicking on the page-number icon inserts a number that increases by one on each subsequent page. (This is the same as the *page number* entry in the Glossary.)

- Clicking on the date icon inserts the current date. Each time you open a Header window or a Footer window that contains an inserted date, Word reads the Macintosh's internal clock and inserts the current date at this location. Each time you print the document, Word prints the current date. (This is the same as the *print date* entry in the Glossary.)

- Clicking on the time icon inserts the current time. Each time you open a Header window or a Footer window containing an inserted time, Word changes the time to match that of the Macintosh's internal clock. Each time you print the document, Word inserts the time of printing. (This is the same as the *print time* entry in the Glossary.)

Word treats each inserted page number, date, or time in a header or a footer as a single character. Although several characters might appear on the screen (especially in a date or a time), you can select the page number, date, or time only as a single character. You can format inserted information by selecting it and applying character formatting to it as you would to any other character.

## PRACTICE
### Entering a header

*Try entering a header for your document:*

1. Choose the Header command from the View menu to open the Header window.

2. Click on the page-number icon to insert a page number. The number *1* appears on the left side of the header field.

3. Press the Tab key to jump to the center-align tab stop in the middle of the line, and then type *Reiteration Report.* The text appears centered on the line.

4. Press the Tab key to jump to the right-align tab stop at the end of the line, and then insert the date by clicking on the date icon. The current date appears right aligned at the right margin.

5. Select the entire first line of the header and turn on bold text formatting.

6. Close the header window by clicking on its close box.

You create a footer in the same way that you create a header except that you enter text in the Footer window instead of in the Header window.

## PRACTICE
### Entering a footer

*Try adding a footer to your document:*

1. Choose the Footer command from the View menu to open the Footer window.

2. Press the Tab key to move to the center-align tab stop, turn on bold text formatting, and type *Redundant Research— Rights Reserved.* (Press Shift-Option-hyphen to produce an *em dash.* The em dash is the typesetter's equivalent of two successive dashes.)

3. Close the Footer window by clicking on its close box.

Note that when you create a header or a footer, pressing Return at the end of the last line adds a blank line below the last line of text, which increases the height of the header or footer and takes space from the main body of text. Don't press Return unless you want that space there.

## PREVIEWING HEADERS AND FOOTERS

When you close the Header window or the Footer window, Word remembers the header or footer you created and adds it to the pages when you print the document. You don't normally see the header or the footer in the main text window. If you'd like to see headers and footers as they appear on the page, you can use Word's Page Layout view. (You will learn how to use Page Layout view in Chapter 13, "Views, Outlines, and Document Windows," but you can sneak a peek and use it here so that you can see your header and footer handiwork.)

### Using Page Layout View

The document view you've seen up to this point is called *Normal view*. It shows all the pages of a document as one long page that you can scroll through. Pages are separated by page-break lines in Normal view. In Page Layout view, the document window changes to show each page of the document, including the edges of each page and any headers and footers you've created. To turn on Page Layout view, simply choose the Page Layout command from the View menu. To return to Normal view, choose the Normal command from the View menu. Try it now on your sample document:

### PRACTICE
#### Using Page Layout view

1. Choose the Page Layout command from the View menu to turn on Page Layout view.

2. Drag the vertical scroll box to the top of the scroll bar. Your viewpoint moves upward so that you can see the top edge of the page and the header you created earlier, as shown in Figure 9-4.

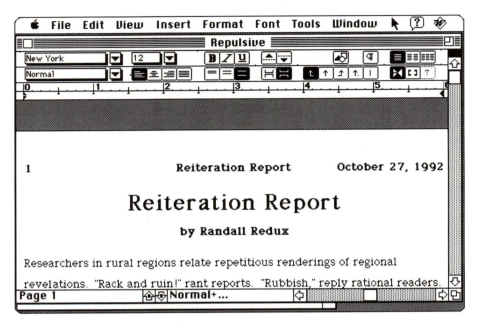

**FIGURE 9-4.** *Page Layout view shows the top or bottom of each page, revealing any header or footer you've created.*

3. Click on the vertical scroll bar below the scroll box to scroll downward one screen at a time until you reach the bottom of the page. You see your footer there, followed by the bottom edge of the page.

4. Click on the scroll bar below the scroll box again to scroll downward another screen. Your viewpoint jumps to the beginning of text on the next page, skipping the header at the top of the page.

5. Click above the scroll box to move the document view to the top of the second page. You see the second-page header there. Notice that the page number is 2.

6. Continue scrolling through the rest of the document, viewing the headers and the footers on each page.

7. When you're finished, choose the Normal command from the View menu to turn off Page Layout view.

*Because Word operates differently when Page Layout view is on, it's important that you return Word to Normal view for the practice sessions in this book unless they specifically ask for Page Layout view.*

## HEADER AND FOOTER OPTIONS

You might want to display different headers and footers on different pages of your document. For example, the title page of a report might look better if you eliminated the header above the report title. Or you might want to display different headers on alternating pages throughout your document. Word allows you to create special treatments for headers and footers by choosing options in the Section and Document dialog boxes. The following sections explain how to do so.

### Creating Headers and Footers for a Title Page

To create a special header and footer for a title page, you first open the Section dialog box, shown in Figure 9-5, by choosing the Section command from the Format menu. The Section dialog box appears. Click on the Different First Page option in the Header/Footer area (in the lower left corner of the dialog box) to turn it on or off; it shows an X in the check box when it's turned on. When the option is set the way you want it, click on the OK button to close the dialog box and apply the option.

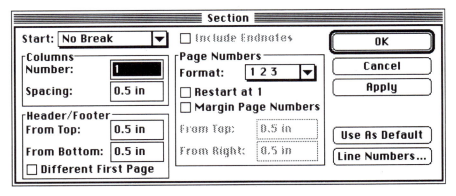

FIGURE 9-5. *Open the Section dialog box to set the Different First Page option.*

If you turn on the Different First Page option, two new commands appear in the View menu: First Header and First Footer. They appear because your document now has two headers and two footers. The first-page header and the first-page footer contain the header and the footer that appear only on the first page of the document. The regular header and footer contain the header and the footer that appear on all subsequent pages.

To create the first-page header, choose the First Header command from the View menu to open the First Header window. You enter text and fields in this window as you do when you create the regular header. Close the window when you've finished entering text for the first-page header. Anything you enter appears as the header on the first page only. If you enter nothing in the text area, no header appears on the first page.

You create the first-page footer by choosing the First Footer command from the View menu to open the First Footer window. Any footer you create in this window appears only on the first page.

## Practice

### Creating a title-page footer

*Try creating a blank header for the title page of the sample report and setting the title-page footer to match the regular footer:*

1. Choose the Section command from the Format menu to open the Section dialog box.

2. Turn on the Different First Page option, and then click on the OK button to close the dialog box.

3. Choose the First Footer command from the View menu to open the First Footer window.

4. Enter the footer used in the rest of the document: Turn on bold text formatting, press the Tab key once to center the text, and then type *Redundant Research—Rights Reserved.*

5. Close the First Footer window.

*Notice that you didn't need to open the First Header window to create a blank header for the first page. The first-page header will be blank unless you enter text in the First Header window. You wanted the first-page header to be blank, so you didn't need to enter anything—you simply went on to the footer. The first-page footer will also be blank unless you enter text in the First Footer window, so you had to open the window and duplicate the footer used in the rest of the document. To see how your first-page header and first-page footer appear on the page, turn on Page Layout view and scroll through the document. After you finish, turn off Page Layout view.*

## Creating Headers and Footers for Facing Pages

If you create a Word document designed to print on facing pages (to be printed on both sides of the paper and then bound together), you can display alternating headers and footers on even-numbered and odd-numbered pages. Displaying different headers and footers on facing pages allows you to place the page number at the outer corner of each page—at the upper right corner of odd-numbered pages and at the upper left corner of even-numbered pages. Headers and footers can also include alternating text on facing pages: You could, for example, display the document title on even-numbered pages and the section title on odd-numbered pages.

To create headers and footers for facing pages, you first open the Document dialog box, shown in Figure 9-6, by choosing the Document command from the Format menu. Click on the Even/Odd Headers option (located in the bottom center of the dialog box) to turn it on or off; it displays an X in the check box when it's turned on. When the option is set the way you want it, click on the OK button to close the dialog box and apply the option.

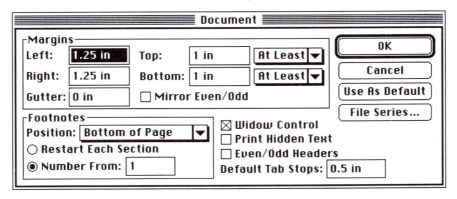

**FIGURE 9-6.** *Open the Document dialog box to set the Even/Odd Headers option.*

If you turn on the Even/Odd Headers option and then open the View menu, you'll find that Word has replaced the Header and Footer commands with four new commands: Even Header, Even Footer, Odd Header, and Odd Footer. As you might suspect, the Even Header and Even Footer commands open windows that allow you to create headers and footers for even-numbered pages, and the Odd Header and Odd Footer commands open windows that allow you to create headers and footers for odd-numbered pages. To enter text and information for these new headers and footers, you open the Header window or the Footer window by choosing the appropriate command from the View menu and then typing text or clicking on the icons in the icon bar as you do for other headers and footers.

## PRACTICE
### Making headers and footers for facing pages

*Now try setting up the report's headers and footers for facing pages:*

1. Choose the Document command from the Format menu to open the Document dialog box.

2. Turn on the Even/Odd Headers option, and then click on the OK button to close the dialog box.

3. Choose the Odd Header command from the View menu to open the Odd Header window.

4. Delete the text currently in the window.

5. Click on the time icon to enter the current time.

6. Press the Tab key to move to the center-align tab stop in the middle of the line and type *Randall Redux*.

7. Press the Tab key to move to the right-align tab stop at the end of the line, and click on the page-number icon to enter the current page number.

8. Select the entire line and turn on bold text formatting.

9. Choose the Even Header command from the View menu to open the Even Header window. (Note that you don't need to close the Odd Header window first; Word replaces it with the Even Header window.)

10. Delete the text currently in the window.

11. Click on the page-number icon to insert a page number on the left side of the header.

12. Press the Tab key to jump to the center-align tab stop in the middle of the line and type *Reiteration Report*. The table appears centered on the line.

13. Press the Tab key to jump to the right-align tab stop at the end of the line, and click on the date icon to enter the date. Today's date appears right aligned at the right margin.

14. Select the entire line and turn on bold text formatting.

15. Close the Even Header window.

16. Save the document with the name "Redundancy" so that you can use it again in later chapters.

*Your document now has an odd-numbered page header with the time of printing at the upper left corner of the page, the author's name centered at the top of the page, and the page number at the upper right corner (the outer corner of an odd page). The even-numbered page header shows the page number at the upper left corner of the page (the outer corner of an even page), the name of the report centered at the top of the page, and the date right aligned at the right margin. To see how your new headers and footers appear in the document, turn on Page Layout view and scroll through the pages. The headers and the footers should look like the ones shown in Figure 9-2, at the beginning of this chapter. Turn off Page Layout view when you finish.*

## ADVANCED HEADER AND FOOTER TECHNIQUES

The header and footer techniques you just learned should serve you well for most multipage documents. However, if you have special header and footer needs, you might want to explore the chapter titled "Numbering Pages" in the *Microsoft Word User's Guide* for some advanced page-numbering options: numbering pages with Roman numerals or the letters of the alphabet; continuing page numbering from one document to another document (such as from one chapter of a book to the next); and placing page numbers in the margins, outside of a standard header or footer.

You'll also find useful information in the chapter titled "Headers and Footers" in the *Microsoft Word User's Guide,* where you can learn to move the top of each header and the bottom of each footer up or down on the page to increase or decrease the white space at the top and bottom of the page.

You've now learned how to add footers and headers to your documents. In the next chapter, you'll learn how to put some pizzazz in a document by adding graphics.

# Chapter 10

# Adding Graphics

A picture on the page pulls in the eye and informs the reader quickly. It breaks up the monotony of the printed word. But drawing the picture and placing it on the page takes some time, which is why it's fortunate that Microsoft Word 5.0 provides its own easy-to-use drawing program. You open Word's drawing program from within a document, draw what you want, and close it to see your graphic inserted in the document.

Because Word's drawing program is just that—an entire program with its own tools found within Word—you'll want to know how to use it. How do you open it? How do you use its tools to draw objects? Can you add text to label objects? How do you place your graphic on the page? Can you put a border around your graphic? And once a graphic is put on the page, can you go back to edit it?

You might also wonder if Word can accept graphics created elsewhere—from your favorite paint program, from a scanner, or a from a graphics file that your friend sent to you. What kind of graphics will Word accept, and how can you import them? How can you get your favorite paint program to send graphics to Word? This chapter answers all of these questions and shows you how to add some graphic splash to your documents.

Before you start working with graphics in this chapter, you should check to be sure that your version of Word is set up to show graphics and includes the drawing program:

1. From the Mac's Finder, open the Word 5.0 folder (probably labeled *Word 5* or something similar).

2. Open the folder within Word's folder labeled *Word Commands* and look for the file named *Picture*. If the Picture file is not in the folder, Word won't be able to run its drawing program. To add the Picture file to the folder, you must run the Word 5.0 installation program again.

3. Start Word.

4. Choose the Preferences command from the Tools menu to open the Preferences window, and then click on the Views icon to show the View preferences.

5. Look at the option labeled *Picture Placeholders* in the Show area to make sure that it's turned off. If it's not off, click on it to turn it off.

6. Close the Preferences window.

Like other features such as the Thesaurus and the spelling checker, Word stores its drawing program as a separate file in the Word Commands folder—you must have it there to be able to use the drawing feature. The Picture Placeholders option controls how Word displays graphics—whether the actual graphics or only placeholders appear. If Picture Placeholders is turned on, you don't see the graphics in your document: You'll see only a shaded box (the placeholder) to show where the graphics will be. The picture placeholder speeds up Word's display, but we don't want it on for this chapter because we want to see the fruits of our graphics work.

## CREATING A NEW GRAPHIC

Word treats each graphic you place in a Word document as a single character. A graphic can occupy its own individual paragraph, or it can fit between other characters in a line of text as shown in Figure 10-1. If you insert text before a graphic, the graphic moves left and then down the page, just as any other character would do. You can cut, copy, and paste the graphic, and if you put the insertion point just to the right of the graphic and press the Delete key, Word deletes the graphic just as it would a character. Word even allows you to apply some character-formatting commands to a graphic, as you'll learn later in this chapter.

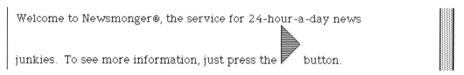

**FIGURE 10-1.** *Word treats each graphic in a document as a single character.*

If you'd like to create a new graphic and place it in a Word document, first move the insertion point to the spot in your text where you want the graphic to appear. It might be in the middle of other text, or it might occupy its own paragraph so that it stands apart. After you've selected the location, click on the graphic button in the Ribbon (shown in Figure 10-2) to open the Insert Picture window.

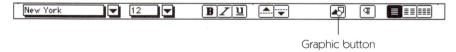

Graphic button

**FIGURE 10-2.** *Click on the graphic button in the Ribbon to open the Insert Picture window.*

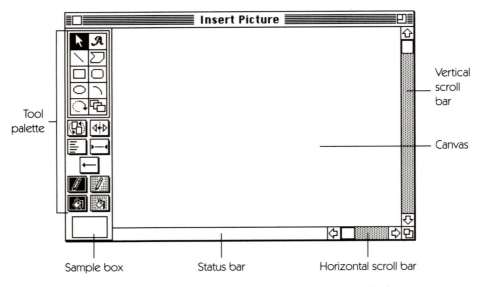

**FIGURE 10-3.** *The Insert Picture window supplies you with Word's drawing tools and drawing area.*

## The Insert Picture Window

The Insert Picture window, shown in Figure 10-3, gives you tools to draw with and a "canvas" to draw on. You can scroll through the canvas using the horizontal and vertical scroll bars—you have more than a full 8½-by-11-inch page of space available for drawing. Don't worry about where on the canvas you draw, because Word automatically trims off any blank space around your drawing before it inserts the graphic into your document.

Word uses the status bar at the bottom of the window to give you information about the size of an object as you draw it. The sample box to the left of the status bar shows you what line width, pattern, and color you're using to draw, as well as the color and pattern you're using to fill in enclosed figures such as rectangles and ellipses.

You'll find three types of tools in the tool palette (shown in Figure 10-4):

- *Creation tools,* which create objects on the canvas.

- *Manipulation tools,* which manipulate an object you've already created. For example, they can duplicate, flip, and rotate objects.

- *Quality tools,* which set the quality of the lines, fill patterns, and text used to create an object.

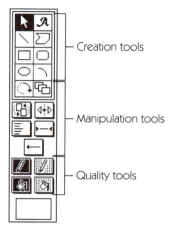

**FIGURE 10-4.** *Word offers three different types of tools to create pictures.*

## PRACTICE

### Opening the Insert Picture window

*Open the Insert Picture window in a new document:*

1. Open a new document if you don't have one already open.

2. Click on the graphic button in the Ribbon. The Insert Picture window opens.

*Feel free to play with the tools in the Insert Picture window as you read through their descriptions in this chapter.*

## Creating Objects

To draw a picture, you create objects with object creation tools, which you'll find in the upper half of the tool palette. Each tool helps you create a different-shaped object. You'll find the tools labeled in Figure 10-5. You can also see the objects they create in the canvas of the window.

### Creating a line

To create a line, click on the line tool and then move the pointer onto the canvas. Drag the mouse (with mouse button held down) from one point to another and then release the mouse button. Word draws a line between the two

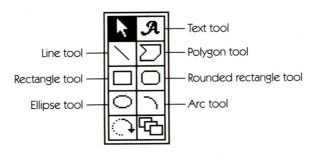

FIGURE 10-5. *The creation tools create objects in the Insert Picture window.*

points. If you want to create a line longer than the visible canvas in the window, you can drag up against the edge of the canvas; Word scrolls the canvas to let you move into hidden areas.

## Creating a rectangle

To draw a rectangle, click on the rectangle tool, and then drag the mouse from one point to another on the canvas as you did to draw a line. Word uses the two points to set the opposing corners of a rectangle, and draws a rectangle defined by those two points.

## Creating a rounded rectangle

You can use the rounded rectangle tool to draw a rectangle exactly as you draw one with the rectangle tool; Word simply rounds the corners of any rectangles you draw.

## Creating an ellipse

An ellipse is a round figure, either a circle or an oval. To draw an ellipse, first click on the ellipse tool, and then drag as you do to create a rectangle. Your dragging defines an ellipse stretched to the proportions of your drag. If you drag horizontally, you create a horizontal oval; if you drag as far to the left or right as you drag up or down, you create a circle.

## Creating a polygon

A polygon is any figure with three or more straight sides that enclose an interior area—a useful type of object for creating irregular shapes. To create a polygon, click on the polygon tool and then begin clicking on a series of locations on the canvas. The first click sets the first point of the polygon; the second, third, and following clicks set the following points of the polygon. Word draws a line from the first point to the second, from the second to the third, and so on until you end the polygon. To end the polygon, you double-click at the last point you want to set. Word then draws a line from the last point to the first point.

## Creating an arc

An arc is a section of an ellipse. The arcs that Word creates cover a quarter of an ellipse, stretching 90 degrees from the top or bottom of the ellipse to the leftmost or rightmost point of the ellipse. To draw an arc, first click on the arc tool, and then drag the pointer on the canvas as if you were drawing a rectangle. Word uses the proportions of your drag to define a quarter of an ellipse, drawing an arc to fit. Which arc of the ellipse you get depends on the direction of the drag—drag down and to the left for the upper left corner, down and to the right for the upper right corner, up and to the left for the lower left corner, and up and to the right for the lower right corner. (If this sounds confusing, just play with the tool. It will soon make sense.)

## Adding text

Although you can put text all around a graphic in a Word document, you might want to add text within the graphic as labels or as an integral part of the graphic. If so, click on the text tool. Then click once in the canvas to place an insertion point, where you can start typing. You can type all the way to the edge of the window, where Word jumps down a line to continue your text just below your first line.

If you'd like to define a rectangular area where your text is inserted, you can click on the text tool and then drag in the canvas just as you do when you create a rectangle. Word shows you the size of the area you're creating with a dotted-line rectangle that disappears as soon as you release the mouse button. When you start typing, your text appears at the top of the text area you defined, and the text's left and right margins fall within the text area's boundaries (as shown in Figure 10-6). If you type more text than the area can contain, Word moves the bottom boundary down to accommodate the text.

## Squares, circles, and other regular objects

There are times when you want to create very regular objects with Word's graphics tools: perfect circles, squares, lines that are absolutely horizontal or vertical. If you don't have a very sure hand on the mouse (or do, but don't want to leave anything to chance), you can use the Shift key as a *constraining key*—that is, a key that forces the objects you create to be perfectly square, circular, vertical, horizontal, and so on.

To constrain an object as you draw it, hold down the Shift key as you drag a creation tool in the canvas. It constrains the line tool to create only horizontal or vertical lines, constrains the rectangle and rounded-rectangle tools to create only squares and rounded squares, constrains the ellipse tool to create only circles, and constrains the arc tool to create only arcs that are "cut" from a perfect circle.

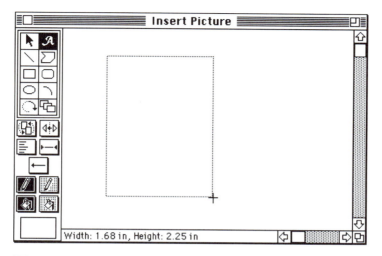

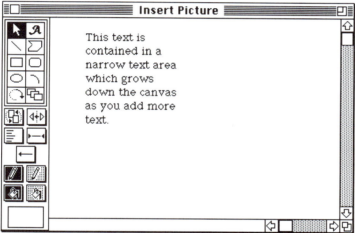

**FIGURE 10-6.** *You can define a text area in the canvas (shown with a dotted line) by dragging the mouse. Any text you then type stays within the text area's boundaries.*

## PRACTICE

### Creating a sample document with graphics

*Try creating the graphics in the sample invitation shown in Figure 10-7. You'll first need to start fresh if you've been playing with the graphics tools and drawing objects in the Insert Picture window.*

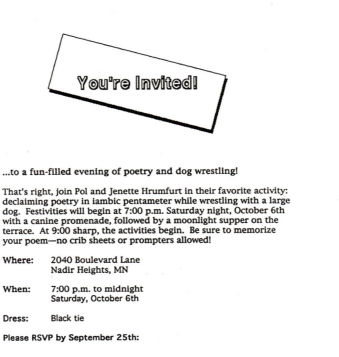

...to a fun-filled evening of poetry and dog wrestling!

That's right, join Pol and Jenette Hrumfurt in their favorite activity: declaiming poetry in iambic pentameter while wrestling with a large dog. Festivities will begin at 7:00 p.m. Saturday night, October 6th with a canine promenade, followed by a moonlight supper on the terrace. At 9:00 sharp, the activities begin. Be sure to memorize your poem—no crib sheets or prompters allowed!

Where:      2040 Boulevard Lane
            Nadir Heights, MN

When:       7:00 p.m. to midnight
            Saturday, October 6th

Dress:      Black tie

**Please RSVP by September 25th:**

☐ I will bring my own dog. (Please, no dogs smaller than a border collie!)

☐ I will require a loaner dog.

☐ Sorry, we won't be able to attend. Besides, we're cat people, and only read novels and self-help books.

**FIGURE 10-7.** *This invitation includes graphical elements that enhance the text.*

1. Click on the close box of the Insert Picture window to close the window and insert the graphic in your new document.

2. Press the Delete key to delete the graphic. Be sure you've deleted everything in the document so that you can start out fresh with an empty document.

3. Click on the graphic button in the Ribbon to reopen the Insert Picture window.

4. Click on the text tool to select it.

5. Move the insertion point about halfway down the canvas, 1 inch from its left border, and click to start typing there.

6. Set your font and character formatting: Choose the Helvetica command from Word's Font menu; choose the 24 Point command, also from the Font menu; and press Shift-Command-D to turn on the outline type style.

7. Type *You're Invited!* across the center of the canvas.

8. Click on the rectangle tool.

9. Drag from the upper left corner of the text to the lower right corner of the text to create a surrounding rectangle as shown in Figure 10-8. Be sure to leave plenty of room around the text as shown. (If you make a mistake, press the Delete key to delete your rectangle and then try again.)

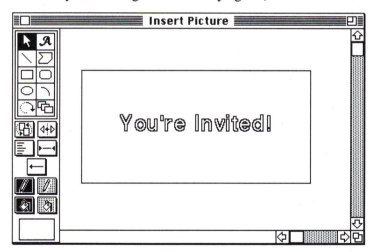

**FIGURE 10-8.** *Create text with a surrounding rectangle.*

## Manipulating Objects

Each time you create an object in the Insert Picture window—a line, rectangle, block of text, or something similar—Word remembers it as an independent object that you can move around and manipulate in many different ways using the manipulation tools shown in Figure 10-9.

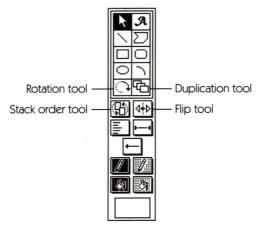

Rotation tool ——— Duplication tool

Stack order tool ——— Flip tool

**FIGURE 10-9.** *Use manipulation tools to select, move, and change the size, shape, and orientation of objects.*

The most important tool for manipulation is the *selection tool,* the arrow located in the upper left corner of the tool palette. Once you click on the selection tool, Word turns the pointer into an arrow that you can use to select or move any object in the canvas.

You can select with the selection tool in three different ways:

- Click directly on an object you want to select as a single object.

- Drag a bounding box around a set of objects to select the set.

- Hold the Shift key down as you click on different objects to select all of the objects you click on (a form of extended selection).

214

## Resizing or reshaping an object

After you've selected an object, Word puts sizing handles around it, as you can see in Figure 10-10. You can drag any one of these handles to resize the object—enlarging it, shrinking it, or even changing its shape by making it narrower, wider, taller, or shorter. If you want to retain a perfect circle, square, or horizontal or vertical line as you reshape or resize, hold down the Shift key to constrain the object during resizing.

**FIGURE 10-10.** *Word adds sizing handles to a selected object in the Insert Picture window.*

## Moving an object

You can move an object or a group of selected objects by moving the selection tool arrow on top of it and dragging in the direction you want to go. You release the mouse button when you want to drop the object at a new location. Note that Word remembers the order in which you created the objects on the canvas, and puts the newer objects on top of the older objects. If you move an older object to the same location as a newer object, the older object slides under the newer object.

## Overlapping objects

If one object on the canvas overlaps another and you'd like to bring the back object to the front or send the front object to the back, you can select either object and then click and hold on the stack order tool in the tool palette, which opens a pop-up menu with two commands: Bring To Front and Send To Back. Bring To Front puts the selected object on top of any other objects; Send To Back puts the selected object behind any other objects. If you have a large object completely covering a second object so that you can't see or select the smaller object, you can select the large object and choose Send To Back from the stack order tool's menu to reveal the smaller object.

### Duplicating objects

If you want to duplicate an object or a group of selected objects, simply click on the duplication tool in the tool palette: Word places a duplicate of the object or group of objects on the canvas next to the original. You can then move the duplicate anywhere you'd like, or duplicate again with the duplication tool for multiple copies of the object.

### Rotating objects

You can rotate any object by first selecting the object and then clicking on the rotation tool. This turns the pointer into a cartwheel shape that you can use to drag one corner of the selected object, rotating the object around the object's center. The status bar in the window tells you how many degrees you've rotated the object; drop the object when you've rotated it as far as you want it rotated. Note that once you've rotated an object you can no longer resize it; Word won't let you drag out the sizing handles as you could before. To get rid of rotation so that you can resize the object, you use the flip tool, as described in the next paragraph.

### Flipping an object

If you'd like to create mirror images of an object, you can duplicate it and then flip the duplicate using the flip tool. Click and hold on the flip tool to open a pop-up menu with three commands: Flip Horizontal, Flip Vertical, and Undo All Flips And Rotations. A vertical flip flips an object upside down around its center, a horizontal flip flips it left to right around its center, and the Undo option returns the object to its original state: unflipped, and with no rotation added, if any was added with the rotation tool. Choose the command you want to affect any selected objects.

### Standard editing commands

Word offers you the use of some of its menu commands for editing graphics; you'll find the Cut, Copy, and Paste commands as well as the Clear, Select All, and Undo commands—all in Word's Edit menu. The Cut command removes any selected objects from the canvas and puts them in the Clipboard; Copy copies any selected objects from the canvas to the Clipboard; and Paste copies the contents of the Clipboard to the middle of the visible canvas. The Clear command completely removes any selected objects from the canvas without putting them into the Clipboard. (Pressing the Delete key will do the same thing.) Select All selects every object on the canvas so that you can do whatever you want with them. And Undo, always your last resort for safety, undoes your last graphics tool action.

## PRACTICE

### Manipulating text

*Try manipulating the rectangle you created, rotating it around the text:*

1. Click on the selection tool and then click on the rectangle to select it. Sizing handles appear on the rectangle to show that it's selected.

2. Click on the rotation tool. The pointer turns into a cartwheel to show that it's ready to rotate the selected rectangle.

3. Drag any of the four rectangle corners in a clockwise rotation, watching the status area to see how many degrees you're rotating. Drop the rectangle when you get to 15 degrees. The canvas should look similar to Figure 10-11.

4. If the text doesn't look centered in your rotated rectangle, use the selection tool to drag the text to a centered location.

**FIGURE 10-11.** *Rotate the rectangle around the text.*

## Setting Object Qualities

When you create objects such as rectangles or ellipses, Word draws them with narrow lines around a hollow center. If you want a filled object, lines of different widths, or other different object qualities, you can use the quality tools shown in Figure 10-12.

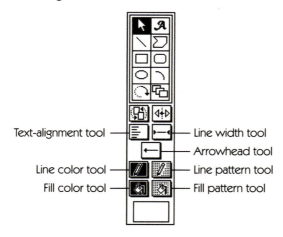

Text-alignment tool ——— Line width tool

——— Arrowhead tool

Line color tool ——— Line pattern tool

Fill color tool ——— Fill pattern tool

**FIGURE 10-12.** *The quality tools set line widths, fill patterns and colors, arrowhead styles, and other object qualities.*

If you use quality tools when you have an object or a group of objects selected, the quality you set affects each of the selected objects. For example, if you select a rectangle on the canvas and then set a very thick line width, the rectangle's border changes to a thick line. If you don't have an object selected, the quality tools don't change anything on the canvas. However, Word uses whatever qualities you set last when you create a new object, so Word will use that thick line you set earlier when you draw a new object.

The sample box at the bottom of the tool palette shows you your current quality settings: Its border shows line width and color, its interior shows the fill pattern and color. Look at the sample box before you create an object so that you'll know what qualities your object will have.

### Setting line width

When you click and hold on the line width tool, you'll see a pop-up menu with a full selection of line widths. Choose the line width you want; the menu

218

closes, and you'll see the line width you chose around the sample box. The line width affects every object you can create except for text.

## Creating arrowheads

Many of the lines people draw in graphics are meant to point to something, and they would look much better if they had arrowheads on them. The arrowhead tool sets the line tool so that it automatically adds arrowheads to the lines you draw. When you click and hold on the arrowhead tool, it opens a pop-up menu with the arrowhead choices shown in Figure 10-13. The first option is the default: It adds no arrowheads. The second option adds an arrowhead at the end of each line you draw, the third option adds an arrowhead at the beginning of each line, and the fourth option adds two arrowheads to each line, one at each end. This tool affects lines only.

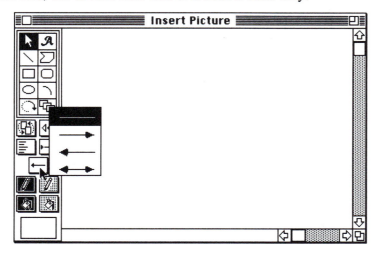

**FIGURE 10-13.** *The arrowhead tool offers various options for lines created by the line tool.*

## Setting line color and line pattern

The line color tool offers you a choice of eight colors for the lines you draw; you won't see the colors on screen unless you have a color Mac (you'll see color names on a black and white Mac) or on paper unless you have a color printer. You can choose any color shown in the menu; note that white is *not* transparent. If you draw with white lines over a black (or other colored) object, you'll see the lines appear over the top of the other object. If you draw white lines on a blank canvas, you won't see the lines.

The line pattern tool just to the right of the line color tool offers a set of patterns that Word uses to fill in your object's lines. If you select a narrow line, chances are that you won't see much of a pattern appear but will get a dotted or dashed line. Thick lines show patterns much better. Note that the line pattern menu (shown in Figure 10-14) offers black (the default), white, and transparent along with a variety of patterns. White shows up above other colors and patterns but not on a blank canvas, whereas transparent doesn't show up anywhere—it lets whatever is underneath it show through. You can see the results of the line colors or patterns you choose in the sample box.

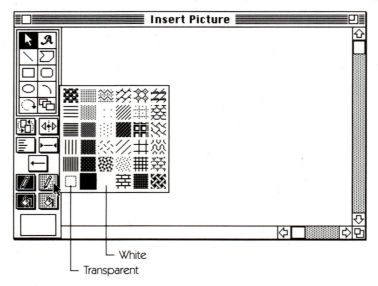

**FIGURE 10-14.** *The white pattern blocks anything behind it, and the transparent pattern allows anything behind it to show through.*

## Setting fill color and fill pattern

The fill color and fill pattern tools work the same way that the line color and line pattern tools work, but they affect the interior of the objects you create or select, not their border lines. You can choose whatever colors and fill patterns you like; the sample box shows you the results.

### Editing, formatting, and aligning text

You control the appearance of text on the canvas. You can set a font, a type style, and alignment for any text areas you create, and you can go back to a text area and edit the text there if you like.

To edit text, click on the text tool and then click on the text where you want to edit. You can then insert new text, delete old text, and make changes where you want. You can also drag over text to select text blocks that you can delete with the Delete key or type new text to replace.

You can format text in a text area using the commands in Word's Font and Format menus. These commands let you set font point size, set type styles, and choose new fonts. One important difference between editing text here and editing standard text in a Word document: Here each text area you create accepts only *one* font, *one* point size, and *one* type style. You can't format just a single character, word, sentence, or other text block; you can format only the entire text area. For example, if you select a text area as an object and then choose Underline from the Format menu, Word underlines all the text in the text area, even if you have only a single character selected there.

To set alignment in a text area, you choose from three options offered by the text-alignment tool's pop-up menu: Align Left (the default), Align Center, or Align Right. Like character formatting in this window, these options affect *all* the text in a text area, not merely a selected block. Word aligns the text using the left and right boundaries of the text area.

Note that if you have a single line of text, Word shrinks the text area boundaries in to fit the text, so alignment has no effect on the text. You can simply drag the text area with the selection arrow to position it wherever you want it.

## Closing the Insert Picture Window

When you're finished working on your graphic, quit the Insert Picture window by clicking on the window's close box. Word closes the window, and your new graphic appears in your document at the location of the insertion point. Word automatically moves the boundaries of the graphic to fit snugly around drawn objects, eliminating any empty space there. If you want extra space, you can add it by using the cropping tools, described later in this chapter.

## PRACTICE

### Manipulating a rectangle

*Try duplicating and changing the qualities of the rectangle to create a shadowed card under the text:*

1. Use the selection tool to select the rectangle.

2. Choose white from the fill pattern tool to turn the interior of the rectangle white. The rectangle now covers the text because it's on top of the text and no longer transparent.

3. Choose the Send To Back command from the stack order tool's pop-up menu to put the rectangle behind the text so that you can see the text.

4. Click on the duplication tool to duplicate the rectangle. A selected copy of the rectangle appears on top of both the rectangle and the text.

5. Choose black from the fill pattern tool to turn the interior of the new rectangle black.

6. Choose the Send To Back command from the stack order tool's pop-up menu to put the black rectangle behind both the text and the white rectangle.

7. Use the selection tool to drag the black rectangle under the white rectangle until it appears as a shadow of the white rectangle, as shown in Figure 10-15.

8. Click on the close box of the Insert Graphic window to close the window. Word inserts your newly drawn graphic in the upper left corner of the document.

**FIGURE 10-15.** *Duplicating the rectangle and setting fill patterns to white and black creates a shadowed backdrop for the text.*

## IMPORTING A GRAPHIC INTO WORD

Many graphics programs are available for the Macintosh, and chances are good you've got some pictures that you or someone else created with one of these programs and that you'd like to put into a Word document. If so, you can use either the Picture command (found in the Insert menu) or the Clipboard to import a graphic from an outside program into Word.

### The Insert Picture Command

If you've saved a picture in an outside graphics program and want to import the entire picture into a document, choose the Picture command from the Insert menu to open the Insert Picture dialog box. It looks just like the Open dialog box you use to open a document because it's the same dialog box—set to show graphics files only. You use it to search disks and folders to find the graphics file you want, and then to open the file. Word inserts the file's contents into your current document; the picture behaves the same way that a Word-created graphic does—like a single large character in a flow of text.

Different graphics programs use a number of graphics formats, and Word will import most of them, including PICT, PICT2, MacPaint, PostScript, EPS, and TIFF. The best test is to try to import the picture. If you're not successful, the picture might be stored in an odd format not supported by Word. You'll find more information about alternative formats in the chapter entitled "Creating and Importing Graphics" in the *Microsoft Word User's Guide*.

## The Clipboard

Often a picture created by another program includes a lot of blank space or extra objects that you don't want inserted into a document. If you use the Mac's Clipboard to insert a picture, you can trim the picture in the other program before you import it into Word.

To use the Clipboard to transport graphics between a graphics program and Word, you run the graphics program and place the graphic in the Clipboard, and then quit the graphics program. You then run Word and paste the graphic into your document.

If your Mac has enough memory, you can run Word and the other program simultaneously to make the job easier. You first run Word, and then choose the Finder command from the Finder menu at the far right of the menu bar to return to the Mac's finder. You then run your graphics program. (If you don't have enough memory in your Mac, you might not be successful. Your Mac will tell you if you don't have enough memory.) Once both programs are running, you can switch back and forth between them by choosing their names from the Finder menu in the far right of the menu bar.

Open the picture you want in the graphics program and select whatever part of the picture you want. Then choose the Copy command from the program's Edit menu to copy the graphic into the Mac's Clipboard. You can then return to Word, move the insertion point to where you want the graphic to appear, and choose the Paste command from the Edit menu to paste the graphic from the Clipboard into the document.

*If you have many graphics to move from a graphics program into Word using the Clipboard, check your Macintosh documentation for information about using the Scrapbook, a useful tool that allows you to move up to 256 different graphics from one program to another—a far stretch from the single graphic that the Clipboard will hold at one time.*

## MODIFYING GRAPHICS

Once you have a graphic in place in a document, you can use Word's graphics-editing features to either trim off unwanted sections of the graphic (a process called *cropping*) or resize the graphic (a process called *scaling*). To revise the contents of the graphic, you can reopen the Insert Picture window (appropriately retitled the Edit Picture window for this purpose) and modify the graphic there. You can also use character formatting to add a border to the finished graphic and use paragraph formatting to position a graphic where you want it in relation to the text around it.

### Selecting and Editing a Graphic

You can select a graphic in a document by simply clicking on it, or you can click and hold the mouse button and drag across the graphic with the pointer to select it as part of a text block. Once it is selected, three small squares—sizing handles—appear on the graphic's right and bottom edges and in its lower right corner, as shown in Figure 10-16. You can drag the sizing handles

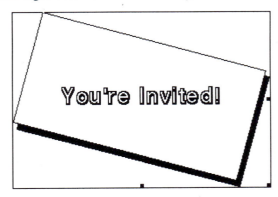

**FIGURE 10-16.** *When a graphic is selected, sizing handles appear on its right and bottom edges and in its lower right corner.*

225

to scale or crop the graphic. The handle on the right edge scales or crops the graphic horizontally, the handle on the bottom edge scales or crops it vertically, and the handle in the lower right corner scales or crops it both vertically and horizontally.

If you click on the graphic button in the Ribbon while a graphic is selected (or if you double-click on the graphic), Word opens the Insert Picture window (now called Edit Picture), offering the tool palette there for you to edit the objects in the graphic. Once you're finished editing the graphic, close the Edit Picture window; your changes appear in the graphic. If you don't like your changes, you can choose the Undo Edit Picture command from the Edit menu, and the graphic will return to its original state.

Note that Word's graphics capabilities are rather limited: If you try to edit a graphic you imported from another program, you probably won't be able to do much to it in the Edit Picture window. The best solution is to use your graphics program to edit the original picture, and then import the graphic into your document.

## PRACTICE

### Editing a graphic

*Try editing the graphic you created earlier, changing the text from outlined type style to shadowed type style to match the shadowed backdrop behind it:*

1. Double-click on the graphic to select it and open the Edit Picture window.

2. Use the selection tool to select the text on the rectangle.

3. Press Shift-Command-D to turn off the outline type style.

4. Press Shift-Command-W to turn on shadow type style.

5. Because the shadow type style creates wider characters, the text doesn't quite fit into the width of the text area, so Word breaks it into two lines. To turn it back into a single line, use the selection tool and drag the sizing handle on the right side out to the right.

6. Click on the close box of the Edit Picture window to close the window. You see the edited graphic in your document.

## Cropping a Graphic

After you insert a graphic, you may decide you want to see only a part of it. If so, you can crop it—move its boundaries in to exclude parts of the picture, much as cutting off sides of a photograph reduces it to the subject matter you want. The difference is that in Word, you can add back what you crop, and can even move the boundaries out further than the original to add white space around a graphic.

To crop a graphic, drag the sizing handles. Dragging a handle inward removes some of the graphic; moving it outward adds white space around the graphic. It's important to note that you can trim parts from only the right and bottom sides of a graphic. However, if you drag a handle outward to add white space to a graphic, Word centers the graphic in the white space, so the effect is the same as adding white space to both sides or to the top and bottom.

## Scaling a Graphic

When you scale a graphic, you stretch or shrink the image to make it wider, thinner, taller, or shorter. To scale a graphic, hold down the Shift key as you drag one of the graphic's sizing handles. The right handle scales the width of the image, the bottom handle scales its height, and the corner handle scales width and height equally to increase or decrease the graphic's overall size. To return a scaled image to its original size, just drag a sizing handle *without* holding down the Shift key. Word automatically returns the graphic to its original size.

## Adding a Border to a Graphic

Sometimes you need a border around a graphic to keep it from looking lost on the page. To add a simple thin-lined border, first select the graphic, and then use the Character dialog box to apply the outline type style to the graphic. If you want to create a thick border, apply the bold type style to the graphic. To add a drop shadow to the border, apply the shadow type style to the graphic. And to add a thick, shadowed border, apply the bold, outline, and shadow type styles to the graphic.

To add extra space between the graphic and its border, drag the sizing handles outward to add extra space around the edge of the graphic.

## Positioning a Graphic

After a graphic is in place within a document, you might want to position it relative to the surrounding text. If you want it to stand alone without text to either side, put it in a paragraph by itself by pressing Return just before and just after the graphic. To move the graphic in that paragraph to the left or right, select the graphic and drag the first-line indent marker on the Ruler—the left edge of the graphic moves left and right with it. If you merely want to center the graphic on the page, you can set the paragraph alignment to centered without having to adjust the first-line indent marker on the ruler.

### PRACTICE

#### Positioning a graphic

*Finish the sample invitation now by centering your new graphic, entering the document text, and adding check boxes by creating a new graphic and duplicating it:*

1. Move the insertion point to the end of the document, which should be just to the right of the graphic you created.

2. Press Return three times to create two blank lines and start a new paragraph.

3. Enter the text in the sample document as shown in Figure 10-7, on page 212. Stop at the beginning of the paragraph with the first check box.

4. Click on the graphic button in the Ribbon to open the Insert Picture window, and then close it immediately. This inserts a blank graphic in the document.

5. Press the space bar two times, type the text of the sentence, and press Return twice to move to a new paragraph.

6. Select the blank graphic you just created.

7. Use the Character command in the Format menu to apply both the outline and shadow type styles to the graphic. This adds a shadowed border to the graphic.

8. Hold the Shift key down, and then drag the corner sizing handle of the graphic up and to the left until you create a small check box. (Using the Shift key ensures that the graphic is absolutely square.)

9. Choose the Copy command from the Edit menu to copy the check box into the Clipboard.

10. Move to the end of the document and choose the Paste command from the Edit menu to insert the copied check box; then finish entering the invitation's text. Use Paste anytime you need another check box.

11. Finish your invitation by centering the graphic at the top. Select it, and then click on the centered alignment icon in the ruler. Word centers the graphic between the margins.

You've now had a chance to create simple graphics from within Word, and you've learned to import graphics from outside of Word. You also know how to edit and position your graphics on the page. If you're interested in more advanced features, you'll find that Word allows you to anchor graphics to the page and force text to flow around the graphics—the graphics don't shift with the text as you enter and edit the text. For more information on this feature, read the chapter entitled "Positioning Frames on the Page" in the *Microsoft Word User's Guide*. And if you're ready to learn about dividing a document into sections and setting up text in two or more columns, move on to the next chapter.

# Chapter 11

# Setting Columns and Document Sections

Some documents that use small font sizes—such as newsletters and brochures—look best when their text is printed in columns. The smaller column width helps the reader's eyes find their way to the next line of text, and a series of columns on the page presents a less formidable-looking block of text to work through. Besides, it's traditional—when you see columns of text, you think of news and magazine articles.

To set the text of your documents in columns, you must learn a new type of formatting: *section formatting.* Section formatting controls headers and footers, page numbering, columns, footnote display, and other characteristics of a document that might pervade the entire document or might appear in only a part of a document.

This chapter answers some questions about section formatting, and about columns in particular: How do you divide a document into sections? How do you select a section and format it? How do you set the text in a section so that it appears in columns? And how do you mix single-column and multicolumn text on a single page?

## PRACTICE

### Creating a practice document

*You need a multipage document for the hands-on sessions in this chapter—use the document you created in Chapter 9 for trying out headers and footers. If you saved it according to the instructions, you should be able to find it under the name "Redundancy."*

1. If you haven't yet started Microsoft Word, do so now.

2. Open the document titled "Redundancy."

*If you can't find or haven't created the document, take a few moments to do so by following the beginning practice sessions of Chapter 9.*

After you work through the section-formatting practice sessions in this chapter, the document will end up looking like Figure 11-1.

## SECTION FORMATTING

What exactly is a section, and what kind of formatting is section formatting? The simple answer is that a section is any part of a document divided from the rest of the document by a section mark. And section formatting is any kind of formatting that can apply to a single section of a document without affecting the rest of the document.

You've already done some section formatting in Chapter 9, where you created headers and footers. Your headers and footers appeared throughout the entire document, which Word perceived as a single section. But, when you

## Reiteration Report

### by Randall Redux

Researchers in rural regions relate repetitious renderings of regional revelations. "Rack and ruin!" rant reports. "Rubbish," reply rational readers. "Rout and remorse" repeat reports. Readers rejected reports; reports relinquished reliability. Repeated reporting rates reservations; recent ratings reveal retreating revenue for rumor rags. Repeating:

Researchers in rural regions relate repetitious renderings of regional revelations. "Rack and ruin!" rant reports. "Rubbish," reply rational readers. "Rout and remorse" repeat reports. Readers rejected reports; reports relinquished reliability. Repeated reporting rates reservations; recent ratings

reveal retreating revenue for rumor rags. Repeating:

Researchers in rural regions relate repetitious renderings of regional revelations. "Rack and ruin!" rant reports. "Rubbish," reply rational readers. "Rout and remorse" repeat reports. Readers rejected reports; reports relinquished reliability. Repeated reporting rates reservations; recent ratings reveal retreating revenue for rumor rags. Repeating:

Researchers in rural regions relate repetitious renderings of regional revelations. "Rack and ruin!" rant reports. "Rubbish," reply rational readers. "Rout and remorse" repeat reports. Readers rejected reports; reports relinquished reliability. Repeated reporting rates

Redundant Research—Rights Reserved

**FIGURE 11-1.** *Column formatting displays the text in this article in two columns.*

divide a document into sections, you can use section formatting to create unique headers and footers, set page-numbering and column-formatting options, and control other aspects of a section's appearance.

## Dividing a Document into Sections

To divide a document into sections, simply place the insertion point where you want the division, and then press Command-Enter. A section marker appears as a double dotted line across the width of the document window. Each section marker you insert contains all the section-formatting information for the section that precedes it, exactly as a paragraph marker contains all the paragraph-formatting information for the paragraph that precedes it. The last paragraph mark contains section formatting for the last (or only) section in the document.

Word treats a section marker as a single character (even though it appears as a double dotted line) that you can select, copy, paste, or delete. When you copy or move a section marker, you copy or move the section-formatting information with the marker. When you delete a section marker, you unify two sections, and all the text in the first section takes on the section formatting of the second section.

## Selecting a Section

To apply section formatting to a section, you must first select the section. Do this by placing the insertion point anywhere in the section, by selecting a text block in the section, or by selecting the section marker at the end of the section. To select more than one section for formatting, select a text block that reaches into each section you want to format.

After you've divided a document into sections, you can tell which section you're looking at by reading the Page-Number area in the lower left corner of the document window. It displays both the page number and the section number of the topmost line in the window. Word displays a section number (if the document contains sections) as a capital letter *S* followed by the section number (for example, *S1*, *S2*, *S3*, and so on).

**PRACTICE**

### Dividing a document into sections

*Try dividing your sample document into two sections—one for the headline of the report, the second for all the text following the headline:*

1. Move the insertion point to the beginning of the first sentence following the headline and byline. (It starts with "Researchers in rural regions....")

2. Press Command-Enter. Word inserts a section mark, dividing the document into two sections as shown in Figure 11-2.

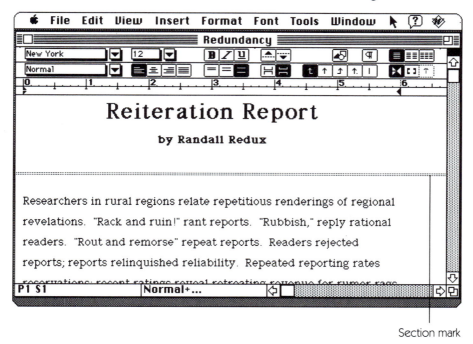

Section mark

**FIGURE 11-2.** *The section mark divides a document into sections.*

*Notice that if you scroll through the text and watch the Page-Number area, it tells you what section is displayed in the top of the window.*

## Types of Section Formatting

The following are some of the different types of section formatting you can apply to a selected document section.

■ *Section starts*—You can force a section to start on a new page, to start on a new even-numbered or odd-numbered page, to start in a new column (if you set more than one column of text), or to start without a break from the text of the preceding section.

■ *Columns*—You can instruct Word to format text in one column (the common method of text layout), two columns, or any number of columns up to 100. You can format each section to use a different number of columns, which is useful for creating newsletters and similar documents.

■ *Headers and footers*—You can create a unique set of headers and footers for each section within a document, which is useful if you've used sections to divide a document into chapters and want each chapter labeled individually. You can set the distance from the top edge of the page to the top of a header and from the bottom of a footer to the bottom edge of the page. You can also create a special first-page header and footer.

■ *Page numbers*—You can place a *margin page number* (a page number created without using a header or footer) anywhere on a page; you can specify the numbering system used to number pages (Roman numerals, Arabic numerals, letters, and other characters and symbols); and you can specify sequential page numbering that runs across sections or section page numbering that starts anew at the beginning of each section. (Page-numbering options aren't discussed in this book, but you can find more information about them in the chapter titled ''Page Numbers'' in the *Microsoft Word User's Guide.*)

■ *Endnotes*—You can set footnotes to appear following selected sections instead of at the bottom of each page or at the end of the document. (Endnotes aren't discussed here, but you can read more about them in the chapter titled ''Footnotes'' in the *Microsoft Word User's Guide.*)

■ *Line numbers*—You can instruct Word to number the lines of text on each page, a convenient feature for contracts or similar documents in which readers need to refer to individual lines. You can turn line numbering on or off, set different line-numbering increments in each section, and control the placement of line numbers. (You'll find more information about line numbers in the chapter titled "Numbering Lines and Paragraphs" in the *Microsoft Word User's Guide*.)

## Setting Section Formatting

You set most section formatting in the Section dialog box (shown in Figure 11-3), which you open by choosing the Section command from the Format menu. The Section dialog box contains list boxes and check boxes you use to set the section-formatting options you want. When you finish setting section-formatting options, click on the OK button to apply the formatting and close the dialog box, or click on the Cancel button to close the dialog box without applying the formatting changes. Click on the Apply button to apply formatting without closing the dialog box; you can see the changes in the document window.

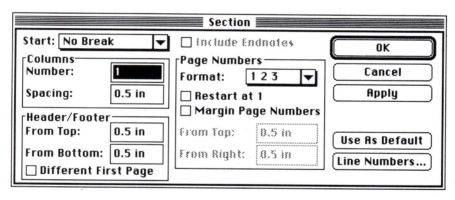

**FIGURE 11-3.** *Open the Section dialog box to format selected sections.*

You should already be familiar with one of the areas in the Section dialog box from your work creating headers and footers in Chapter 9: the Header/Footer area.

You can also set section formatting outside of the Section dialog box: Simply create headers and footers in the Header and Footer windows, and use the column buttons in the Ribbon to set columns (as you'll learn to do later in this chapter).

## SETTING COLUMNS

The most dramatic type of section formatting available in Word is *snaking columns*. Snaking columns divide each page into parallel vertical strips that Word treats as narrow pages; Word fills each column with text and then moves to the top of the next column to continue. If you change, add, or delete text, Word simply adjusts the text from column to column. Magazine and newspaper text is typically set in snaking columns.

To set columns in a section, you first select the section. You can then set columns using either the column buttons in the Ribbon (shown in Figure 11-4) or the Section dialog box. Using the column buttons in the Ribbon is the simpler method—you simply click on the button that sets the number of columns you want in the section: one column (the default), two columns, or three columns.

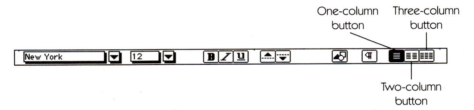

**FIGURE 11-4.** *Set simple columns using the column buttons in the Ribbon.*

The Section dialog box offers more column options than the column buttons in the Ribbon. In the Section dialog box you'll find a Columns area, shown in Figure 11-5, in which you can set the number and spacing of columns.

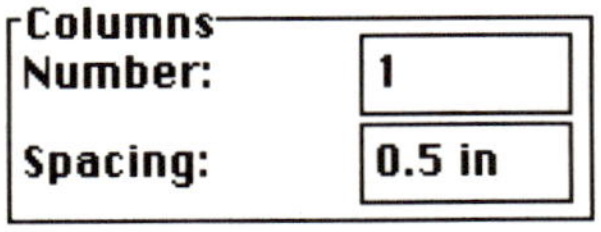

**FIGURE 11-5.** *Set the number of columns and column spacing using the Columns area of the Section dialog box.*

To set the number of columns, you enter a number from 1 to 100 in the Number text box. Two or three columns work well in most documents; you might want to use more columns if you plan to print on wide paper. If you set too many columns for a given page width, the columns will be too narrow, resulting in excessive hyphenation if you hyphenate your document or large gaps in text if you don't hyphenate. (Hyphenation is an advanced Word feature you can read more about in the *Microsoft Word User's Guide*.)

You set the amount of space between columns in the Spacing text box. The default setting is 0.5 inch, but you can increase or decrease this width by entering a new value in inches. Again, use good judgment. Spacing too wide leaves little room for text in the columns, and spacing too narrow runs the columns so close together that it becomes difficult to read the text.

## Mixing Column Formats on a Page

Occasionally you might want to mix the number of columns on one page. For example, the "Redundancy" document shown at the beginning of the chapter includes a title and byline that extend the width of one page (a single column) and appear above text displayed in two columns. To mix column formats, you insert a section break where you want to change the number of columns, and then format the second section to use a No Break start (explained in the section "Setting a Section Start" later in this chapter) and a different number-of-columns setting.

 **Practice**

### Mixing column formats

*The title, byline, and following text in your document are currently all set in single-column formatting. Change the following text to appear in three columns:*

1. Move the insertion point into the second section, if it isn't already there, so that the second section is selected.

2. Click on the three-column button in the Ribbon to set the second section in three columns. You'll notice that the text appears in a single narrow column at the left side of the document window. The right side of the document window is empty.

## Viewing Columns

You don't see columns lying side by side in Word's Normal view; instead, you see the text as one continuous column so that you can scroll downward to view the entire document. To see the columns side by side, turn on Page Layout view by choosing the Page Layout command from the View menu.

### PRACTICE

#### Viewing columns side by side

*Turn on Page Layout view now to see the columns you set in your document, and then set the text in two columns:*

1. Choose the Page Layout command from the View menu. You see the text set in three columns across the width of the document window.

2. Format the second section to use two columns by clicking on the two-column button in the Ribbon. (Be sure you have the insertion point in the second section.) Word changes the text to lie in two columns across the width of the document window.

3. Leave Page Layout view turned on for the next practice session.

## SETTING A SECTION START

Whenever you create a new section in a document, Word formats the section to start without a break from the previous section. This is a useful default, but you might want other options. For example, if you're dividing a long document into chapters, one chapter to each section, you might want to set each section to start on a new page to ensure that each chapter starts on a fresh page. To control how a section starts, choose an option from the Start list box in the upper left corner of the Section dialog box.

The five options in the Start list box offer these section starts:

- *No Break* instructs Word to start the section as a new paragraph on the same page on which the previous section ended (unless the section starts at the end of a page).

- *New Column* instructs Word to start the section at the top of the next column, but only if the selected section and the previous section are formatted with the same number of columns. If both follow a one-column format and you choose this option, Word starts the section at the top of the next page.

- *New Page* instructs Word to start the section at the top of the next page following the last page of the previous section.

- *Even Page* instructs Word to start the section at the top of the next even-numbered page (adding a blank, odd-numbered page to the previous section if necessary).

- *Odd Page* instructs Word to start the section at the top of the next odd-numbered page (adding a blank, even-numbered page to the previous section if necessary).

## PRACTICE

### Setting a section start

*Try setting the second section in your document so that it starts on the next page following the first section—so the title will be separated from the text that follows it—and then return the section start to No Break:*

1. Move the insertion point to the second section to select that section.

2. Choose the Section command from the Format menu to open the Section dialog box.

3. Choose New Page from the Start list box.

4. Click on the OK button to close the dialog box. If you scroll through the document in Page Layout view, you'll see that the text after the byline now starts on a new page, leaving the title and byline on page 1 by themselves.

5. Choose the Section command once again from the Format menu to open the Section dialog box, choose No Break from the Start list box, and click on the OK button to close the dialog box and return the text to the same page as the title and byline.

6. Choose the Normal command from the View menu to return to Normal view. You see the text set in a single narrow column on the left side of the document window.

## SETTING HEADERS AND FOOTERS

Whenever you create a new section, Word duplicates any existing headers or footers and inserts them in the new section. Word then *links* the headers and footers of the new section to the headers and footers in the following section. This link keeps the headers and footers consistent throughout the document; whenever you change a header or footer, you change the linked headers and footers in the sections that follow.

For example, if you create a document with a header that reads "Main Document" and then divide the document into five sections, every header of each section also reads "Main Document." If you select the first section and change the header to "Chapter One," the headers in all subsequent document sections also change to "Chapter One."

To create a section header or footer that isn't linked to the preceding section's header or footer, position the insertion point in the section you want, and then choose the Header or the Footer command from the View menu. The Header or Footer window opens, as shown in Figure 11-6, showing the header or footer contents. Change the contents as you want, and then click on the close box to close the window and set the header or footer.

After you change a section header or footer, Word breaks the link between that section and the preceding section so that any changes in the preceding sections won't affect the new header or footer you set. Of course, if the new header or footer is linked to sections that follow, the following headers or footers change to include revisions to the new header or footer.

For example, consider the five-section document we just discussed. Each of the five sections has a header that reads "Chapter One." If you change the

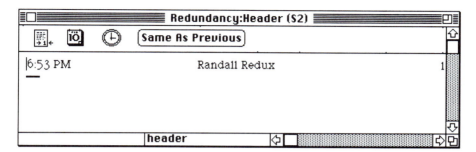

**FIGURE 11-6.** *A Header window shows the header for the currently selected document section.*

header in the third section to "Chapter Three," you break the link between the second and third sections. The first two sections are still headed by "Chapter One" because the second section is still linked to the first. The third section is headed by "Chapter Three" because it's no longer linked to the second section. And sections four and five are now headed by "Chapter Three" because they're still linked to section three.

You can reestablish a link between sections by opening a Header or Footer window and clicking on the Same As Previous button. After you break the link between a section and the preceding section, the Same As Previous button becomes active. When you click on the button, the contents of the header or footer change to match the preceding section's header or footer, and the link is reestablished between the two sections.

If you set even and odd headers in the Document dialog box (which sets even and odd headers in every section of the document), you should note that a link exists between the odd and even headers in a section. The even header displays the contents of the odd header of the section unless you break the link by setting new even-header contents. If you click on the Same As Previous button in an Even Header window, you link the header to the even header of the previous section. The same relationship is true for even and odd footers.

One more important linking feature: If you click on the Same As Previous button for a header or footer and there is no previous header or footer, Word searches the preceding section, and continues searching back to the beginning of the document until it finds a header or footer with contents that it can use. It then links the current section to that header or footer.

## SETTING DEFAULT SECTION FORMATTING

The Section dialog box includes OK, Cancel, and Apply buttons as the Character and Paragraph dialog boxes do, but it also includes a new button: Use As Default. Click on this button to set *default section formatting*.

Every time you create a new document, Word sets the default section formatting for the document. You can change the default section formatting, of course, but you always start with the default formatting when you create a new document.

The default section formatting might not be the section formatting you want to use. For example, if you prepare legal documents, you might want to begin with line numbering turned on. To change the default formatting, open the Section dialog box, set the section format options you want, and then click on the Use As Default button. Word remembers your settings and uses them whenever you create a new document. Word also stores the default settings on disk so that the new default settings remain set even after you quit Word and restart later.

You've now learned how to divide a document into sections and apply section formatting. In the next chapter you'll learn about another type of Word formatting: document formatting.

Chapter 12

# Margins and Document Formatting

Page margins control the amount of white space around the text on each page of your document. They provide space above and below for headers and footers, and space to the side to keep your document from looking too cluttered. By setting margins, you can control the visual weight of your entire document.

This chapter shows you the ins and outs of margin settings. It also introduces you to *document formatting,* settings that change the appearance of an entire document. You'll find answers to some of the questions you'll have if you're involved in creating documents for publication: How can I create offset margins? How can I set up margins for documents printed on both sides of the page? And how can I format a document so that the words on the page won't get lost in binding?

## PRACTICE

### Preparing the document

*Once again, you'll need a multipage document for the practice sessions in this chapter. Use the document you created in Chapter 9, which you should have saved under the name "Redundancy." Remove its headers and footers, which you don't need for these sessions.*

1. If you haven't yet started Microsoft Word, do so now.

2. Open the document "Redundancy."

3. If you formatted the document in Chapter 11 to have two columns, change the formatting back to a single column.

4. Choose the First Footer command from the View menu to open the First Footer window.

5. Delete the contents of the window, and then close the window.

6. Repeat steps 4 and 5 for the Odd Header, Odd Footer, Even Header, and Even Footer windows.

*If you can't find or haven't created the document, take a few moments to go through the practice session titled "Creating a Sample Document" in Chapter 9.*

As you work through the practice sessions in this chapter, you'll change the document so that its margins are greatly increased in size and include extra space along the inner edge of the page for binding, as shown in Figure 12-1.

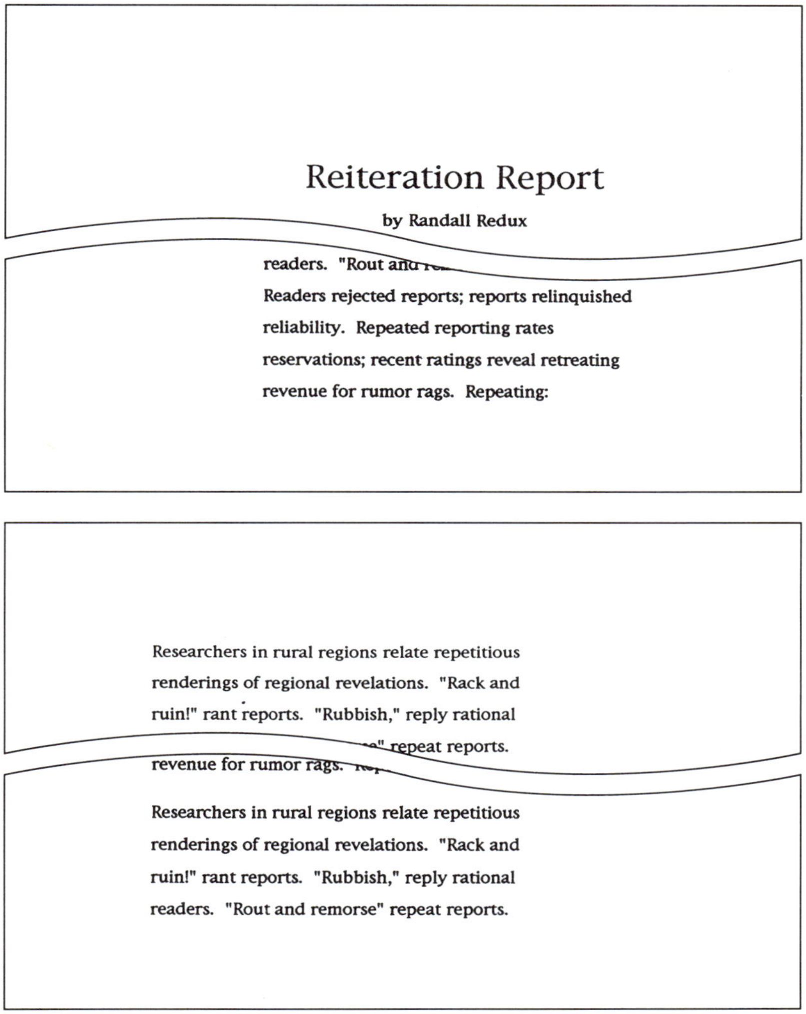

## Reiteration Report

by Randall Redux

readers. "Rout and re...

Readers rejected reports; reports relinquished
reliability. Repeated reporting rates
reservations; recent ratings reveal retreating
revenue for rumor rags. Repeating:

Researchers in rural regions relate repetitious
renderings of regional revelations. "Rack and
ruin!" rant reports. "Rubbish," reply rational
...e" repeat reports.

revenue for rumor rags. Re...

Researchers in rural regions relate repetitious
renderings of regional revelations. "Rack and
ruin!" rant reports. "Rubbish," reply rational
readers. "Rout and remorse" repeat reports.

**FIGURE 12-1.** *The margins in this document include extra space along the inner edge of the page (the left edge of the first page, the right edge of the second page) for binding. When the document is bound, the first page will be a right-hand page.*

# DOCUMENT FORMATTING

Setting margins is a type of document formatting—formatting that applies to all sections of a document, controlling its overall appearance. You've already done some simple document formatting: In Chapter 9, you created odd and even headers. Word offers many types of document formatting:

- Setting a document's top, bottom, left, and right margins.

- Creating a *gutter*, extra space that appears on the inside margin of each page. Adding a gutter to a document provides extra white space for binding.

- Setting mirror margins, which turn left and right margins into inside and outside margins. You use mirror margins for documents printed on both sides of the page; you can then control inside and outside margins, which swap sides from page to page.

- Controlling *widows* and *orphans*, which are single lines of text broken off from the rest of a paragraph when Word paginates a document.

- Setting a document to print out hidden text, which you learned to create in Chapter 3.

- Setting odd and even headers (which you learned to do in Chapter 9), which creates a header and a footer for even-numbered pages and a separate header and footer for odd-numbered pages.

- Setting the distance between default tab stops on the Ruler (the tab stops that appear along the measure before you set your own tab stops).

- Controlling the position of footnotes on the page, an advanced feature not covered in this book but discussed in the chapter titled "Footnotes" in the *Microsoft Word User's Guide*.

- Creating a series of files, an option that links one document with other documents so that you can continue page and line numbering from one document to the next. This type of formatting isn't discussed here, but you can read more about it in the chapter titled "Setting Up Long Documents" in the *Microsoft*

*Word User's Guide.* You'll also find information there about starting page numbering with numbers other than 1.

You set most document formatting by using the Document dialog box (shown in Figure 12-2), which you open by choosing the Document command from the Format menu. You can also set margins using the Ruler or the Print Preview window, as you'll see later in the chapter.

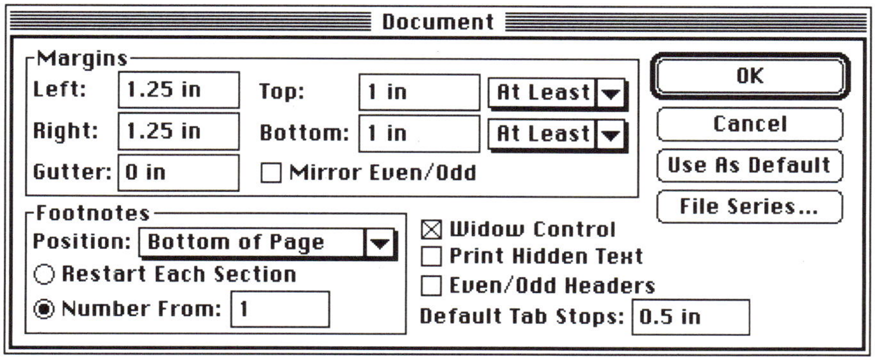

**FIGURE 12-2.** *Use the Document dialog box to set document formatting.*

## MARGINS

Word uses the margin values you enter to set the amount of space surrounding the body text on each page. The size of the text area equals the size of the page minus the size of the margins. You can change the page size in the Page Setup dialog box (which varies according to your printer) to accommodate many common paper-stock sizes—8½-by-14-inch or 11-by-17-inch sizes, for example, if your printer can use them. Although Word creates a default margin setting for all of these page sizes, you might want to alter the margin setting to get the particular look you're after.

To see how margins work, consider Word's default page size, which is 8.5 inches by 11 inches—the size of a standard (U.S.) sheet of paper, as shown in Figure 12-3. Word normally sets left and right margins at 1.25 inches and top and bottom margins at 1 inch. The remaining text area measures 6 inches wide (8.5 inches minus 2.5 inches) and 9 inches high (11 inches minus 2 inches). In Word's default setting, then, you have 6 inches across a page and 9 inches down a page as your work space.

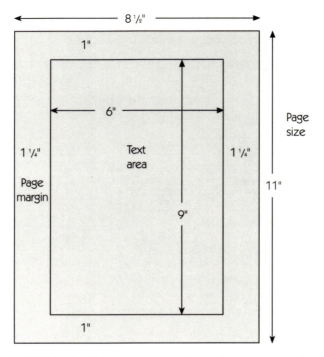

**FIGURE 12-3.** *The text area on a sheet of paper equals the page area minus the page margin area.*

## Setting Top and Bottom Page Margins

The Margins area of the Document dialog box, shown in Figure 12-4, includes four text boxes labeled *Left*, *Right*, *Top*, and *Bottom*, in which you can enter values to set the margins you want. These values are the margins from the edges of the paper. The Margins area also contains a text box labeled *Gutter* that sets the amount of extra white space you add to the inside margin of each page.

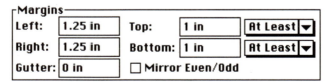

**FIGURE 12-4.** *To set the document's margins, enter values in the text boxes in the Margins area of the Document dialog box.*

The Top and Bottom margin settings determine how much white space you see at the top and bottom of each page, and also set the position of headers and footers. Headers and footers usually appear above and below the top and bottom margins. If you use *flexible* margins (which you get if you choose At Least from the list boxes to the right of the Top or Bottom text boxes), Word moves the top or bottom margin of the body text toward the center of the page to accommodate a lengthy header or footer. For example, if you set a flexible top margin of 1 inch and then create a header that descends 1.5 inches from the top of the page, Word moves the top margin downward to avoid overlapping the document text and the header text.

If you want to set a top margin that remains at a constant distance from the top of the page regardless of the size of the header, set a *fixed* margin by choosing Exactly from the list box next to the Top text box. And if you want to set a bottom margin that remains at a constant distance from the bottom of the page, choose Exactly from the list box next to the Bottom text box. Be aware that if you create a 1.5-inch header in a document with a fixed 1-inch top margin, the header text will overlap the document text.

Fixed margins are useful if you want to create a sidebar header such as one used in an organizational letterhead that includes a list of board members' names extending down the left margin of the page. You can create this type of letterhead by entering the list of names as a header with its left and right indents both set to the left of the body text's indents (to form a column). You then set a fixed 1-inch margin in the Top text box so that the header and the document text can overlap vertically. When you turn Page Layout view on or print the document, the list of names appears to the left of the document text.

## Setting Left and Right Page Margins

To set left and right page margins using the Document dialog box, enter the margin values in inches in the Left and Right text boxes. Because there are no side equivalents of headers and footers, both the left and right margins are fixed margins.

When you change left and right margins, the Ruler shows the new constraints of the text area. The left margin marker always remains at the 0 mark on the Ruler's measure, showing the edge of the left margin. The right margin marker, shown in Figure 12-5 as a dotted vertical line, moves to the left or right to show the total width of the text area. (Because the right indent marker usually sits on top of the right margin marker, you must move the right indent marker aside to see the full right margin marker.)

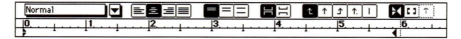

FIGURE 12-5. *The Ruler shows the width of the text area. The left margin marker always remains at the 0 mark, and the right margin marker moves to the left or right to show the edge of the right margin. (Notice that the right indent marker has been moved slightly to reveal the full right margin marker.)*

You can also set left and right margins using the scale icons in the Ruler. Click on the page scale icon in the Ruler to turn on page scale, as shown in Figure 12-6. The margin markers appear as square brackets on the left and right sides of the Ruler and indicate the actual margin measure from the left and right page edges. To change the margins, simply drag the margin markers to new locations along the measure. When you've finished, click on the normal scale icon to return the Ruler to normal.

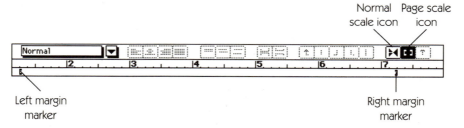

Normal Page scale
scale icon icon

Left margin
marker

Right margin
marker

FIGURE 12-6. *The Ruler in page scale shows the actual margin measures from the left and right edges of the page.*

 ## PRACTICE

### Changing margins

*Try changing the left, right, top, and bottom margins of the "Redundancy" document so that each increases in size by 1 inch. Use the Document dialog box to set the top and bottom margins and the Ruler to set the left and right margins:*

1. Choose the Document command from the Format menu to open the Document dialog box.

2. Type *2* in the Top and Bottom text boxes of the Margins area to increase the top and bottom margins to 2 inches.

3. Click on the OK button to close the dialog box and set the new margins. If you scroll through the text on the page, you'll notice that the first page break now appears earlier in the text than it did previously because there is now 2 inches less of vertical text space on each page.

4. Click on the page scale icon to turn page scale on. The margin markers appear in the Ruler.

5. Drag the left margin marker from the 1.25-inch mark to the 2.25-inch mark and the right margin marker from the 7.25-inch mark to the 6.25-inch mark. The text of the document narrows in width to reflect the new text width of 4 inches (6 inches minus 1 inch from each of the two margins).

6. Click on the normal scale icon again to return the Ruler to normal. The right margin marker now appears at the 4-inch mark, showing that the text width is now 4 inches.

## Setting paragraph indents using margin markers

As you changed the margin settings in the last example, you probably noticed that the paragraph indents moved with the margins. Indents are set as constant distances from the left and right margins. For example, because the right indent in this example was set at 0 inches from the right margin, when the right margin moved in 1 inch, the right indent moved in with it, maintaining its fixed distance of 0 inches.

Although you normally keep indents within the document text area, you can extend paragraph indents into the margins if you want to display text in the margins. To move a right indent marker into the right margin, drag the right indent marker to the right of the right margin marker. To move a left indent marker into the left margin, drag its marker to the left of the 0 mark into the negative numbers on the measure. (To do so, drag the marker to the left end of the Ruler; the Ruler scrolls right to let you move the marker.) You can also set indents inside the margins by entering negative values in the Indentation text boxes in the Paragraph dialog box.

## Creating a Gutter

Whenever you bind printed pages together—whether you have them stitched at a bindery, insert them in a folder, or simply staple them together along one edge—you lose part of the inside edge of each page to the binding. If your text falls too close to the binding, the reader is forced to pry the pages apart to read them. A *gutter* is an extra margin on the inside (binding) edge of each page. By adding a gutter, you ensure that text won't be caught in the binding. To add a gutter, enter a value in the Gutter text box of the Document dialog box to specify (in inches) the gutter size you want. Word adds the gutter space to the inside edge of each page, further reducing the width of the text area.

## Creating Mirror Margins

When you print a document on both sides of each sheet of paper and then bind the sheets together (like the pages of this book), your pages require different treatment than when you use only one side of each sheet. The gutter must alternate on odd-numbered and even-numbered pages in order to remain on the inside edge of each sheet, and any unequal left and right margins you set must alternate to maintain their inequality.

Word offers a *mirror margins* feature to accommodate double-sided printing. When you turn on the Mirror Even/Odd option in the Document dialog box, the Left and Right text boxes become Inside and Outside text boxes. The Inside box controls the left margin of odd-numbered pages and the right margin of even-numbered pages; the Outside box controls the right margin of odd-numbered pages and the left margin of even-numbered pages. Word adds to the inside margin of the page any gutter measure you set. Turn on the Mirror Even/Odd option whenever you print a document for reproduction on both sides of a page.

## PRACTICE

### Using mirror margins and gutters

*Try setting up mirror margins and a gutter for the "Redundancy" article as follows:*

1. Choose the Document command from the Format menu to open the Document dialog box.

2. Click on the Mirror Even/Odd check box to turn on the option.

3. Type .5 in the Gutter text box to specify a 0.5-inch gutter.

4. Click on the OK button to close the dialog box and apply your document formatting. Because the gutter uses another 0.5 inch of the page width, the text width is reduced now to 3.5 inches. The right margin marker in the Ruler now appears at the 3.5-inch mark.

5. Choose the Print Preview command from the File menu to open the Print Preview dialog box and see the "Redundancy" article as it appears on the full page.

*Notice that the gutter appears as a shaded vertical strip on the inside edge of each page. Notice also that the gutter appears on the right side of even-numbered pages and on the left side of odd-numbered pages, as shown in Figure 12-7.*

## Setting Margins Using the Print Preview Dialog Box

The Print Preview dialog box, which you just opened in the last practice session, provides a view of your document as it will be printed on the page. You'll learn more about the Print Preview dialog box in the next chapter, so for now just take a look at one convenient feature: an easy way to set all four page margins.

When you open the Print Preview dialog box, it displays the margin edges as four dotted lines on the page, as shown in Figure 12-7. You can reset a margin by simply dragging a margin line to a new location, which you do by dragging its margin handle (the small black box at the end of the margin line). As you drag the line, you can see the margin's measure at the top of the Print Preview dialog box, shown as a distance in inches from the edge of the page. Once you have set the margins as you want them, click on the Close button to exit the Print Preview dialog box.

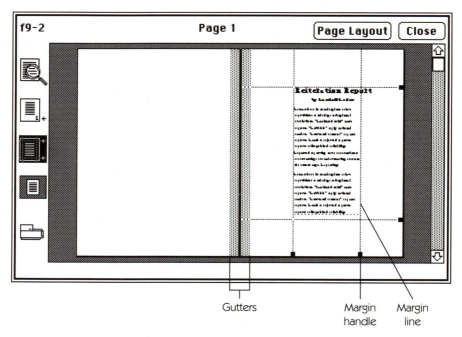

Gutters        Margin handle     Margin line

**FIGURE 12-7.** *Set a margin using the Print Preview dialog box by dragging a margin handle.*

## PRACTICE

### Changing margins with Print Preview

*Change the margins of the "Redundancy" article once again, this time using the Print Preview dialog box:*

1. Use the margin handle at the bottom right of the page to drag the outside margin out by one-half inch. The measurement at the top of the window shows how far you have it set; stop dragging when you reach 1.75 inches.

2. Click on the Close button to close the Print Preview dialog box. Notice that the right margin marker in the Ruler has now moved out by half an inch.

## SETTING DEFAULT TAB STOPS

Word normally sets default tab stops every half inch along the Ruler. The default tab stops remain in effect until you set your own tab stops (as you learned to do in Chapter 6, ''Aligning Text with Tabs''). To change the default tab-stop interval, enter a new interval value in inches in the Default Tab Stops text box of the Document dialog box. Word changes the default tab stops in the Ruler to fall at the interval you set.

## CONTROLLING WIDOWS AND ORPHANS

When Word paginates a document, it normally checks to be sure it doesn't create *widows* and *orphans*. A widow is a single line of text separated from the end of a paragraph and placed alone at the top of the next page. An orphan is a single line separated from the beginning of a paragraph and left standing alone at the bottom of the preceding page.

To avoid creating widows and orphans, Word checks the lines it creates when it splits a paragraph. If an orphan exists, Word moves the page break upward by one line, moving the orphan to the beginning of the next page, where the line rejoins the paragraph. If a widow exists, Word moves the page break upward by one line, moving another line of the paragraph to join the widow on the next page.

If you don't want Word to protect against widows and orphans, simply turn off widow control by deselecting the Widow Control check box in the Document dialog box.

That's it for margins and document formatting! In the next chapter, you'll learn how to look at your handiwork using the many different document views that Word offers.

# Chapter 13

# Views, Outlines, and Document Windows

We often look at documents in different ways for different information. We might read through the text closely for content, look at the way the print lies on the page for form, or scan the headings quickly for structure. We might also compare one part of the document to another, or compare the contents of one document with those of a second document. To help you look at your documents in different ways, Microsoft Word offers you several different document views.

This chapter introduces you to Word's document views and also to Word's abilities to present many documents at once. You'll find answers to viewing questions: What views do Word offer? How do I change from one view to another? How do editing and scrolling change from view to view? How can I see the entire page at one time? How can I create an outline in Outline view? How can I look at two different documents at the same time? And how can I look at two widely separated parts of the same document at one time?

As you work through the practice sessions in this chapter, you'll use two documents. One is the "Redundancy" report you created in Chapter 9, "Creating Headers and Footers," which you'll look at in Page Layout view. The second is an outline you'll create in Outline view that shows the structure of a user's manual for a piece of entertainment software called "Stellar Sawbones," a science-fiction medical-adventure program. Figure 13-1 shows the outline document.

## DOCUMENT VIEWS

Word offers three different views for any document:

- Normal view
- Page Layout view
- Outline view

Normal view is the view you've used throughout most of this book. Normal view shows full character and paragraph formatting but not all the document elements as they appear on the page. For example, Normal view doesn't show footnotes, headers or footers, or the edges of the page. In return for the limited view of the page and document elements, Normal view offers faster display speed—you can scroll through a document more quickly than you can in Page Layout view, and Word doesn't take occasional pauses to update the screen as you type. Most people use Normal view for entering the text of a document.

You've used Page Layout view in previous chapters to view formatting and document elements that aren't visible in Normal view: headers, footers, multiple columns, and the like. Although Page Layout view displays a much more accurate picture of your document as it will print, you give up display

**Introduction**

Welcome to a world of medical thrills and excitement! As Dr. Thralnor Fefnikal of the Assimilated Lowculture Planetary Association, you will have the opportunity to practice surgery and larceny on unsuspecting denizens of planets throughout the known galaxy. Before you begin your career, take a few minutes to fill in the warranty card.

**The Warranty Card**
**Other Digidilly Games**

**Setting Up**
**Computers with the IRS Card**
With Depreciation Accelerators
With Itemized Raster RAM
With File Extension
**Computers with the GTI Card**
With Bitstream Injection
With Radial Disks
With Molded Graphics Primitives

**Playing the Game**
**Choosing a Planet**
Ice Planets
Desert Planets
Fixer-Upper Planets
**Finding a Patient**
Listening to the Police Scanner
Waiting Around the Race Track
The Bad Part of Town
**Your Surgical Tools**
The Laser Scalpel
The Superglue Sutures
The Neutrino Nail Clipper
**Malpractice Insurance**
Cut-Rate Firms
Forging Coverage Certificates
**Intergalactic Flight**
Avoiding Police
Paying Bribes
Your Safe Hiding Place
**Scoring**

**FIGURE 13-1.** *Using Word's Outline view makes creating document outlines easy.*

speed when you use it. Word takes longer to scroll from page to page in Page Layout view and often pauses in order to display the document elements on screen as you scroll. If Page Layout view seems too slow for you, then use it only to view a document after you've entered its text and to make small editing and formatting changes to your final document.

Outline view isn't intended for page layout or for extensive text editing, but instead shows the underlying structure of a document. Outline view displays different levels of headings indented in outline form. Outline view recognizes nine levels of headings and displays them indented at 0.5-inch levels. It also recognizes document text accompanying headings, displaying each block of text indented slightly under its heading.

Word offers another, "unofficial," view: Page Preview. Page Preview shows you the entire page at one time on the screen so that you can get a feel for the overall page layout. And as you learned in the last chapter, you can set some of the document's formatting in Page Preview.

## PAGE LAYOUT VIEW

As you learned in previous chapters, you choose the Page Layout command from the View menu to turn on Page Layout view. Once Page Layout view is turned on, you see your document as close to the way it will appear when printed as your monitor screen allows. Although you probably won't be able to see an entire page at one time (unless you have a large-screen monitor), you can scroll to see all parts of the page. In addition to character and paragraph formatting (which you also see in Normal view), you see section and document formatting as you scroll. You see the edges of the page and the page margins you set. You also see footnotes, headers, and footers where they appear on each page. A page break appears not as a dotted line across the width of the document window but as an actual break from one page to another, complete with page edges and top and bottom page margins. If you create multiple columns, you see them side by side in Page Layout view.

Scrolling in Page Layout view works a little differently from the way it does in other views. The bottom of the screen in Page Layout view, shown in Figure 13-2, includes two additional controls: the *page-back icon* and the *page-forward icon*. Click on the page-forward icon to move the view forward to the top of the next page; click on the page-back icon to move the view backward to the top of the preceding page. Use the vertical scroll bar as you do in Normal view to scroll to the top and bottom of each page to see the page edges and any headers, footers, or footnotes there. You can also use the vertical scroll bar to scroll to the preceding or following page.

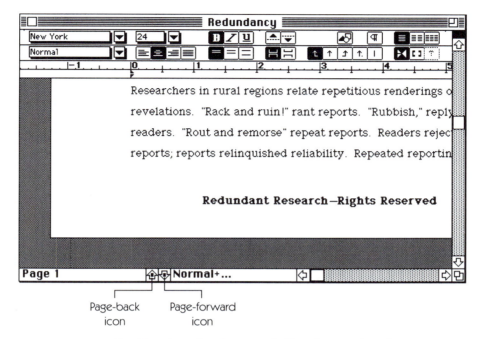

Page-back icon    Page-forward icon

**FIGURE 13-2.** *Scrolling through a document in Page Layout view shows you all elements of the document, including headers, footers, footnotes, and multiple columns. It also shows the edges of the page.*

You use the cursor keys in Page Layout view as you do in Normal view to move up, down, left, and right through the text. When working with multiple columns on a page, you'll find that the insertion point doesn't jump to the right or left to a neighboring column as you use right-arrow or left-arrow cursor keys; the insertion point moves upward or downward to the next line of text in the same column, a useful feature for retaining the thread of text as you entered it. You'll also find that moving the insertion point upward or downward with cursor keys doesn't always move the insertion point upward or downward into a header, footer, or footnote if it exists. To move to any of these document elements, it's best to click on the desired element and then use the cursor keys to move the insertion point.

Editing in Page Layout view has its own conventions. Although you edit document text as you do in Normal view, you don't need to open separate windows to edit headers and footers as you do in Normal view. Because these elements appear on the page, you simply select the text in a header or footer where it appears on the page and then change it as you want. If you change a header or footer that's linked to other headers or footers, the text in the linked headers or footers changes accordingly.

Adding headers or footers to a document in Page Layout view is similar to the process of adding them in Normal view: You set the types of footers you want (for example, odd and even, special first page) in the Section and Document dialog boxes and then choose the Header command (or the appropriate command) from the View menu. But instead of opening a special window for the header or footer, Word creates space at the top or bottom of the page and then moves the insertion point there so that you can enter the text you want. When you've finished, you simply click elsewhere on the page to move out of the header or footer area.

When you work on a document that has multiple columns in Page Layout view, the Ruler (when displayed) functions differently from the way it does in Normal view. When you move the insertion point to a column, the 0 mark on the Ruler moves to the left margin of the column. For example, if you select the right column of a pair of columns and the right column begins halfway across the width of a standard page, the 0 mark moves to the middle of the document window. This convention makes it easier to set indentions in columns.

Word offers an additional Page Layout view tool for working with multiple columns: multiple selection bars. In Normal view, the selection bar is a thin (and invisible) vertical strip along the left side of the window, in which you can move the pointer to easily select lines, paragraphs, or the entire document. In Page Layout view, Word places a selection bar along the left side of each column so that you can select lines and paragraphs within each column. You use the column-selection bars in the same way you use the selection bar in Normal view: Move the insertion point into the selection bar to the left of a line, and click the mouse button to select the line; to select a paragraph, double-click to the left of the paragraph.

**PRACTICE**

### Viewing the document

*Try viewing the "Redundancy" document in both Normal view and Page Layout view. First set the document to include multiple columns. Once in Page Layout view, view the columns, and then move to edit a footer. Look, also, at the way the Ruler shows indents for columns of text.*

1. Start Word if you haven't already done so.

2. Open the document named "Redundancy." It appears on the screen in Normal view.

3. Move the insertion point to the beginning of the first paragraph of document text ("Researchers in rural regions....") and press Command-Enter to divide the document into two sections.

4. Click on the two-column button in the Ruler to set the document text in two columns.

5. Scroll downward to the end of the document. Notice that the text appears in a single narrow column on the left side of the document window and that page breaks appear as horizontal dotted lines.

6. Choose the Page Layout command from the View menu to turn on Page Layout view.

7. Use the vertical scroll bar to scroll upward to the beginning of the document. You'll now see two columns per page. You'll also see the breaks between pages, and when you reach the top of the document, you'll see the top edge of the first page. (Click on the up scroll arrow of the scroll bar to see the top of the page.)

8. Choose the Footer command from the View menu to move to the footer. The insertion point jumps to the footer at the bottom of the page. You can edit the footer if you want.

9. Move the insertion point up into the right column of body text. Notice that the 0 mark on the Ruler moves to match the left edge of the column, as shown in Figure 13-3.

10. Choose the Normal command from the View menu to return to Normal view.

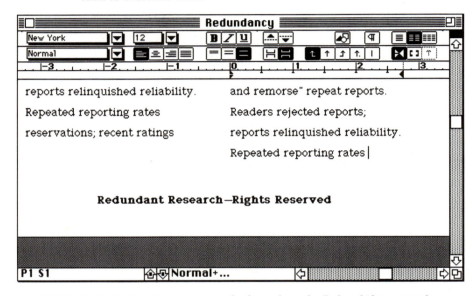

**FIGURE 13-3.** *In Page Layout view, the 0 mark on the Ruler shifts to match the insertion point at the edge of the column.*

## OUTLINING WITH OUTLINE VIEW

An outline is a traditional form for arranging concepts in hierarchical order. Main (higher-level) concepts align at the left margin, and lesser (lower-level) concepts are indented to the right below the concept under which they are subsumed. You can easily see the main points of an outline by reading only the higher-level-concept headings. Outlines make it easy to rearrange concepts in priority order. To promote a lower-level concept to a higher level, you simply move the concept heading to the left; to demote a concept to a lower level, you move the heading to the right.

Outline view offers many useful features for creating and changing outlines. You can use Outline view to do the following:

- Enter concepts as different levels of headings

- Add associated text (called *body text*) to any heading

- Change a heading's level by moving the heading to the left or right

- Change the order of concepts by moving headings, subheadings, and body text upward or downward in the outline (without using the Cut and Paste commands)

- Hide all subheadings and body text so that you can view only the main points of an outline

- Set the display level to hide all body text and any headings below a certain level so that you can view only the selected levels of an outline

You can use Outline view for many tasks, but you might find the following three uses to be particularly helpful:

- *Creating an outline from scratch.* Use Outline view to create a hierarchical order of headings and to set the basic structure of your document. You then return to any other view to fill in text below each heading.

- *Viewing the structure of an existing document.* Turn on Outline view for an existing document to show its headings in their hierarchical order and the body text below each heading. By setting the display level to show only important concepts, you can quickly see the overall document structure.

- *Scrolling quickly through a document.* Turn on Outline view and set it to show only headings at and above a certain level. Doing so ''shortens'' a long document considerably. You can quickly scroll to the location you want and then switch to another view to see all the text.

## Using Outline View

To turn on Outline view, choose the Outline command from the View menu. When Outline view is on, the *Outline icon bar* appears at the top of the document window where the Ruler usually appears. *Outline-selection icons* appear to the left of each paragraph, and paragraphs are indented according to their heading levels. Note that you can't display the Ruler when you're in Outline view; all indentions are set strictly by heading structure and can't be changed using the Ruler. Figure 13-4 shows this chapter's sample document as it appears in Outline view.

You click on the icons in the Outline icon bar to perform actions on selected paragraphs:

- The *movement icons* move paragraphs upward or downward in the outline or to the left or right to promote or demote them.

- The *demote-to-body-text icon* demotes a heading to body text.

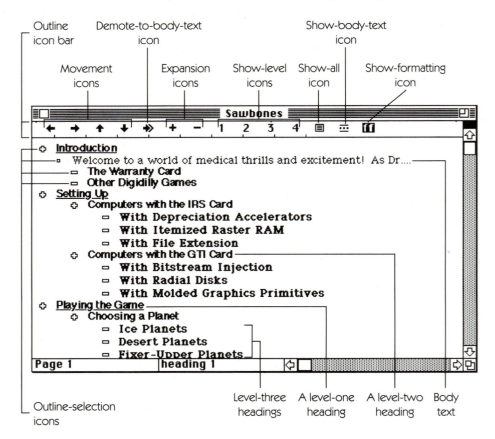

**FIGURE 13-4.** *Outline view shows the structure of headings in a document.*

- The *expansion icons* hide or display subheadings and body text below a selected heading.

- The *show-level icons* hide all headings and body text below the level you select.

- The *show-all icon* shows all headings, subheadings, and body text.

- The *show-body-text icon* shows the full text of each body-text paragraph or reduces the paragraph to a single line of text.

- The *show-formatting icon* shows the character formatting in each paragraph or turns character formatting off so that all characters appear in a uniform typeface, point size, and type style.

The outline-selection icon to the left of each paragraph in the outline shows a paragraph's status. If the icon is a plus sign, the paragraph is a heading that has subheadings or body text below it. If the icon is a minus sign, the paragraph is a heading that has no subheadings or text. If the icon is a small square, the paragraph is body text. Outline-selection icons also let you drag a paragraph upward, downward, or to the left or right. They also let you hide or reveal any subheadings or body text associated with a paragraph. You'll learn more about these features later in this chapter.

## Entering Text

You enter text in Outline view as you do in other views. Each time you press Return, you start a new paragraph at the same heading level as the previous paragraph. The Style area at the bottom of the window tells you the heading level of the paragraph you're entering.

## Selecting Text

You select text in Outline view as you do in other views. If you select a text block that includes more than one paragraph, Word selects *all* the text of the paragraphs in your selected text block. This makes it impossible (fortunately) to promote, demote, or move only part of a paragraph. To select a heading with all its subheadings and associated body text, simply click on its outline-selection icon.

## Promoting or Demoting a Paragraph

To promote or demote a paragraph to a new heading level, you drag its outline-selection icon to the left or right. If the paragraph has subheadings, they are promoted or demoted along with the paragraph's main heading. Associated body text also moves to the left or right to match the new heading positions.

You can also promote or demote paragraphs by first selecting them and then clicking on either the promote (left-arrow) or demote (right-arrow) icon. If you prefer the keyboard, you can promote or demote a selected paragraph by pressing Option–left-arrow cursor key or Option–right-arrow cursor key on the keyboard.

To change a paragraph into body text, you demote it in a different way from the way you demote a paragraph to a lower level—you click on the demote-to-body-text icon (the right-pointing arrow with the double head). You can also demote a paragraph to body text by pressing Command–right-arrow cursor key. When you demote a paragraph to body text, it is associated with the first heading above it.

To promote body text to a heading, first select the paragraph or paragraphs; then click on either the left arrow or right arrow in the Outline icon bar or press Option–left-arrow cursor key or Option–right-arrow cursor key.

### PRACTICE

#### Outlining

*Try your hand with outlining by starting an outline for a software manual. This particular manual is for the new medical-adventure computer game "Stellar Sawbones" (published by Digidilly, Inc.). In this first session, you'll enter headings and change their levels.*

1. Open a new document, and choose the Outline command from the View menu to turn on Outline view; the Outline icon bar appears. The insertion point is in the first paragraph, a "level-one" paragraph that has a minus (–) outline-selection icon to its left.

2. Type *Introduction*, and then press Return to begin a new paragraph.

3. Type two more paragraphs: *Setting Up* and *Playing the Game*. Each paragraph you type appears as a level-one heading. You have now defined the three major parts of your manual.

4. Now type a level-two subheading under ''Introduction'' by moving the insertion point to the end of the ''Introduction'' line and pressing Return to begin a new paragraph.

5. Drag the new paragraph's outline-selection icon to the right by one position (or click on the right arrow in the Outline icon bar) to demote the new paragraph to a level-two heading. Notice that the outline-selection icon to the left of ''Introduction'' changes to a plus sign to show that the paragraph now has a subheading.

6. Type *The Warranty Card*, press Return, and then type *Other Digidilly Games*. Two subheadings now appear below the heading ''Introduction.''

7. Now add subheadings below ''Setting Up.'' Move the insertion point to the end of ''Setting Up,'' press Return to begin a new paragraph, and demote it to a level-two heading.

8. Type *Computers with the GTI Card*, press Return, and then demote the new paragraph to a level-three heading.

9. Type three new paragraphs as level-three headings: *With Bitstream Injection*, *With Radial Disks*, and *With Molded Graphics Primitives*.

10. Continue typing outline elements, promoting and demoting paragraphs as necessary until the outline matches that shown in Figure 13-5.

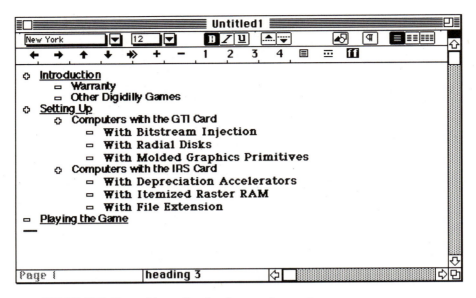

**FIGURE 13-5.** *Enter this outline for the practice session.*

## Changing Paragraph Order

To move a paragraph upward or downward in the outline without promoting or demoting it, drag the paragraph's outline-selection icon upward or downward to the new location. If the paragraph is a heading with subheadings and associated body text, the subheadings and body text move with the paragraph.

You can also move a selected paragraph (or paragraphs) upward or downward by clicking on the up-arrow or down-arrow movement icon in the Outline icon bar or by pressing Option–up-arrow cursor key or Option–down-arrow cursor key on the keyboard.

### ▲ PRACTICE

#### Changing an outline

*Try changing paragraph order in the outline you just created, and then go on to fill out the rest of the outline:*

1. Switch the order of two second-level headings—"Computers with the IRS Card" and "Computers with the GTI Card"— so that the "IRS" heading and all its subheadings appear

before the ''GTI'' heading. Drag the ''IRS'' outline-selection icon upward until it appears directly above the ''GTI'' heading, and then drop it there.

2. Type the rest of the outline as you see it in the sample document in Figure 13-1 at the beginning of the chapter, but for this step leave out the body-text paragraph following ''Introduction.''

3. To create the body-text paragraph, move the insertion point to the end of ''Introduction,'' press Return, and then demote the new paragraph to body text by clicking on the demote-to-body-text icon in the Outline icon bar.

4. Type the text of the paragraph.

## Collapsing or Expanding a Heading

If you don't want to see subheadings or body text beneath a heading, you can *collapse* the text so that only the heading shows. Word adds a thick, dotted bar below the heading to show that the heading has subheadings or body text beneath it, even though the elements are hidden.

To collapse subheadings and body text one level at a time from below a heading, first move the insertion point into the heading and then click on the minus (−) icon in the Outline icon bar. Each click on the minus icon collapses the lowest visible level of heading or body text beneath the selected heading. For example, if you put the insertion point in a level-one heading that contains level-two, level-three, and level-four subheadings, the first time you click on the minus icon the level-four headings disappear, collapsing into the level-three headings above them. The next click collapses the level-three headings, and the following click collapses the level-two headings into the main heading.

To expand a heading that contains collapsed subheadings, move the insertion point into the heading and then click on the plus (+) icon in the Outline icon bar. Each click expands the next lower level of heading following the selected heading. If you were to expand the heading you collapsed in the last example, the first click would reveal the level-two subheadings, the next click would show the level-three subheadings, and another click would show the level-four subheadings.

To collapse all levels of subheadings and body text with one action, double-click on the heading's outline-selection icon. Double-clicking on the heading's outline-selection icon a second time expands all levels of subheadings under that heading.

## Setting the Display Level

To set the display level of an outline, click on any of the show-level icons in the Outline icon bar—1, 2, 3, or 4—or click on the show-all icon at the right of the show-level icons. When you click on a show-level icon, Outline view shows only the headings at and above the level you choose, collapsing lower-level headings and body text into the headings above them. When you click on the show-all icon, Outline view shows all headings and body text.

## Showing Formatting and Full Text

When you first turn on Outline view, Word is set to show the full text of each body-text paragraph in the document and to show all character formatting. If you want to turn off character formatting so that all text on the screen appears in uniform typeface, point size, and type style, click on the show-formatting icon (marked "ff") in the Outline icon bar. To return to full character formatting, click on the show-formatting icon again.

You might find that showing the full text of each body-text paragraph bloats the outline so that it's difficult to discern the main ideas contained in its headings. Clicking on the show-body-text icon (marked with an ellipsis) truncates each body-text paragraph so that only the first line shows. If a paragraph contains more than one line of body text, Word appends an ellipsis at the end of the line to show you that more text exists. To see body-text paragraphs in full, click on the show-body-text icon a second time.

## Returning to Normal View

If you return to Normal view after creating an outline in Outline view, you'll find that the outline looks different: The headings are no longer indented, and the body text beneath each heading is set flush against the left page margin—as you can see in Figure 13-6. In Normal view, your outline looks more like a standard document, a good option for an outline you want to flesh out with more body text and print as a regular document.

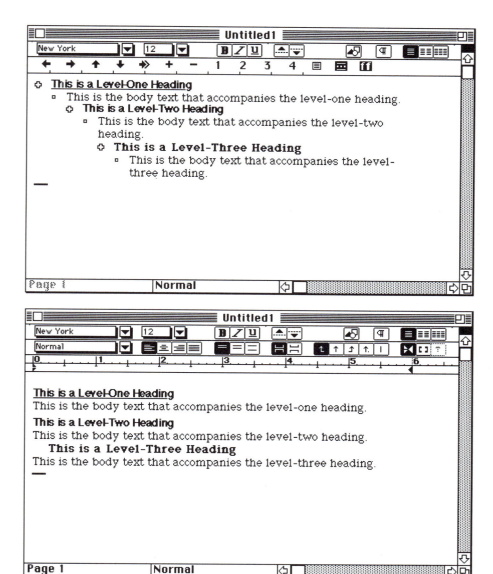

**FIGURE 13-6.** *An outline created in Outline view (shown on top) appears in more conventional form in Normal view (shown on bottom).*

Word sets the appearance of the different heading paragraphs in Normal view using *styles*, an advanced feature that controls the paragraph and character formatting of related paragraphs throughout a document. If you learn how to use styles, you'll be able to change the headings' appearance in Normal view to something you might like better than Word's defaults. You can also learn to create documents in Normal view that easily convert to a structured outline in Outline view (a matter of using "level-one," "level-two," and other styles as you write). You'll find styles described in the chapter titled "Formatting with Styles" in the *Microsoft Word User's Guide*.

### ◣ PRACTICE

#### Viewing an outline

*Try viewing your outline at different levels, with text shown truncated and with no character formatting. Then change to Normal view and look at your outline there.*

1. To view the outline with only level-one and level-two headings, click on the 2 icon in the Outline icon bar. The outline shows only the first two levels of headings, with a thick, dotted line below each heading that contains hidden subheadings or body text (as shown in Figure 13-7).

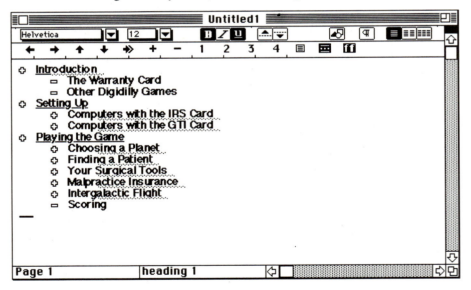

**FIGURE 13-7.** *Click on the 2 icon in the Outline icon bar to see only first- and second-level headings in an outline.*

2. Click on the show-all icon to view all the subheadings and body text again.

3. To view the outline with all character formatting turned off, click on the show-formatting icon.

4. To reduce the body-text paragraph to a single line, click on the show-body-text icon.

5. Now look at your outline in Normal view. Choose the Normal command from the View menu. The document appears with headings, subheadings, and body text all in place. All you need to do to write the manual is fill in more (much more!) body text. Good luck!

## USING PRINT PREVIEW

Unless you have a large-screen monitor, you won't see an entire page at a time in any of Word's three regular views. If you'd like to see the entire page, use Word's Print Preview command, which reduces the page in size until Word can fit the entire page (including white space around the edge) on the screen.

When you choose the Print Preview command from the File menu, the Print Preview dialog box, shown in Figure 13-8 (the ever-popular "Redundancy" document), displays your document as it will appear when printed. The pages are reduced to fit in the dialog box. Because the pages are reduced, you probably won't be able to read the text, but you can see where the body, headers, footers, and footnotes appear on the pages. You can adjust some aspects of page layout in the Print Preview dialog box, or you can close the Print Preview dialog box and adjust the layout in the document window.

### Paging Through the Document

To page through the document in the Print Preview dialog box, use the scroll bar located on the right side of the dialog box: Scrolling downward advances you through the pages; scrolling upward sends you backward through the pages. The page-number display at the top of the dialog box shows the current page location.

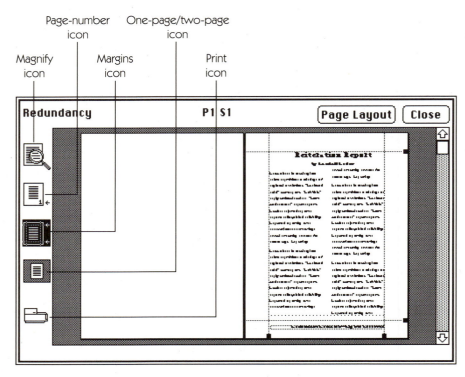

**FIGURE 13-8.** *The Print Preview dialog box displays the full-page layout of your document pages.*

## Magnifying the Page

If you need to see details on the page—to read the tiny print, for example— you can click on the *magnify icon* in the upper left corner of the Print Preview dialog box. Clicking on the magnify icon turns the pointer into a small magnifying glass. Move the pointer over the part of the page you'd like to see up close and then click the mouse button. Word expands that part of the page to full size, and fills the dialog box with it. You can scroll through the page using the vertical and horizontal scroll bars and read what you'd like, but you can't edit. To edit, click on the Page Layout button to exit the Print Preview dialog box and view the document in Page Layout view. To turn off magnification, simply click on the magnify icon again.

## Adding a Page Number

The second icon on the left side of the Print Preview dialog box window is the *page-number icon*; use it to add page numbers to your document. When you click on the page-number icon, the pointer turns into the number "1." You can move the pointer onto the page in the dialog box and click where you want to insert a page number. Word inserts a page number at that location on each page of your document. Adding a page number by clicking on this icon has the same effect as turning on the Margin Page Numbers option in the Section dialog box—it adds a page number without creating a header or a footer.

## Changing Page Breaks and More

The third icon in the Print Preview dialog box is the *margins icon*. When you click on this icon, Word shows dotted lines in the dialog box, as shown in Figure 13-9. The dotted lines show the location of the page margins, the header and the footer (if they exist), the automatic page number (if there is one), page breaks, and other page elements described in the Viewing Documents section of the *Microsoft Word User's Guide*. You can drag these elements to new locations with the pointer; when you do, the Page-Number area changes to show the new location in inches from the upper and left edges of the page.

If you added an automatic page number to the document, the number appears as a small dotted rectangle. To change the position of an automatic page number, click on the margins icon and drag the rectangle to the new position. Click outside the limits of the page to update the screen image. To remove the page number completely, drag the rectangle off the page and then click outside the limits of the page.

A manual page break appears across the width of the page as a closely spaced dotted line. An automatic page break appears as a widely spaced dotted line, often so close to the bottom margin line that the two lines merge together, appearing as a dashed line. If you want to change the location of a page break, you can drag the page-break line upward or downward to a new location. If you drag an automatic page break upward on a page, it turns into a manual page break. To remove a manual page break, drag it below the bottom margin and drop it. Click outside the edges of the page to update the screen.

Margin        Header
lines         box

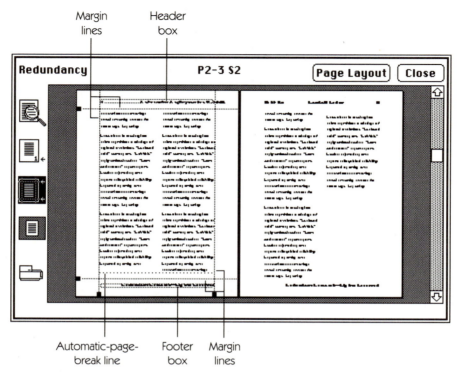

Automatic-page-    Footer    Margin
break line         box       lines

**FIGURE 13-9.** *When you click on the margins icon, the Print Preview dialog box shows the location of page margins, the header and the footer (if they exist), the automatic page number (if one exists), page breaks, and other page elements.*

Headers and footers appear inside long, dotted rectangles at the top and the bottom of the page. To reposition them, drag them upward or downward. You can't drag them below the top margin line or above the bottom margin line; if you could, you might cover the main text, with messy results. Click outside the edges of the page to update the screen.

The page margins appear on all four sides of the page. As you learned in the last chapter, you can drag the margins to new positions. If you don't want to see margins and other elements on the page, click once again on the margins icon.

## One-Page and Two-Page Displays

The Print Preview dialog box can show one or two pages of a document at a time. You can switch between the two display modes by clicking on the *one-page/two-page icon*, located below the margins icon. When the dialog box displays a single page, the vertical scroll bar moves through a document one page at a time. When the window displays two pages, the vertical scroll bar moves through a document two pages at a time if the document is set for facing pages (when the Mirror Even/Odd option is selected in the Document dialog box); otherwise, it scrolls one page at a time.

## Printing from the Print Preview Dialog Box

The last icon in the Print Preview dialog box is the *print icon*. If you click on it, Word opens the Print dialog box so that you can print your document without leaving the Print Preview dialog box.

## Exiting the Print Preview Dialog Box

Clicking on either of the two buttons in the upper right corner of the Print Preview dialog box closes the Print Preview dialog box. Clicking on the Page Layout button closes the dialog box, returns you to the document window, and turns on Page Layout view so that you can see the details of your page layout. In Page Layout view, you can read the text on the page and make editing changes.

Clicking on the Close button closes the Print Preview dialog box and returns you to your most recent view of the document in the document window.

### PRACTICE

#### Viewing the sample report

*Use the Print Preview command now to view the "Redundancy" report:*

1. Return to the "Redundancy" document. If you closed it, reopen it. If you left it open but it's now covered by the outline document, choose *Redundancy* from the list at the bottom of the Window menu.

2. Choose the Print Preview command from the File menu. A blank page and page 1 of your document appear in the Print Preview dialog box.

3. Click on the down arrow of the scroll bar. Pages 2 and 3 of your document appear in the dialog box.

4. Scroll back to page 1.

5. Click on the magnify icon. The pointer turns into a small magnifying glass.

6. Click on the title of the document. Word draws the title full size in the Print Preview dialog box.

7. Click on the magnify icon once again to turn off magnification.

8. Move the pointer to the automatic-page-break line at the bottom of the page, and drag it up the page. As you drag, the Page-Number area shows the exact location of the page break in inches from the top of the page.

9. Drag the page break to a new location, higher on the page, and then drop it. Word repaginates the entire document to show you the page break and clears all the text from below the page break.

10. Drag the manual-page-break line down below the bottom margin line, and then drop it. Word repaginates the entire document.

11. Click on the Close button to close the Print Preview dialog box.

## DOCUMENT WINDOWS

Word lets you open up to 23 documents on the screen at one time to compare text and formatting and to cut, copy, and paste text in and among the documents. Each document you open appears in its own document window; as you open new documents without closing the windows already on the screen, Word displays the document windows in layers, one on top of another, with the most recently opened document on top.

## Activating a Document Window

When you open more than one document window in Word, the windows overlap, usually with the top window completely covering underlying windows. You can move or resize document windows so that you can see more than one window at a time, but if you do, only one window is active—the window on top if they overlap, the window you worked on most recently if they don't overlap. Only the active window has an insertion point and an operating scroll bar, so it is the only window in which you can enter text. To make an inactive window active, click on the desired window (if any part of it is visible), or press Option-Command-W to activate each window in turn and bring it in front of the others.

If you open the Window menu, you'll find a list of all open Word documents at the bottom of the menu. Choose the name of any window you want to make active; Word brings the document window to the top of any other open document windows and makes it the active document window.

## Opening a New Window for an Open Document

You can open more than one window for a document by first opening the document as you would normally and then choosing the New Window command from the Window menu. This opens a second document window that displays the same document as the first document window. Both the original window and the new window show the same document title in their title bars, but Word numbers the windows with title extensions—:1, :2, :3, and so on.

When Word shows the same document in two or more windows, you can use the windows to view different locations in the document simultaneously, or you can set the windows to display their contents in different formats. For example, one window can show a document with its hidden text hidden, and another window can show the same document with its hidden text visible. No matter how many windows you open to show a document, Word still treats their contents as a single document. If you edit the contents of the document in one window, the contents change in all the other windows as well.

## Splitting a Window

To compare different sections of the same document without opening a second window, you can split a window in two, creating an upper and a lower window within the document window. These two subwindows (which we'll call *panes* for clarity) are separated by a *split bar*, a horizontal double line across the width of the text area of the document window.

When you split a window, each resulting pane has its own vertical scroll bar. You can set each pane to show a different view, so you can use a split window to look simultaneously at different locations in a document, using different document views for each pane. For example, one pane can show the Outline view of a document while the second pane shows the Normal view of the same document; or one pane can show the beginning text of a document while the second pane shows the ending text—many pages away—of the same document.

To split a window into panes, find the *split-bar drag box,* a small, black box at the top of the vertical scroll bar. Drag it downward. As you drag, the split bar moves downward in the window. When you've dragged the split bar to the location you want, release it to split the window into panes, as shown in Figure 13-10. You can also split the window into roughly equal panes by double-clicking on the split-bar drag box.

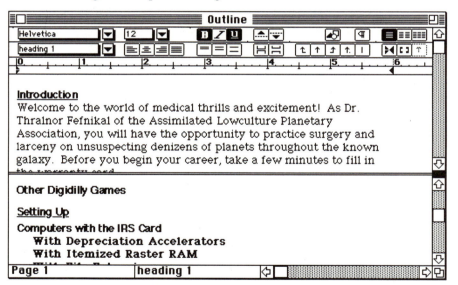

**FIGURE 13-10.** *When a window is split into two panes, each pane can show a different section and a different view of the same document.*

To change the location of the split bar, simply drag the split-bar drag box to a new location. If you drag the box all the way to the top or bottom of the document window and release it, you close one pane and remove the window split. You can also close a split window by double-clicking on the split-bar drag box.

After you split a window into two panes, you can move the insertion point between panes by simply clicking in whatever pane you want. If you want to change the view in a pane, place the insertion point in that pane and then set either Page Layout view, Outline view, or Normal view. For example, if both panes show Normal view, you can move the insertion point to the bottom pane and turn on Outline view by choosing the Outline command from the View menu. The top pane shows the document in Normal view (as it did before), and the bottom pane now shows the same document in Outline view.

Word normally allows independent scrolling of each pane to let you see a different section of a document in each pane. However, if you set one pane to show Outline view and the other to show Normal view or Page Layout view, the second pane scrolls to match the location of the Outline view. You can use this idiosyncrasy to your advantage: You can scroll the Outline view pane to find a location you want and then jump to the other view pane (which will be in the same location) to edit or add text. Note that it's the top paragraph shown in the Outline view pane that sets the document location; other paragraphs that you can see toward the end of the outline might be much farther along in the full document (because of an outline's condensed nature), so they won't appear in the other pane's view.

## PRACTICE
### Using a split document window

*Try working in a split document window with the game-manual outline you created. Start with the document in Normal view:*

1. Choose the document's name from the Window menu to bring its document window in front of the document you worked with in the last practice session.

2. Split the window into two panes by double-clicking on the split-bar drag box.

3. Choose the Outline command from the View menu. The lower pane (where the insertion point is located) appears in Outline view, and the upper pane remains in Normal view.

4. Scroll the bottom pane downward by one screen. The upper screen scrolls to match. The top line of the Outline view pane controls the view location of the Normal view pane.

5. Close the window split by double-clicking on the split-bar drag box. The entire document now appears in Outline view because the document window retains the view of the pane that contains the insertion point.

6. Choose the Normal command from the View menu to return to Normal view.

You've now learned how to handle Word's document views—Normal, Page Layout, Outline, and Print Preview—and to control document windows. In the next chapter you'll learn how to use an extremely useful Word feature for organizing complex text: tables.

# Chapter 14

# Creating Tables

If you arrange information in a table, you're guaranteed to draw your reader's eye to it. You might spend a good deal of time putting the table together, however, using text in lines of tabbed columns. Fortunately, Microsoft Word makes the job much easier with its table features, which offer special grids that you can insert in a document to keep information separated in discrete rows and columns.

This chapter teaches you the fundamentals of using Word's tables and answers some beginning questions: How do you insert a table in a document and set the table's dimensions? How do you enter, edit, and format text in a table? How can you move material from one part of a table to another part, and how can you add or delete rows and columns in a table? Finally, how can you control a table's appearance, setting column widths and adding borders to emphasize different parts of the table? At the end of the chapter, you'll read about advanced table features that you can explore on your own.

## PRACTICE

### Turning on gridlines

*Before you begin working with the examples in this chapter, check to be sure that Word shows table gridlines so that you can see the rows and columns of your table as you work on it:*

1. If you haven't done so already, turn your computer on and start Word.

2. Choose the Preferences command from the Tools menu to open the Preferences window.

3. Click on the View icon to see the View preferences.

4. If the Table Gridlines option in the Show area isn't turned on, click on its check box to turn it on.

5. Click on the close box to close the Preferences window.

The sample document for this chapter, shown in Figure 14-1, is a single-page letter that solicits subscriptions for a national newspaper. The document includes a table that compares the newspaper's features to those of other newspapers; you'll create the table, enter information, and edit it by using Word's table features.

## AN OVERVIEW OF TABLES

In Chapter 6, ''Aligning Text with Tabs,'' you learned to arrange information in columns by setting tab stops, a method that works well provided you don't insert more than a few words of text in each location. Revising column text can be quite difficult; if you add or delete too much text, entries might jump

1/9/92

Dear Friend:

The midwinter doldrums—we all get them! That's why Leander Mylarivek, the man who brought you mail-order pizza, is expanding his services to include home delivery of *The New Midnight Star Tattler.* You might know the *Star Tattler* as the weekly newsmagazine guaranteed to deliver the stories you want, but did you know that it now has double the writing staff to bring even more of these great stories to you? From Mr. Alzorno, our spirit-channeling astrologist/hairdresser columnist, to Zachary Ansadahl, our roving reporter on the lookout for Elvis, we've beat the competition across the board when it comes to giving you the features we *know* you want to read. The table below tells it all:

Number of Features from October through December 1991

| | The New Midnight Star Tattler | The Gossip Rag | USA Enquirer | Lifestyles of the Sinful and Wicked |
|---|---|---|---|---|
| Psychic predictions of natural catastrophes and changing presidential hairstyles | 22 | 19 | 6 | 11 |
| Inspiring stories of recovery from drug dependency, psoriasis, or a vague feeling of unrest | 35 | 8 | 29 | 13 |
| I-was-there accounts of UFO abductions for interstellar checker tournaments | 12 | 2 | 4 | 7 |
| Accurate reports on Elvis's new career as a topless mud wrestler in Motley, Minnesota | 49 | 37 | 26 | 47 |

Well, what are you waiting for—more hours of tedious boredom?! Get out your Visa or MasterCard and call us *now* at the number on the enclosed subscription card. Your copies of the *Star Tattler* will be on their way *immediately!!!!*

Yours sincerely,


James T. Ardentheffer
Subscription Manager

**FIGURE 14-1.** *You use Word's table features to create the table in this sales letter.*

forward or backward by a tab stop, misaligning information and moving it from the end of one line to the beginning of another. By creating tables with Word's table features, you can avoid these problems.

A table is a grid that divides a page into rows and columns, as shown in Figure 14-2. If you're familiar with spreadsheet software such as Microsoft Excel, you'll notice that a table looks like a small spreadsheet. Each location

Column       Cell

| | The New Midnight Star Tattler | The Gossip Rag | USA Enquirer | Lifestyles of the Sinful and Wicked |
|---|---|---|---|---|
| Psychic predictions of natural catastrophes and changing presidential hairstyles | **22** | 19 | 6 | 11 |
| Inspiring stories of recovery from drug dependency, psoriasis, or a vague feeling of unrest | **35** | 8 | 29 | 13 |
| I-was-there accounts of UFO abductions for interstellar checker tournaments | **12** | 2 | 4 | 7 |
| Accurate reports on Elvis's new career as a topless mud wrestler in Motley, Minnesota | **49** | 37 | 26 | 47 |

Row       Gridlines

**FIGURE 14-2.** *A table divides the page into rows and columns of cells.*

within the table is called a *cell*; you can move the insertion point from cell to cell in a table and enter text or insert graphics in each cell.

Each cell in a table is an independent text-entry area; it has its own margins, indents, and tab stops. You can set character and paragraph formatting within a cell exactly as you do outside the table. You set the width of each cell when you create or modify the table. The height of each cell is determined by its contents; as you enter text and graphics, the cell, along with all the other cells in the same row, extends downward to accommodate the contents of the cell requiring the greatest height.

After you enter text or insert graphics in a cell, you can easily edit the contents of a cell and move the contents from one cell to another. You edit a cell's contents by moving the insertion point into the cell and editing in the same way you edit regular text. To move the contents of one cell to another, you use the Cut, Copy, and Paste commands. You can also add or delete rows and columns of cells. And you can control the appearance of a table by changing the width of its columns and by adding borders either around groups of cells or around the entire table. When you print the table, only the borders and contents of the table print; the dotted gridlines don't.

## Inserting a Table

To insert a table in a document, move the insertion point to the location where you want the table to appear. Choose the Table command from the Insert menu to open the Insert Table dialog box, shown in Figure 14-3.

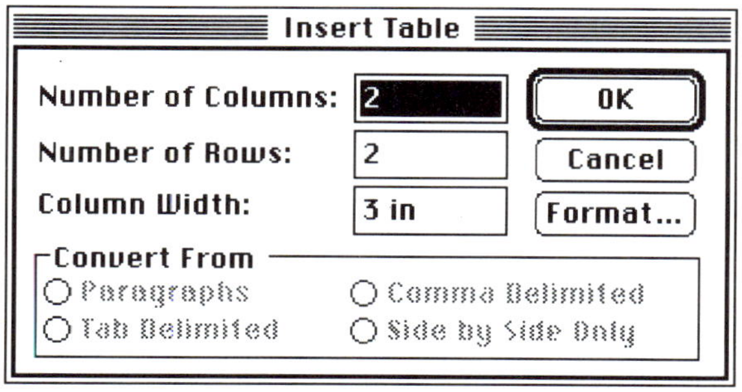

```
╔══════════════ Insert Table ══════════════╗
║                                           ║
║  Number of Columns: [2        ]  ┌────────┐ ║
║                                  │   OK   │ ║
║  Number of Rows:    [2        ]  └────────┘ ║
║                                  ┌────────┐ ║
║  Column Width:      [3 in     ]  │ Cancel │ ║
║                                  └────────┘ ║
║  ┌─Convert From──────────────┐   ┌────────┐ ║
║  │ ○ Paragraphs  ○ Comma Delimited│Format…│ ║
║  │ ○ Tab Delimited ○ Side by Side Only│ ║
║  └──────────────────────────┘             ║
╚═══════════════════════════════════════════╝
```

**FIGURE 14-3.** *Set the dimensions of a new table in the Insert Table dialog box.*

Word's default values create a table that stretches across the width of the page, with two columns across and two rows down. To set different table dimensions, change the values in the Number Of Columns and Number Of Rows text boxes.

The Column Width text box controls the width of each column. Its default value is determined by the number of columns you set in the Number Of Columns text box. Word divides the distance between the left and right page margins by the number of columns to calculate a column width that fills the space between margins. For example, if your page has 6 inches of text area between margins (the default Word setting) and you set three columns, Word offers 2 inches as the default column width (three columns of 2 inches fill up a 6-inch page width).

To set a column width, enter a value in inches in the Column Width text box. If the width you enter creates columns that don't fill the width of the page, Word inserts the remaining space to the right of the table. If the width is too wide for the page, the right side of the table runs off the page.

The Convert From area at the bottom of the dialog box governs conversion of regular text into a table. If you select a text block and then choose the Text To Table command from the Insert menu, you can choose one of four available options.

- *Paragraphs*, which converts each paragraph of the text block into a separate cell

- *Tab Delimited*, which converts each string of text separated by a tab into a separate cell

- *Comma Delimited*, which converts each string of text separated by a comma into a separate cell

- *Side By Side Only*, which converts side-by-side paragraphs into separate cells

Refer to the *Microsoft Word User's Guide* to learn more about these four options.

Click on the buttons on the right side of the Insert Table dialog box to move out of the dialog box. The OK button closes the dialog box and inserts the table, applying the dimensions you set; the Cancel button closes the dialog box without inserting a table; and the Format button opens the Table Cells dialog box, from which you can control the table's appearance. (You'll learn to use this dialog box later in this chapter.)

## Practice

### Creating a table

*Try including a table in the sample letter:*

1. Open a new document. Set paragraph formatting to include a blank line before each paragraph, set the font size to 10 points, and then type the first three paragraphs of the sample letter, ending with the sentence ''The table below tells it all.'' (It isn't important that you enter this text verbatim.) When you finish, press Return to begin a new paragraph.

2. Set paragraph formatting to centered alignment and character formatting to bold, and then type the table's title: *Number of Features from October through December 1991.* Press Return.

3. Set paragraph formatting to left alignment, with no blank line before the paragraph. (Word applies the paragraph formatting of the current paragraph as the paragraph formatting for each cell of the table.)

292

4. Press Return to add one blank line below the title.

5. Choose the Table command from the Insert menu to open the Insert Table dialog box.

6. Set a table dimension of five rows by five columns by entering 5 in both the Number Of Columns and the Number Of Rows text boxes.

7. Press Return to close the dialog box and insert the table. The table appears below the title paragraph, and the insertion point appears in the top left cell.

## MOVING THE INSERTION POINT WITHIN A TABLE

Any text you type in a cell fills only that cell—it doesn't extend to adjacent cells. When you reach the right border of the cell, the insertion point jumps to the beginning of a new line within the cell instead of moving to the next cell. To move to another cell using the mouse, simply click in that cell. The insertion point appears there, and you can begin entering text.

To move the insertion point from cell to cell with the keyboard, press the Tab key. Each time you do so, the insertion point jumps one cell to the right unless it's at the end of a row, in which case it jumps to the beginning (left end) of the row below. To jump in the opposite direction, press Shift-Tab. Note that if you press the Tab key when the insertion point is in the lower right cell, Word creates a new row of cells and moves the insertion point to the beginning of the new row. This is an easy way to expand the size of your table.

You can also use the cursor keys to move from cell to cell: If you press the up-arrow cursor key when the insertion point is at the top of the cell or if you press the down-arrow cursor key when the insertion point is at the bottom of the cell, the insertion point moves upward or downward into the adjacent cell. If the insertion point is at the beginning of the first line of the cell's contents, press the left-arrow cursor key to move it to the cell to the left; if the insertion point is at the end of the last line of the cell's contents, press the right-arrow cursor key to move it to the cell to the right.

To leave the table entirely, simply click outside the table. To reenter the table, click in any cell. To leave the table using the keyboard, press the up-arrow or down-arrow cursor key until the insertion point moves out of the table. To reenter the table, use the up-arrow or down-arrow cursor key to move back into the table.

# WORKING WITHIN A CELL

After you move the insertion point into a cell, you can enter text and graphics there as you do in other parts of the document. The Ruler shows the indents and margins of the cell you're in. As you type, the text fills in from the left to the right indent and then begins a new line below the current line. If the cell isn't large enough to accommodate the new line, the cell extends downward and all the other cells in the row extend with it to maintain the same height across the entire row.

You can set character formatting within a cell just as you do outside the table by choosing different fonts, point sizes, and type styles. You can also set paragraph formatting by choosing alignment and spacing and by setting tab stops. To jump from tab stop to tab stop within a cell, press Option-Tab; pressing the Tab key alone moves the insertion point to the next cell, not to the next tab stop.

## Setting Cell Margins and Indents

You set paragraph indents within a cell relative to *cell margins* rather than to page margins. Cell margins are very much like page margins; in the same way in which Word sets page margins to prevent text from running off the edge of the page, Word sets cell margins within each cell to prevent text from running into the border of the cell. These left and right cell margins usually measure only a fraction of an inch. The Ruler shows their location with margin markers, shown in Figure 14-4. The first-line indent and left indent of each paragraph are set relative to the cell's left margin, and the right indent is set relative to the cell's right margin. To set paragraph indents in a cell, select the paragraph(s) you want, and then drag the indent markers on the Ruler or set the indents using the Paragraph dialog box.

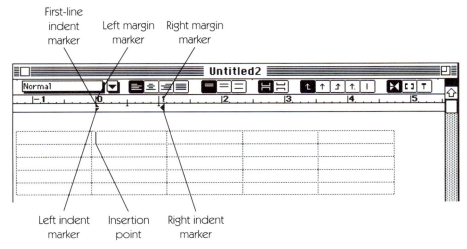

**FIGURE 14-4.** *The Ruler shows the margins and indents for the currently selected paragraph in the selected cell. The 0 mark is set at the cell's left margin.*

## Editing and Formatting Cell Contents

After you've entered text in a cell, you can edit and format it. First select a text block and then apply editing or formatting commands to alter the text. Your text selection must remain within the cell; if you extend the selection to an adjacent cell, Word selects the entire contents of both cells. Any editing or formatting command you choose affects the entire text block.

### PRACTICE

#### Entering text in cells

*Enter some text in the cells of your table. Begin by moving the insertion point to the upper left cell of the table. Then take the following steps:*

1. Move to the right by one cell (click in the cell to the right or press the Tab key) and type *The New Midnight Star Tattler.* The row expands vertically to accommodate the text.

2. Move to the right by one cell and type *The Gossip Rag.*

3. Move to the right by one cell and type *USA Enquirer.*

4. Move to the right by one cell and type *Lifestyles of the Sinful and Wicked.*

5. Move to the first cell of the next row (click in it or press the Tab key) and type *Psychic predictions of natural catastrophes and changing presidential hairstyles.*

6. Move through the rest of the cells and type their contents as shown in the sample document in Figure 14-1. (To center the numbers in their cells, turn on centered alignment, and then press Return once before typing each number.)

7. Move to the end of the document (out of the table) and type the rest of the letter.

## EDITING AND FORMATTING MULTIPLE CELLS

To edit or format the contents of more than one cell at a time, you must first select all the cells you want:

- To select the entire contents of a single cell, move the pointer into the left margin of the cell (the pointer turns into a right-pointing arrow) and click the mouse button.

- To select a row of cells, move the pointer into the left page margin beside the row you want (the pointer turns into a right-pointing arrow) and double-click the mouse button.

- To select a column of cells, move the pointer to the top border of the top cell in the column you want. When the pointer turns into a small down-pointing arrow, click the mouse button. You can also select a column by moving the pointer anywhere within the column of cells, holding down the Option key, and clicking the mouse button.

- To select a block of cells, drag the pointer from one corner of the block to the opposite corner of the block.

- To select the entire table, move the pointer anywhere within the table, hold down the Option key, and double-click the mouse button.

After you select a block of cells, you can cut, copy, and paste the cells' contents. If you choose the Cut command, the contents of the cells in the block are cut and placed in the Clipboard, leaving empty cells behind. If you choose the Copy command, the contents of the cells are copied into the Clipboard, leaving the cell contents intact. To paste the contents of multiple cells from the Clipboard into the table, select a single cell and then choose the Paste command. Word pastes the contents of the Clipboard into the table, using the selected cell as the upper left cell of the block and working to the right and down as it pastes. The pasted cell contents replace any previous cell contents.

Note that if you extend the selection to include part of the table *and* part of the document above or below the table, cutting cell contents also cuts the actual cells along with the contents.

## PRACTICE

### Formatting multiple cells

*Format the* Star Tattler's *column so that the text appears in boldface. Begin by selecting the second column from the left. Then take the following steps:*

1. Move the pointer to the top of the second column from the left, where the pointer turns into a small down-pointing arrow.

2. Click the mouse button to select the column.

3. Turn on bold character formatting. All the characters in the column appear in bold.

## CHANGING THE TABLE LAYOUT

After you create a table, you can add or delete cells. To do so, first select a cell or block of cells, and then choose the Table Layout command from the Format menu to open the Table Layout dialog box, shown in Figure 14-5.

The first three options in the upper left quarter of the dialog box set the type of table section that your editing actions affect. If you turn on the Row option, Word works on full rows; if you turn on the Column option, Word works on full columns; and if you turn on the Selection option, Word works only on the selected cells. If you turn on the Row option or Column option

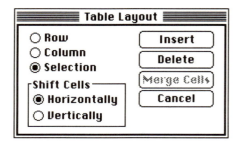

**FIGURE 14-5.** *Insert and delete cells in a table by selecting options in the Table Layout dialog box.*

when you don't have a full row or column selected, Word extends your selection to include the full row or column. For example, if you select two side-by-side cells in the middle of the table and then turn on the Column option, Word extends the selection to include the full columns containing both cells.

Clicking on the buttons on the right side of the dialog box initiates editing actions. The Insert button inserts a new column if the Column option is on, a new row if the Row option is on, or a new block of cells next to the selected block if the Selection option is on. The Delete button cuts the columns containing the selected cells if the Column option is on, the rows containing the selected cells if the Row option is on, or the selected block if the Selection option is on.

The options in the Shift Cells area determine how Word inserts and deletes around a selected cell block. If you turn on the Horizontally option, Word moves existing cells to the right of the selected block to make room for new cells or moves existing cells to the left to fill in a deleted block. If you turn on the Vertically option, Word moves existing cells downward from the selected block to make room for new cells or moves existing cells upward to fill in a deleted block.

## FORMATTING TABLE CELLS

To change the appearance of cells within a table, select the cells you want to format, and choose the Table Cells command from the Format menu to open the Table Cells dialog box, shown in Figure 14-6.

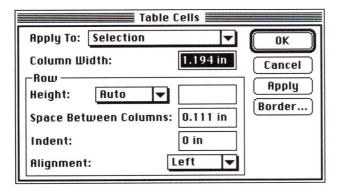

**FIGURE 14-6.** *Set cell formatting in the Table Cells dialog box.*

The Apply To list box at the top of the dialog box lets you choose how much of the table you want to affect when you format:

- *Selection*, which formats only the cells you have selected in the document

- *Each Cell In Table*, which formats the entire table

- *Entire Columns Selected*, which formats all columns in the table that contain a selected cell

- *Entire Rows Selected*, which formats all rows in the table that contain a selected cell

The Column Width text box just below the Apply To list box controls the width of selected table columns; you simply enter a value in inches.

The Row area contains a set of controls that affect the properties of selected table rows. The Height list box and text box control the height of a row exactly as the Line list box and text box in the Paragraph dialog box control the height of lines of text in a paragraph: You first choose Auto, At Least, or Exactly to determine how flexibly or rigidly Word controls the row height. You then enter a height in points in the text box to set a height if you chose At Least or Exactly.

The Space Between Columns text box sets the cell margins. Any value you enter here in inches determines the cell margins in the selected cells. Word divides the Space Between Columns value by 2 to set the cell margins.

299

For example, if you enter a value of 0.2 inch in the Space Between Columns text box, Word inserts 0.1 inch of space at both the left and right edges of the cell. Figure 14-7 shows the relationship between cell width and cell margins.

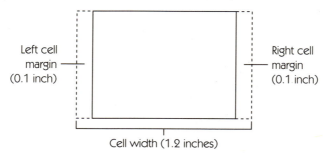

Left cell margin (0.1 inch)     Right cell margin (0.1 inch)

Cell width (1.2 inches)

**FIGURE 14-7.** *A 1.2-inch cell with a Space Between Columns setting of 0.2 inch has 0.1-inch cell margins.*

The Indent and Alignment text boxes allow you to create tables that are offset from body text surrounding the tables; you'll find more information about these advanced features in the chapter titled ''Tables'' in the *Microsoft Word User's Guide.*

## Adding Cell Borders

Click on the Border button to open the Border dialog box, shown in Figure 14-8. You should be familiar with this box from its use in adding borders to paragraphs (discussed in Chapter 5, ''Working with Paragraphs''). The Border dialog box offers border style options and a border box that you can click on to set border lines where you want them.

To set cell borders, first select a border style from the Line area in the middle of the dialog box. Click on the border you want, and apply it to any one of the four exterior border sides of the Border area by clicking on the side you want. Word adds a border line there using the line style you selected in the Line area. If you've selected a block of cells, you can add interior lines between the cells by clicking in the center of the Border area. To remove a line from the Border area, select the line by clicking on it (a small wedge appears at each end of the line to show that it's selected), and then click on the None option in the Line area.

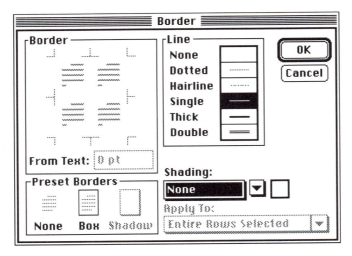

**FIGURE 14-8**. *Set cell borders in the Border dialog box.*

Once you've finished setting the borders you want, click on the OK button to close the Border dialog box and accept your borders, or click on the Cancel button to close the dialog box without effect. When the Border dialog box closes, you return to the Table Cells dialog box.

## Applying Cell Formatting

Once you've set row properties, column width, borders, and any other cell formats you might want to apply, you can apply them without closing the Table Cells dialog box (so you can see their effect) by clicking on the Apply button. To close the dialog box and accept your formatting, click on the OK button. To close the dialog box without accepting any of the formatting you set, click on the Cancel button.

## Viewing the Table

To view the table without gridlines (which you made sure were turned on at the beginning of the chapter), choose the Preferences command from the Tools menu to open the Preferences window. Click on the View icon to see the View preferences, turn the Table Gridlines option off in the Show area, and click on the close box to close the window. The table appears as it will print— without gridlines.

# PRACTICE

## Adding borders and changing column widths

*Add borders to your table to improve its readability, and then change column widths to more easily accommodate the text in the first column:*

1. Select the entire top row of the table.

2. Choose the Table Cells command from the Format menu to open the Table Cells dialog box.

3. Select the Each Cell In Table option from the Apply To list box so that your border settings will affect the whole table.

4. Click on the Border button to open the Border dialog box.

5. Click on the Thick line in the Line area.

6. Click on the four outside borders (left, right, top, and bottom) of the border box to set a thick-line border around the outside of the entire table.

7. Click on the center of the Border area.

8. Click on the Single line in the Line area to set thin-line borders between interior cells of the table.

9. Click on the OK button to close the Border dialog box.

10. Click on the OK button to close the Table Cells dialog box. The table is now framed with a thick border, and the interior cells are divided by single thin lines.

11. Select the rightmost four columns of the table. (Leave the leftmost column unselected.)

12. Choose the Table Cells command from the Format menu to open the Table Cells dialog box.

13. Type *1* in the Column Width text box to reduce the cell width of the columns to 1 inch.

14. Select the Entire Columns Selected option from the Apply To list box.

15. Click on the OK button to apply the column width and close the Table Cells dialog box.

16. Select the leftmost column of the table.

17. Choose the Table Cells command from the Format menu to reopen the Table Cells dialog box.

18. Type *2* in the Column Width text box to set the cell width to 2 inches.

19. Click on the Border button to open the Border dialog box.

20. Click on the Double line in the Line area.

21. Click on the right border of the Border area to add a double line to the right border of the first column.

22. Click on the OK button to close the Border dialog box, and then click on the OK button to close the Table Cells dialog box. The table now appears with the first column 2 inches wide and the other four columns 1 inch wide. The right side of the first column has a double-line border.

23. Select the entire top row of the table.

24. Choose the Table Cells command from the Format menu to open the Table Cells dialog box once again.

25. Click on the Border button to open the Border dialog box.

26. Click on the Double line in the Line area, and then click on the bottom border of the Border area to add a double-line border to the bottom of the top row.

27. Click on the OK button to close the Border dialog box, and then click on the OK button again to close the Table Cells dialog box. The table now appears with a double-line border along the bottom of the first row. You've duplicated the table as it appears in Figure 14-1, at the beginning of the chapter.

## MORE TABLE FEATURES

The table features you've read about so far are only the basics. If you explore tables more fully in the *Microsoft Word User's Guide,* you'll find you can do much more—for example:

- Convert existing text into a table (including a text file generated by a database program)
- Convert a table into text
- Set table cell widths using the Ruler
- Place tab stops within a cell
- Split a table into two parts
- Insert a page break in the middle of a table
- Set a minimum row height to expand rows with minimal contents
- Merge the contents of several cells into a single cell
- Split a previously merged cell into several separate cells
- Position a table on the page so that text flows around it
- Create irregular tables containing partial rows and columns

You've now learned how to create a simple table and to format its contents and cells. And with this, you've reached the end of the book! You should feel comfortable creating most standard documents with Word and should know how to create a few exotic documents as well. You'll find, as you continue to use Word, that it has many more powerful features to make your work easier and to create very specialized documents. Take some time to play around—there's no telling what you might discover.

# Appendix

# Setting Up Word

This appendix guides you through the steps you take to install Microsoft Word 5.0 on your Macintosh. But first it describes the hardware and software Word requires to run, provides a brief overview of what happens during installation, and helps you prepare for installation. If you've already installed Word but need to restore one or more of Word's files on your hard disk, the last section of this appendix shows you how to use installation procedures to restore files.

# REQUIRED HARDWARE

To successfully run Word 5.0, you need a Macintosh with at least 1 megabyte (MB) of RAM and a hard-disk drive with at least 8.5 MB of free space. Word will run better if you have 2 or more MB of RAM. One of Word's features, the grammar checker, won't run with less than 2 MB of RAM. Word's other features don't require 2 MB, but they will run faster and more efficiently with the extra memory. And if you intend to run Word simultaneously with other programs using System 7 software or MultiFinder, you must have enough extra memory to accommodate those other programs.

Although Word runs on most Macintosh models—including the Mac IIs, the Mac Portables, the Mac Classics, the Mac SE's, and the Mac Pluses—a few older models, such as the original Macintosh, won't run Word without major modifications. Check with a Macintosh dealer or service center to find out what those modifications are; you might find that it's less expensive to buy a newer model than to modify an older Mac.

## Printers

To print Word documents, you must have a printer attached to your Mac. Apple makes printers for the Macintosh that range from humble dot-matrix printers to high-end LaserWriters. Other manufacturers such as Hewlett-Packard also make Macintosh-compatible printers. Word works with any Macintosh-compatible printer.

The quality of printed documents depends on the quality of the printer. For best results, print on a laser printer such as the Apple LaserWriter II. For more economical printing, use a dot-matrix printer such as the Apple Image-Writer II or—for better results at a still-low price—use an ink-jet printer such as the Hewlett-Packard DeskWriter printer.

# REQUIRED SOFTWARE

The Mac on which you run Word must run up-to-date system software: either System 6 or System 7 software. To find out what system software your Mac runs, open the Apple menu in the upper left corner of the screen, and then choose either About The Finder or About This Macintosh to open a window. You'll find the system software version number displayed there. If the version number is lower than 6.0, you must upgrade the system software on your Mac before you install Word. If the version number is 6.0 or higher (6.0.2, 7.0, or similar numbers), you don't need to upgrade for installation.

System 7 is the latest version of the Macintosh operating-system software; it offers many advantages over earlier versions, including improved printing quality on many printers. This book assumes that your Mac is running System 7, and the examples show System 7 screens. If you're running System 6, Word works (for the most part) the same way it does under System 7. But there are a few differences that will make Word's response in the tutorials diverge slightly from the described results.

## Printer Drivers

To print Word documents on an attached printer, your Mac must have an appropriate *printer driver*. A printer driver is a piece of software that translates the Mac's standard printing output into the specific codes and data that your printer needs to print each document page. Apple provides Apple printer drivers with its system software; other manufacturers provide an appropriate printer driver on a disk that comes with the printer. To install a printer driver on your Mac, copy the printer driver from its floppy disk into the System Folder on your hard disk.

To see what printer drivers are installed on your Mac, choose the Chooser command from the Apple menu. The Chooser window opens (shown in Figure A-1) and shows each printer driver in the left half of the window. If you don't see the appropriate printer driver for your printer, you must find one (check with your dealer) and install it on your Mac.

## INSTALLING WORD

To install Word, you use a special program—Installer—that takes care of all the details of installation. It first checks your Mac to see if you have the appropriate hardware to run Word and sufficient disk space to install Word. If you don't, Installer notifies you and stops installation. If you do, Installer asks you for the name of a folder where you want to install Word, and creates a new folder if you need one.

Once you've set a destination folder, Installer copies files from the Word floppy disks into that folder. It also copies a few files into the System Folder. These files are all in compressed form—they've been through a compression

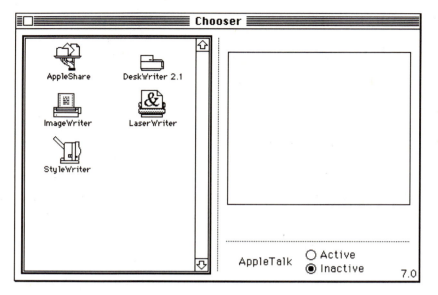

**FIGURE A-1.** *The Chooser window shows you the printer drivers installed on your Mac.*

program that reduces their size by more than half. Compression allows all the Word files to fit on only five floppy disks. Your Mac can't read or run compressed files until they've been decompressed, which is why you can't simply copy files from the floppy disks onto your hard-disk drive without using Installer. Installer runs each copied file through a decompression program. When it has finished, Installer asks you to set a default font for Word to use, and then restarts your Macintosh.

## Preparing for Installation

Before you install Word, take time to protect the original Word disks so that they won't accidentally be erased or altered: Set the write-protect tab on each disk so that the disk is write-protected. To see the tab, look at the back of the disk (the unlabeled side). You'll see a small plastic tab that you can slide up and down to either cover or reveal a square hole. Slide the tab so that the hole is revealed; this write-protects the disk, and the Mac can't write on or erase it.

Installer copies files into the System Folder, so some virus-protection programs, such as GateKeeper, will not allow installation; they see Installer as a possible virus trying to write unauthorized files into the System Folder. You must therefore deactivate any such virus-protection programs before you install Word. To do so, drag the program's icon out of the System Folder and onto the desktop; then restart your Macintosh.

The last matter to take care of before you start Installer is to decide on the folder where you'll install Word. If you have your own folder system on your Mac, you'll know just where Word should go. If not, consider creating a new folder named "Word 5.0" for installation. You don't need to create it now; Installer will create it for you during installation.

## Installation

To install Word, run Installer and follow its instructions:

1. Turn on your Macintosh if it isn't already on, and wait for the desktop to appear.

2. Insert the first of the Word disks. It's labeled "Install."

3. Double-click on the Install disk's icon to open the disk's window.

4. If you see a file on the disk labeled "Read Me Before Installation," double-click on it to open it and read it. This file contains last-minute comments on installing Word and might contain information you should know before installation. When you've finished reading, choose Quit from the File menu to close the file and quit TeachText, the application that displays it.

5. Double-click on the Installer 3.3 icon to run Installer. A Registration dialog box appears on the screen, reminding you to register your version of Word with Microsoft.

6. Click on the OK button to close the Registration dialog box. A dialog box appears (shown in Figure A-2), asking you to personalize your copy of Word.

7. Type your name in the Name text box and, if you want, an organization in the Organization text box. (Press the Tab key to move from text box to text box.) When you're finished, click on the OK button to close the dialog box. A new dialog box appears to ask if you've turned off all virus protection.

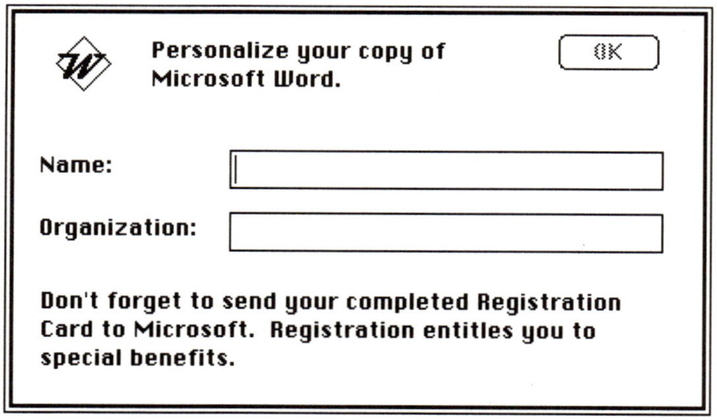

**FIGURE A-2.** *This dialog box asks you to personalize your copy of Word.*

8. If you haven't turned off virus protection, click on the Quit button to stop installation so that you can turn virus protection off. If you have turned virus protection off, click on the Continue button to close the dialog box and continue installation. The Easy Install dialog box (shown in Figure A-3) appears. It shows you what files Installer will install and the disk drive on which it will install them (which should be your main hard-disk drive).

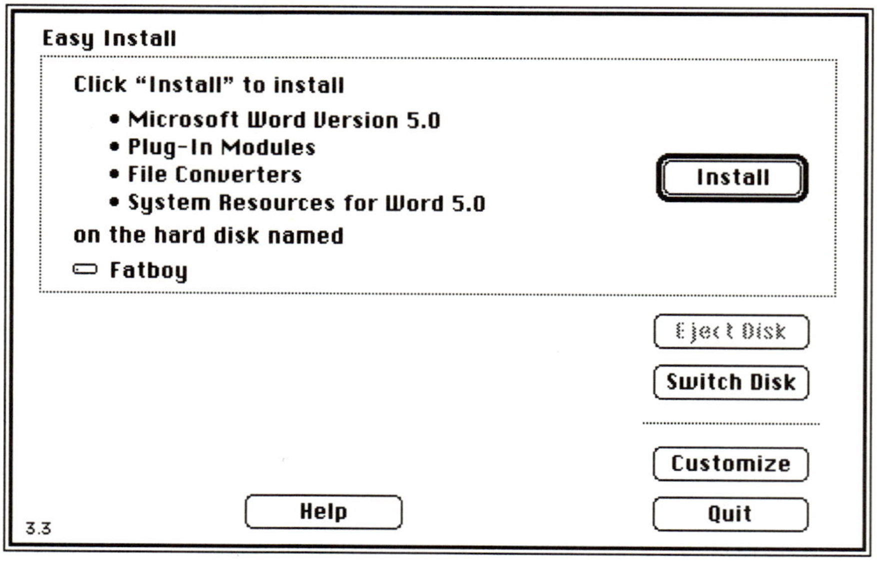

**FIGURE A-3.** *The Easy Install dialog box.*

9. If you have more than one hard-disk drive on your Mac and you don't want to install Word on the proposed drive, click on the Switch Disk button to open a Disk dialog box, where you can choose another disk drive. Once you've selected the drive, click on the OK button to return to the Easy Install dialog box.

10. Click on the Install button to start installation. The Easy Install dialog box closes, and the Folder dialog box (shown in Figure A-4) appears, asking you for the name of the folder where you want to install Word.

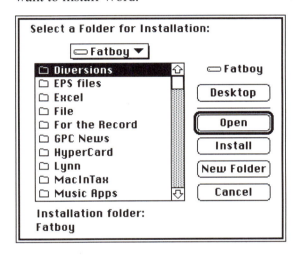

**Select a Folder for Installation:**

⊡ Fatboy ▼

☐ **Diversions**
☐ EPS files
☐ Excel
☐ File
☐ For the Record
☐ GPC News
☐ HyperCard
☐ Lynn
☐ MacInTax
☐ Music Apps

⊡ Fatboy

Desktop

Open

Install

New Folder

Cancel

**Installation folder:**
**Fatboy**

**FIGURE A-4.** *In this dialog box, choose a folder in which to install Word.*

11. If you have a folder ready for installing Word, find its name in the list box and double-click on the folder to select it. Its name appears in the box above the list box. If you don't have a folder ready for Word, click on the New Folder button to open a small dialog box in which you can enter a new folder name. Type *Word 5.0* or any other name you want, and then click on the Create button to go back to the Folder dialog box.

12. Click on the Install button to start installation. Installer displays a dialog box that shows you how the installation is progressing. It prompts you to insert the other Word disks one at a time.

13. Insert each Word disk when prompted. Installer copies the files from those disks into the destination folder and the System Folder. When Installer is finished copying files, it displays a message that advises you to take a break while it decompresses the files. Decompression can take as long as half an hour, so this is a good time to go out for lunch or coffee. While you're gone, a series of decompression windows appear and disappear, one for each file being decompressed. When all files are decompressed, the Select Default Font dialog box (shown in Figure A-5) appears.

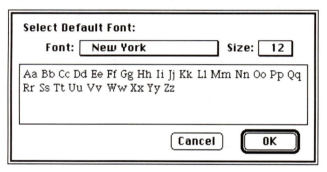

**FIGURE A-5**. *Set a default font and size for new Word documents in the Select Default Font dialog box.*

14. Click on the OK button to accept the 12-point New York font as Word's default font. (The tutorials in this book assume 12-point New York as Word's default font. You can change the default font later from within Word if you want to.) The dialog box closes, and Install asks you to insert the Install disk.

15. Insert the Install disk in the floppy drive. Installer finishes its work and displays a dialog box that tells you the installation was successful.

16. Click on the Restart button to restart your Mac. The Mac restarts, and displays the desktop once again.

## After Installation

After you've installed Word, take a few minutes to reinstall your virus protection and check out Word:

1. If you disabled virus protection before installation, drag the virus-protection program's icon from the desktop and drop it in the System Folder. Choose the Restart command from the Special menu to restart the Mac with virus protection in place.

2. Open the folder in which you installed Word and look at its contents. You should see a Word document icon there named "ReadMe." Double-click on this document icon to start Word and open the document.

3. Read through the document for last-minute information about Word 5.0 that isn't in the Word manuals.

4. Choose the Quit command from the File menu to quit Word and return to the desktop.

5. Put the Word disks away in a safe place so that you can reinstall Word later if it or any of its files are erased from your hard disk.

## REINSTALLING DELETED WORD FILES

If you accidentally or deliberately deleted Word files from your hard disk and want to restore them from the Word disks, use Installer. Because all the files on the Word disks are compressed, you can't simply copy them onto the hard disk; Installer must decompress them before your Mac can work with them.

To use Installer to reinstall specific Word files:

1. Follow steps 1 through 9 of the installation instructions earlier in this appendix. They start Installer and take you to the Easy Install dialog box.

2. Click on the Customize button in the Easy Install dialog box to open the dialog box shown in Figure A-6.

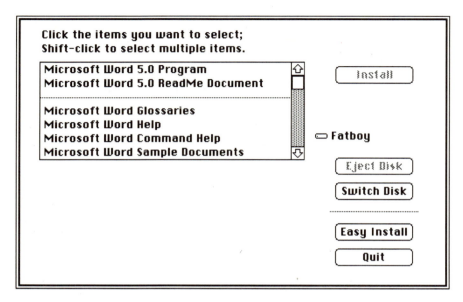

**FIGURE A-6.** *Choose the files you want to restore in this dialog box.*

3. To select the files, click on the names of the files in the list box that you want to restore. If you want to select more than one file, hold down the Shift key as you click.

4. Click on the Install button to install the selected files. The rest of the installation continues as it does during full installation.

# Index

Page numbers in *italics* refer to figures or tables.

## Special Characters

^ (caret), use of in searches, 89–90
, (comma), as delimiter for table cells, 292
... (ellipsis), *208,* 209, 210

## A

addition, operators for, 140. *See also* Calculate command
aligning text, 39–40
alphabetizing, 158–61
antonyms, 136–37
Apple Macintosh
    limitations of certain models, 306
    requirements for Microsoft Word, 306–7
Apple menu, 10
AppleTalk, printing and, 178
Application menu, *5,* 13
applications, using simultaneously, 9
arcs, *208,* 209–10
arrowheads, *218,* 219
ASCII (text-only) format, 170
At Least line spacing option, 106–8
author, finding file by, 175
auto line spacing, 106–8
automatic paper feed, 181

## B

bar-marker button, 120
Best print quality, 182
bitmap fonts, 52–53
Bitstream fonts, 53
blocks, text, 31. *See also* text
body text, in outlines, 267
boldface
    format command for, 35, 58
    keyboard shortcut for, *62*
    with Ribbon, 35, 57
Border dialog box, 99
borders
    cell, 300–303
    graphics, 227
    paragraph, 110–13
bottom margin, 250–51, 252–53

## C

Calculate command, 139–43
canvas, in Insert Picture window, 206

caps, small, *62*
Caps Lock key, 20–21
caret (^), use of in searches, 89–90
case
    changing, 35, *58,* 59–60
    matching in searches, 86
    sorting and, 160
    spell checking and, 153
cells in tables. *See* tables
center alignment, 39, 104, 120
Change Case command, 35, *58,* 59–60
Character dialog box, 60–61
character keys, 19–21
characters. *See also* fonts
    formatting (*see* formatting, characters)
    invisible, 66–68
    measuring for point size and line spacing, 54, 106
    printed vs. on-screen, 53–54
    special (*see* special characters)
    wildcard, 86–87
character sets, 50
Chooser, 178–79, 307, *308*
circles, 209, 210
Clear key, 23
Clipboard
    calculations and, 141
    defined, 33–34
    graphics and, 216–17, 224–25
close box, *5*
close-line button, 109
closing documents, 44–45
collapsing outline headings, 273–74
color
    general control of, 36–37, 61
    line, *218,* 219–20
column buttons, *7*
columns
    example, *233*
    in Page Layout view, 264
    Ribbon buttons, 238
    section formatting and, 236
    setting, 238–39
    in tables
        formatting, 299
        layout, 297–98
        width, 291, 302–3
    viewing, 240

## U–V

## W–Z

## MICHAEL BOOM

Michael Boom is the author of three other Microsoft Press books: *Learn Word for Windows Now, Music Through MIDI,* and *The Amiga.* He has published numerous other books and magazine articles and served as a columnist for *Computer Currents.* He currently lives in the Bay area, where he writes what he claims are understandable manuals for C programmers working on UNIX workstations.

The manuscript for this book was prepared and submitted to Microsoft Press in electronic form. Text files were processed and formatted using Microsoft Word.

Principal editorial compositor:  Barb Runyan
Principal proofreader:  Alice Copp Smith
Principal typographer:  Lisa Iversen
Interior text designer:  Kim Eggleston
Interior illustrator:  Lisa Sandburg
Cover designer:  Lani Fortune
Cover photographer: Ben Kerns
Cover color separator:  Color Control, Inc.

Text composition by Microsoft Press in Times Roman with display type in Kabel Bold, using the Magna composition system and the Linotronic 300 laser imagesetter.

*Printed on recycled paper stock.*